Empowering the UN Security Council

Empowering the UN Security Council

Reforms to Address Modern Threats

Edited by
MONA ALI KHALIL
MAK LAW International

FLORIANE LAVAUD
Withers

OXFORD
UNIVERSITY PRESS

OXFORD
UNIVERSITY PRESS

Oxford University Press is a department of the University of Oxford. It furthers the University's objective of excellence in research, scholarship, and education by publishing worldwide. Oxford is a registered trade mark of Oxford University Press in the UK and certain other countries.

Published in the United States of America by Oxford University Press
198 Madison Avenue, New York, NY 10016, United States of America.

Library of Congress Cataloging-in-Publication Data
Names: Khalil, Mona Ali, editor. | Lavaud, Floriane, editor.
Title: Empowering the UN Security Council : reforms to address modern threats /
[edited by] Mona Ali Khalil, Floriane Lavaud.
Other titles: Empowering the United Nations Security Council
Description: New York : Oxford University Press, 2024. | Includes bibliographical references and index.
Identifiers: LCCN 2024024717 (print) | LCCN 2024024718 (ebook) |
ISBN 9780197780602 (hardback) | ISBN 9780197780626 (updf) |
ISBN 9780197780619 (epub) | ISBN 9780197780633 (online)
Subjects: LCSH: United Nations. Security Council | United Nations. Charter. |
International Court of Justice. | Security, International.
Classification: LCC KZ5036 .E47 2024 (print) | LCC KZ5036 (ebook) |
DDC 341.23/23—dc23/eng/20240604
LC record available at https://lccn.loc.gov/2024024717
LC ebook record available at https://lccn.loc.gov/2024024718

DOI: 10.1093/oso/9780197780602.001.0001

Printed by Integrated Books International, United States of America

Note to Readers

This publication is designed to provide accurate and authoritative information in regard to the subject matter covered. It is based upon sources believed to be accurate and reliable and is intended to be current as of the time it was written. It is sold with the understanding that the publisher is not engaged in rendering legal, accounting, or other professional services. If legal advice or other expert assistance is required, the services of a competent professional person should be sought. Also, to confirm that the information has not been affected or changed by recent developments, traditional legal research techniques should be used, including checking primary sources where appropriate.

(Based on the Declaration of Principles jointly adopted by a Committee of the American Bar Association and a Committee of Publishers and Associations.)

MIX
Paper
FSC
FSC® C183721

To all those who believe in the Charter of the United Nations

Contents

Foreword ix
Mohamed ElBaradei
Acknowledgments xiii
List of Abbreviations xv
List of Contributors xvii

Introduction 1

PART I EMPOWERING THE MEMBERSHIP

1. Respecting the UN Charter 9
Tareq Albanai

2. Empowering the Elected Members 23
Syed Akbaruddin

PART II FULFILLING THE RESPONSIBILITY

3. Improving the UN Response to Aggression and Mass Atrocities 41
Axel Marschik

4. Ensuring Criminal Accountability 55
Adama Dieng

PART III RESTRAINING THE VETO

5. Restoring the Legitimacy of the Security Council 73
Ian Johnstone

6. Restraining the Use of the Veto 91
Juan Manuel Gómez-Robledo and Pablo Arrocha Olabuenaga

PART IV REIMAGINING THE PARTNERS

7. Tapping the Full Potential of the General Assembly 109
Mona Ali Khalil

8. Reinforcing the International Court of Justice 127
Catherine Amirfar and Floriane Lavaud

9. Enforcing the Rome Statute and the Geneva Conventions 145
Fatou Bensouda

10. Strengthening Regional Cooperation 161
Boštjan Malovrh

Conclusion 179

Index 181

Foreword

Mohamed ElBaradei[*]

The book you are about to read could not be more timely or important.

As I and many others have observed, many if not all of the pillars of the post–World War II global order seem to be crumbling. Violent conflict has become the default method to settle disputes between states and within them. The permanent members' use of the veto to willfully block the Security Council from fulfilling its "primary responsibility for the maintenance of international peace and security" is not only morally unconscionable, but it also threatens to slide the multilateral security system into irrelevance. The erosion of respect for the fundamental principles and customary norms of international law is itself a threat to international peace and security.

Our world's geostrategic power structure is undergoing rapid and transformational change. Globalization and interdependence are the hallmark of our time. Existential threats like climate change, nuclear proliferation, pandemics, and artificial intelligence are global in nature and require global solutions. The United Nations and other UN system organizations provide the necessary fora for states to craft the solutions and set the rules for multilateral cooperation, to prevent and resolve conflicts, and to ensure accountability.

At a time when the fortitude of these multilateral institutions is absolutely imperative, it is ironic and dangerous that we find them losing authority and sometimes relevance. The Security Council, the jewel in the crown of the post–World War II architecture and the body entrusted with the primary responsibility to maintain international peace and security, has remained in a state of paralysis, unable to address the most pressing international crises of our time. Its composition reflects a bygone era, and its working methods are

[*] Mohamed ElBaradei served as Director General of the International Atomic Energy Agency (IAEA) from 1997 to 2009. He received the Nobel Peace Prize in 2005, jointly with the IAEA, "for their efforts to prevent nuclear energy from being used for military purposes and to ensure that nuclear energy for peaceful purposes is used in the safest possible way."

held hostage by the veto wielded by the permanent five members (P5). The Council's inability to act at crucial moments is nothing short of distressing.

In his remarks to the UN Human Rights Council on February 26, 2024, UN Secretary-General António Guterres recently lamented the Council's inability to act and said that it "has severely—perhaps fatally—undermined its authority." Calls for reforming the Council to meet changing circumstances date back decades. Despite a plethora of declarations and exhortations, little has been achieved. The sad reality is that amending the Charter of the United Nations in a way that is sufficient to meet the realities of today's world is possible but not plausible in the near future. Even if a two-thirds majority of UN member states could agree on the desired amendments to the Charter and ratify them in their respective constitutional processes, the Gordian knot lies in the difficulty (and more likely, impossibility) of getting all P5 members to ratify any such amendments in their respective constitutional processes as required by Article 108 of the Charter. As long as some or even all of the P5 members prefer to maintain the status quo, they will stand in the way of any amendment that would diminish their privileged position.

This book seeks to answer the question: Without amending the UN Charter, what steps can UN member states, UN organs, and UN partners take to maintain international peace and security in the face of such Council paralysis?

The authors—a group of prominent scholars and practitioners of international law and diplomacy, intimately familiar with the workings of the Security Council—understand that there can be no "ideal" structural reform of the Council without amending the Charter. But, like me, they understand that the best is the enemy of the good, and that there are still a few significant steps and important measures that could be taken to "fix" the Council processes and procedures to make it more representative and effective without amending the Charter.

The Council, as provided for in the Charter, performs its duties and responsibilities on behalf of all the members of the United Nations and adopts decisions that are legally binding on the entire UN membership. However, there is often a dichotomy between the views of the overwhelming majority of UN members and the views of one or more of the permanent members of the Council, often expressed through the veto power. The fear is that this trend of frustrating the will of the majority could lead over time to the Council losing further authority and relevance, and the world descending deeper into confusion and chaos.

With this in mind, the recommendations included in this book become ever more important to stop the Council's decline. They include improving the Council's representative character to align it with today's global power structure; empowering the nonpermanent members of the Council to be more than "birds of passage" elected for two years; restoring the Council's legitimacy and improving its transparency and accountability to public scrutiny; restraining thc use of the veto power, which often cripples the Council's ability to act, to the detriment of its legitimacy; improving the UN's ability to respond to crimes of aggression and other mass atrocity crimes through preventive measures, prompt responses, and by making use of preauthorized sanctions mechanisms; and by invoking the "Responsibility to Protect."

The authors have also understood and made it clear that for the Security Council to better function, it needs the support of other organs and organizations—primarily, the UN General Assembly and international courts. The General Assembly can tap the full potential of the "Uniting for Peace" resolution, as it has done in the past, to authorize peacekeeping missions or to adopt sanctions when the Council is paralyzed due to the veto power. The International Court of Justice (ICJ) could also play a mutually reinforcing role as foreseen in the UN Charter. The Security Council can seek ICJ advisory opinions, encourage states to accept the ICJ's jurisdiction, and enforce the ICJ's judgments when states fail to comply. The Council can also refer situations involving aggression and mass atrocity crimes to the International Criminal Court to uphold criminal accountability and end impunity. Finally, regional arrangements also have an invaluable role to play in preventive diplomacy; in the peaceful settlement of disputes; and in the implementation of collective measures, from peacekeeping to peace enforcement.

The book reinforces the symbiotic relationship between international law and international diplomacy to ensure that the Security Council can fulfill its primary responsibility as the cornerstone of the collective security system.

For those who wish to see the Security Council play its intended role in creating a more just, peaceful, and secure world based on international legitimacy and anchored in the rule of law, this book is a must-read.

Acknowledgments

We wish to thank His Excellency Mr. Mohamed ElBaradei for agreeing to write the foreword to our book; for capturing the essence of our message so clearly; and for reminding us that the erosion of respect for international law is itself a threat to international peace and security.

We are grateful to our distinguished contributors from every region of the world for their unity of purpose despite their diversity of perspectives and above all for their concrete proposals to empower the UN Security Council to be more effective in addressing modern threats.

We also wish to express our appreciation to Emma MacFarlane, Becca Murphy, Allison Perlin, and Caroline Wallace for their valuable assistance in ensuring the works are properly cited.

Abbreviations

ACT	Accountability, Coherence, and Transparency Group
AMIB	African Mission in Burundi
AO	advisory opinion
ASEAN	Association of Southeast Asian Nations
AU	African Union
A3	referring to the three elected African members
A3+1alliance	referring to the three elected African members plus SVG
CAR	Central African Republic
CARICOM	Caribbean Community
CIS	Commonwealth of Independent States
ECOWAS	Economic Community of West African States
EES	emergency extra session
ESS10	tenth emergency special session
ESS11	eleventh emergency special session
E10	referring to the nonpermanent or elected ten members of the UN Security Council
EUFOR	European Union Force
g7+	Group of Seven Plus
HRDDP	Human Rights Due Diligence Policy
IAEA	International Atomic Energy Agency
ICJ	International Court of Justice
ICC	International Criminal Court
ICISS	International Commission on Intervention and State Sovereignty
ICTR	International Criminal Tribunal for Rwanda
ICTY	International Criminal Tribunal for the Former Yugoslavia
IGN	intergovernmental negotiations
IIIM	International, Impartial, and Independent Mechanism
ILC	International Law Commission
IO	international organization
ISAF	International Security Assistance Force
ISIL	Islamic State of Iraq and the Levant
IWG	Informal Working Group on Documentation and Other Procedural Questions
LAS	League of Arab States
LDCs	least developed countries
MINUSTAH	the United Nations Stabilization Mission in Haiti

NAM	non-aligned movement
NATO	North Atlantic Treaty Organization
NPMs	nonpermanent members (of the Security Council); an older term for the E10
OAS	Organization of American States
ONUB	UN Operation in Burundi
OPT	Occupied Palestinian Territory
OSCE	Organization on Security and Co-operation in Europe
OTP	Office of the Prosecutor
PRP	Provisional Rules of Procedure
P5	referring to the permanent five members of the UN Security Council
RSF	Rapid Support Forces
R2P	Responsibility to Protect Doctrine
SAF	Sudanese Armed Forces
SIDS	small island developing states
SVG	Saint Vincent and the Grenadines
UDHR	Universal Declaration of Human Rights
UNAMID	United Nations–African Union Hybrid Operation in Darfur
UNCIO	United Nations Conference on International Organization
UNEF	UN Emergency Force
UNGA	UN General Assembly
UNOMIG	UN Observer Mission in Georgia
UNROD	UN Register of Damage
UNSC	UN Security Council
VCLT	Vienna Conventions on the Law of Treaties
WEOG	Western European and Other States Group

Contributors

Syed Akbaruddin Dean of the Kautilya School of Public Policy in Hyderabad, India, and former Permanent Representative of India to the United Nations (UN) in New York

Tareq AlBanai Permanent Representative of Kuwait to the UN in New York and Co-chair of the Intergovernmental Negotiations on Security Council Reform

Catherine Amirfar Partner at Debevoise & Plimpton and Co-chair of its International Dispute Resolution Group and Public International Law Group

Pablo Arrocha Olabuenaga is a Mexican diplomat, specialized in public international law, and an Affiliate of the Harvard Law School Program on International Law and Armed Conflict

Fatou Bensouda High Commissioner of the Gambia, former Prosecutor of the International Criminal Court , and former Minister of Justice of the Gambia

Adama Dieng President of the Pan-African Alliance for Transparency and Rule of Law, and former UN Special Advisor on the Prevention of Genocide

Juan Manuel Gómez-Robledo Judge of the International Court of Justice and former Deputy Permanent Representative of Mexico to the UN in New York

Ian Johnstone Professor of International Law at the Tufts Fletcher School of Law and Diplomacy and former adviser in the Executive Office of the UN Secretary-General

Mona Ali Khalil Director of MAK LAW, Affiliate of the Harvard Law School Program on International Law and Armed Conflict, and former UN Senior Legal Officer

Floriane Lavaud Senior Partner at Withersand Co-chair of the Arbitration Committee of the American Branch of the International Law Association

Boštjan Malovrh Permanent Representative of Slovenia to the UN in New York and former Deputy Head of Mission at the Slovenian Embassy in Beijing

Axel Marschik Permanent Representative of Austria to the UN in New York and Co-chair of the Intergovernmental Negotiations on Security Council Reform

Introduction

The international community looks to the United Nations Security Council (UNSC) to prevent aggression and mass atrocity crimes. As the principal organ entrusted with primary responsibility for the maintenance of international peace and security under the Charter of the United Nations, the Security Council's record since the turn of the millennium has been largely defined by failure and paralysis.

Three main challenges prevent the UNSC from fulfilling its primary responsibility more effectively as envisioned in the UN Charter. First, the composition of the membership of the UNSC is not regarded as representative of the broader membership of the UN or reflective of current geopolitical realities of the new world order. Second, the UNSC's failure to prevent and resolve conflict and to enforce its own resolutions has further undermined its credibility and legitimacy. Third, the five permanent members (P5) have used, or in fact misused, their veto power in a manner inconsistent with the Charter and customary international law.

The UNSC's Composition

The lack of equitable geographic representation is among the most-cited criticisms of the UNSC, in respect of both the permanent members as well as the nonpermanent or elected members (E10). The P5, namely China, France, Russia, the United States, and the United Kingdom, were accorded permanent seats and veto power as the Great Powers in 1945. These five are not necessarily the most economically, politically, or militarily powerful states in today's world, nor do they represent the majority of the world's population.

The permanent members do not include any states from Africa or from Latin America and the Caribbean. The current distribution of the ten elected seats magnifies the UNSC's lack of geographic representation. Article 23(1) of the UN Charter sets out explicit criteria for membership, mandating "due

Mona Ali Khalil and Floriane Lavaud, *Introduction* In: *Empowering the UN Security Council*. Edited by: Mona Ali Khalil and Floriane Lavaud, Oxford University Press. © Oxford University Press 2024.
DOI: 10.1093/oso/9780197780602.003.0001

regard" for "equitable geographic distribution" as well as for candidates' contributions to the maintenance of international peace and security and the other purposes of the UN.[1]

A 1963 resolution of the UN General Assembly (UNGA) provides the current distribution of the ten elected seats.[2] Pursuant to that resolution, the Western European and Other States Group (WEOG) holds two of the ten elected seats in addition to its three permanent seats. With one-seventh of the world's population, WEOG holds a total of five of the fifteen seats—a full third of the UNSC membership. The African Group and the Asian Group, which together make up five-sevenths of the world's population, hold five elected seats, in addition to China's permanent seat—nearly an equal proportion to WEOG, despite the disparity in population. The Latin American and Caribbean Group holds two elected seats, and the Eastern European Group holds one elected seat, in addition to Russia's permanent seat.

Moreover, the UNSC lacks equitable gender representation. Notwithstanding, Security Council resolution 1325 (2000)[3] promoting the participation of women in peace and security, , less than 25% of the current permanent representatives of UNSC members are women and less than 20% of the chairpersons of the UNSC committees and working groups are women.[4]

The UNSC's Failures

In its first forty-five years, the UNSC routinely fell into gridlock on account of the Cold War. In the 1990s and into the 2000s, the UNSC saw a surge of activity. The UNSC unanimously condemned Iraq's invasion of Kuwait in 1990 and authorized an international coalition to reverse the aggression; in the same decade, the UNSC established an unprecedented number of peacekeeping operations and sanctions regimes. However, in the last two decades, violations of the UN Charter by the P5 themselves have often impeded or even paralyzed the UNSC's broader efforts to maintain international peace and security. The impacts of the US and UK invasion of Iraq in 2003 and

[1] UN Charter art. 23(1).
[2] UN General Assembly, Resolution 1991 (XVIII), A/RES/1991 (XVIII) (Dec. 17, 1963).
[3] UN Security Council Resolution 1325 (2000), S/RES/1325 (2000) (Oct. 31, 2000).
[4] United Nations Security Council, "Women at the Security Council," accessed June 16, 2024, https://www.un.org/securitycouncil/content/women-security-council.

the Russian invasions of Ukraine in 2014 and 2022 are compounded by the UNSC's failure to take meaningful action in response to the mass atrocities in Syria, Myanmar, Palestine, Sudan and elsewhere.

The P5's Veto

The veto derives from Article 27(3) of the UN Charter, which states that decisions of the UNSC on all matters aside from procedural matters "shall be made by an affirmative vote of nine members including the concurring votes of the permanent members." This provision also imposes certain parameters on the use of the veto, stating that "in decisions under Chapter VI, and under paragraph 3 of Article 52, a party to a dispute shall abstain from voting."[5] Contrary to this absolute limitation, the P5 have nonetheless voted on and even vetoed resolutions under Chapter VI relating to disputes to which they are a party.[6] Most notably, Russia has repeatedly exercised the veto in respect to resolutions concerning its invasions of Ukraine, where it is undoubtedly a party to the dispute within the meaning of Article 27(3). In 2014, Russia vetoed a resolution condemning its annexation of Crimea in the Ukrainian peninsula.[7] Russia again wielded the veto in 2022, blocking a resolution that declared its invasion of Ukraine a violation of territorial integrity and calling for its immediate withdrawal.[8] The P5 have also vetoed resolutions related to disputes involving their allies. For example, since October 7, 2023, the United States has vetoed successive resolutions calling for humanitarian ceasefires in the conflict between Hamas and Israel in the Occupied Palestinian Territory.[9]

The exercise of the veto power by the P5—not only in respect of their own actions, but also on behalf of their allies—undermines the P5's credibility in upholding the UN Charter and impedes the UNSC responsibilities es under the Charter; doing so in situations involving genocide, war crimes and

[5] UN Charter art. 27(3).

[6] Security Council Report, "Article 27(3) and Parties to a Dispute: An Abridged History" (Apr. 2014), accessed June 16, 2024, https://www.securitycouncilreport.org/atf/cf/%7B65BFCF9B-6D27-4E9C-8CD3-CF6E4FF96FF9%7D/article_27_3_and_parties_to_a_dispute.pdf.

[7] UN Security Council, Draft Resolution S/2014/189 (Mar. 15, 2014).

[8] UN Security Council, Draft Resolution S/2022/720 (Sept. 30, 2022); UN Security Council, 9143rd mtg., UN Doc. S/PV.9143, 4 (Sept. 30, 2022).

[9] See, e.g., UN Security Council, Draft Resolution S/2023/773 (Oct. 18, 2023); UN Security Council, Draft Resolution S/2023/970 (Dec. 8, 2023).

crimes against humanity violates their *erga omnes* obligations under customary international law.

Section IV: Overview

To overcome the challenges and to empower the Security Council to be more effective, this book offers proposals to reform the Council without amending the UN Charter. In their Declaration on the Commemoration of the UN's Seventy-Fifth Anniversary, the heads of state and government unanimously recognized that "[t]here is no other global organization with the legitimacy, convening power, and normative impact of the United Nations. No other global organization gives hope to so many people for a better world and can deliver the future we want. The urgency for all countries to come together, to fulfil the promise of the nations united, has rarely been greater."[10]

In order to succeed in addressing modern challenges and existential threats, the UNSC and its members must fulfill their responsibility to act promptly and effectively to maintain international peace and security in a manner consistent with the purposes and principles of the United Nations. Many have written about the flaws and failures of the UN in general, and the Security Council in particular. This book focuses not on the problems, but on the solutions. In each of its four parts, the book and its distinguished authors from every region of the world set forth reforms and measures to empower the membership; to uphold the responsibility of the permanent members, including with respect to the exercise of their veto; to restore the legitimacy of Security Council action; and to reimagine the partners in the effort to maintain international peace and security and uphold the international rule of law.

Part I seeks to empower the voices and improve the composition of the E10. Its proposals bring to life the principles embedded in the UN Charter. Part I contains two chapters. Chapter 1 recalls the duties and responsibilities of the Security Council, acting on behalf of the UN membership, for the maintenance of international peace and security and the other purposes of the United Nations. Chapter 2 discusses reforms and working methods that empower the ten elected members to fulfill the UNSC's mandate.

[10] UN General Assembly, Resolution 75/1, A/RES/75/1 (Sept. 28, 2020).

Part II proposes tools to uphold the primary responsibility of the UNSC in accordance with Article 24 of the UN Charter. These tools cover the prevention of, response to, and accountability for threats to international peace and security and violations of international law. Part II contains two chapters. Chapter 3 considers improvements to the UN's response to aggression and mass atrocity crimes, including through a preauthorized sanctions mechanism. Chapter 4 examines how UN member states may ensure criminal accountability for violations of international law.

Part III discusses waysto restrain the use of the veto. The veto power prevents the UNSC from fulfilling its responsibility to address serious threats to international peace and security. Absent a renewed commitment to applicable legal principles and norms, the misuse of the veto power foretells a diminishing role for the UNSC in the new world order. Part III contains two chapters. Chapter 5 discusses how to restore the legitimacy of the UN Security Council. Chapter 6 analyzes the existing initiatives seeking to set voluntary limits on the exercise of the veto and explores how the customary international law of *jus cogens* applies to the veto power.

Part IV reimagines the internal and external partners for peace and justice. Part IV contains four chapters. Chapter 7 focuses on the untapped powers of the UN General Assembly (UNGA) under the "Uniting for Peace" Resolution to ensure a more robust UN response to aggression and mass atrocity crimes when the UNSC is unable to act due to a veto..[11] Chapter 8 focuses on UNSC tools to reinforce the International Court of Justice (ICJ), such as encouraging states to accept its jurisdiction and refer their legal disputes for adjudication, requesting advisory opinions, and enforcing its judgments. Chapter 9 calls for the enforcement of the Rome Statute of the International Criminal Court and the Geneva Conventions. Chapter 10 describes opportunities for strengthening cooperation with regional organizations and other security arrangements in accordance with Chapter VIII of the UN Charter.

This book reflects the practical perspectives of authors from every region of the world: diplomats who have played key roles in the Security Council, senior officials who have worked at the highest levels of the UN Secretariat, international lawyers who have appeared before the ICJ and a former prosecutor of the ICC, as well as notable scholars..

[11] UN General Assembly, Resolution 377 (V) (Nov. 3, 1950).

We have come together to offer a roadmap to a more legitimate and effective Security Council—one that is willing and able to address modern threats to international peace and security. In light of the converging crises and existential threats, we believe that there is a realistic possibility borne out of the imperative of necessity to meaningfully reform the Security Council so that it can better serve current and future generations of humankind.

PART I

EMPOWERING THE MEMBERSHIP

1
Respecting the UN Charter

*Tareq Albanai**

Introduction

At the heart of the United Nations, the Security Council stands as the pinnacle of collective efforts to maintain the global order. In upholding the principles enshrined in the UN Charter—specifically, Articles 23, 24, and 25 that set out its composition, functions, and decision-making processes—the Security Council wields the most power and assumes primary responsibility for the maintenance of international peace and security. This chapter sets forth the foundational understanding of the Council's composition and mandates as envisioned in the Charter, serving as a prelude to the broader discourse on reform.

The international landscape has evolved dramatically since the founding of the UN, presenting new challenges that test the limits of the Security Council's original design and capabilities. The demands for a Council reflective of the current geopolitical realities are growing louder, calling into question not only the legitimacy but the viability of the Council to carry out its mandate. Since its inception, UN membership has increased from 51 to 193 member states, while Council reform has hardly kept apace. Membership in the Council expanded only once, changing from six elected members to ten in 1965; there was no corresponding change to the permanent membership.

A frustrated membership resents the paralysis borne of the five permanent members' (P5) exercise of the veto to block necessary Security Council action. An increasing number of governments and people around the world see the Council as both ineffective and unfair, controlled by unaccountable powers that are more likely to exploit their authority than to safeguard peace.

* The views expressed in this chapter are exclusively the author's views in his personal capacity and do not reflect any opinion of or attribution to the State of Kuwait's Ministry of Foreign Affairs.

Tareq Albanai, *Respecting the UN Charter* In: *Empowering the UN Security Council*. Edited by: Mona Ali Khalil and Floriane Lavaud, Oxford University Press. © Oxford University Press 2024.
DOI: 10.1093/oso/9780197780602.003.0002

The UN membership has sought to reform the Security Council—both its composition and its working methods—to restore its credibility and effectiveness. However, UN member states have deadlocked over the shape of any reform. There are many obstacles to reform, including the difficulties in amending the UN Charter and the lack of consensus among UN member states about the number and nature of new seats and whether the veto should extend to any new permanent members. Most significantly, reform of the Council's composition or voting rules requires approval of two-thirds of UN member states and ratification within their respective domestic legal systems, including those of the P5. This chapter focuses on practical solutions to Security Council reform, moving beyond efforts to change the composition or voting rules of the Council, which require amending the Charter. Through an analytical lens, the chapter elucidates the procedural nuances and multifaceted dynamics at play in the Council's processes. It navigates the complexities of international diplomacy, revealing how procedural elements and other factors influence the Council's responses to global crises and challenges.

Section I delves into the vital contributions of both permanent and nonpermanent members of the Security Council, examining their roles under Article 23 of the Charter in the Council's deliberations and decision-making. Section II discusses how the Security Council may more effectively carry out its mandate under Article 24, focusing on horizon scanning, targeted missions, and other forms of regional arrangements. Section III discusses Article 25, the cornerstone of the collective international security system, which obliges member states to accept and carry out the decisions of the Council. Finally, the chapter concludes with some forward-looking thoughts on reform and the Council's role in today's geopolitical climate.

Section I. The Composition and Dynamics of the UN Security Council under Article 23

Article 23 of the UN Charter lays out the composition of the Security Council, stipulating that the Council shall consist of fifteen members of the United Nations. It establishes five permanent members, namely China, France, Russia, the United Kingdom, and the United States. Article 23 also states that the General Assembly shall elect ten other UN member states to serve two-year terms as nonpermanent members, "due regard being specially paid, in the first instance to the contribution of Members of the United Nations to the maintenance of international peace and security and to the other purposes of the Organization, and also to equitable geographical distribution."[1]

A. Equity and accountability in Security Council membership: evaluating contribution and commitment

A 1965 General Assembly resolution dictates the current composition of the ten elected seats, wherein the Western European and Other States Group (WEOG), with one-seventh of the world's population, holds five of the fifteen seats, including three of the five permanent seats; Africa and Asia, which together make up five-sevenths of the world's population, hold six seats, including one permanent seat; Latin America and the Caribbean hold three seats, with no permanent seat; and Eastern Europe holds two seats, including one permanent seat. While the General Assembly cannot expand the number of seats without amending the UN Charter, it can adopt a new resolution redistributing the ten seats in a more equitable manner to enhance the Council's representativeness and responsiveness to the new global order.

The question of who is eligible to sit on the Security Council is an even more provocative and contentious issue. What does "contribution . . . to the maintenance of international peace and security" truly entail? Does it include states that participate in military operations under Chapter VII, peacekeeping deployments under Chapter VI, or peaceful settlement of disputes also under Chapter VI of the UN Charter? Does it exclude states that violate the UN Charter or commit gross violations of international law; states that are aggressor states or occupying powers; states that commit genocide or other mass atrocity crimes? How can such states be eligible for a role that is fundamentally about maintaining peace? The current geopolitical dynamics often see such countries not only participating in the Security Council but wielding significant power within it.

The "other purposes of the Organization" mentioned in Article 23 may include promoting human rights, encouraging the peaceful settlement of disputes, fostering social and economic development, and upholding international law. Each of these is a vital purpose of the UN and should arguably be a prerequisite for membership in its most powerful principal organ. As a

[1] UN Charter art. 23.

matter of principle, member states should not support the election of states to the Security Council that have poor human rights records or have been responsible for aggression or mass atrocity crimes. However, the practice is far removed from principle, and often geopolitical alliances and strategic interests overshadow the foundational values of the UN. It is a complex issue, but one that requires urgent attention if the Security Council is to remain credible and effective in the face of twenty-first-century challenges.

The criteria set out in Article 23 of the UN Charter for the nonpermanent members implicitly acknowledge that a state's actions in support of peace and security, human rights, and the other purposes of the United Nations are vital considerations for election to the Council. Indeed, these are the principal factors influencing the legitimacy and effectiveness of member states' actions undertaken pursuant to their Council duties. If such contributions are a measure of legitimacy and effectiveness for nonpermanent members, then logically, these considerations are even more pertinent for the permanent members given their greater power and permanent responsibility. Holding a permanent seat on the Council should come with the expectation of upholding the highest standards in contributing to international peace and security. The permanent members must be cognizant of the impact that their contributions to peace and security, and their violations of international law, have on their own legitimacy and effectiveness, as well as on the legitimacy and effectiveness of the Security Council as a whole.

The Charter's requirement that nonpermanent members must contribute to peace and security suggests that their eligibility is dynamic, based on ongoing actions and their commitment to the UN's goals. This dynamic approach stands in stark contrast to the static nature of the permanent seats, which are held without regard to the changing international landscape or the current actions of the permanent members. It is counterintuitive to exempt permanent members from the very criteria that are deemed essential for nonpermanent members, especially considering their significant influence on the Council's deliberations and decision-making.

A reformed Security Council may require the General Assembly to establish a mechanism to assess the eligibility of member states running for a seat. The UN membership should only consider states who have demonstrated a commitment to the UN's principles and contributed to the UN's purposes. This mechanism could take into account not just the candidate state's contributions to international peace and security, but also its human rights and humanitarian record. After all, a member state's actions both within and beyond its borders speak volumes about its willingness to abide by the principles of the United Nations and its ability to carry out the duties of the Security Council.

B. E10 unity: power in numbers

The unity of the ten elected nonpermanent members (E10) of the Security Council is crucial in ensuring that the Council operates not merely as a reflection of the interests of its permanent members but as a body that represents the entire membership of the United Nations. The ten elected members, by virtue of their election by the General Assembly, carry the voice of the international community. They represent not just their regional interests, but also the collective interest in maintaining international peace and security.

E10 unity takes on a significant role in the geopolitical theater, where the balance of power can be disproportionately skewed by the P5's veto power. The veto enables any of the P5 to unilaterally block any substantive resolution, potentially paralyzing the Council's ability to fulfill its duties and responsibilities. A concerted stance by the E10, potentially leading to a collective boycott of the decision-making process by denying the required majority of nine affirmative votes, can therefore serve as a powerful statement against the use of the veto in circumstances where it may undermine the very principles and purposes of the United Nations. Such a boycott would not be without precedent or risk, but it would underscore the need for the Security Council to act as a unified body dedicated to the maintenance of international peace and security rather than one beholden to the interests of a few powerful states.

Through this unique collective power, the E10 may leverage their moral and political authority to challenge the status quo. The decision to collectively boycott the decision-making process is a radical yet potent form of protest. This action can send a resounding message to the international community and the permanent members themselves: that the democratic spirit of the United Nations must prevail over the interests of a select albeit powerful few.

A boycott could manifest in various forms, from abstaining en masse during votes to a coordinated withdrawal from certain discussions, thereby stalling the Council's proceedings. In the short term, the risk here is considerable: the boycotting members could face political backlash, both from the veto-wielding power and from allies of that power. Moreover, a boycott could compromise the effectiveness of the Security Council in addressing urgent international crises. However, the long-term implications of a successful boycott could inspire more responsible use of the veto by the P5 and, at a minimum, could initiate a much-needed dialogue on reforming the veto system.

The underlying intent of the proposed E10 boycott would not be to create a permanent rift within the Security Council, but to reaffirm the fundamental principles upon which the UN was founded: to maintain international peace and security through a collective rather than selective approach. It is a call for the Security Council to operate as a truly representative organ reflective of the international community's aspirations, not merely the strategic interests of its permanent members.

The E10 could also unite to push for a broader reform of the Security Council, advocating for changes that would address the current asymmetries of power within the body and making the use of the veto a matter of last resort, only in the most exceptional circumstances, as originally conceived by the architects of the UN Charter.[2] Furthermore, such an action would highlight the need for a mechanism within the UN General Assembly that addresses the perceived misuse of the veto power. It could propel the United Nations toward a more democratic process, where the use of the veto would be subject to international scrutiny and the concerns of the nonpermanent members would carry more weight in the decision-making process. The standing mandate for a General Assembly debate when a veto is cast in the Security Council is a first step toward such a mechanism.[3]

In essence, the unity and potential collective action of the nonpermanent members serve as a safeguard against the misuse of the veto power. E10 unity is also a powerful catalyst for the evolution of the Security Council into a body that upholds the universal values and collective will of the international community for peace and security, as well as for justice and human rights. It is a reminder that while the Security Council is tasked with the maintenance of international peace and security, it must also adhere to the most

[2] "The Secretary of State to the United States Representative at the United Nations," *in Foreign Relations of the United States*, Diplomatic Papers, 1945, General: The United Nations, Volume I, eds. Velma Hastings Cassidy et al. (1967),1133–34 ("It is not to be assumed, however, that the permanent members, any more than the nonpermanent members, would use their 'veto' power wilfully to obstruct the operation of the Council"); Arthur Boutellis, "Lessons from E10 Engagement on the Security Council," *International Peace Institute* (November 2022): 5.

[3] See UN General Assembly, Resolution 76/262, A/RES/76/262 (Apr. 28, 2022).

basic of principles enshrined in the Charter, including the sovereign equality of states. This evolution would contribute to making the Council a more equitable and democratic body—one that is better equipped to fulfill its responsibilities under the UN Charter in the twenty-first century.

Section II. The Balancing Act: The Security Council's Mandate under Article 24

Article 24 of the UN Charter outlines the obligations of the Security Council in its efforts to maintain international peace and security, through three main aspects:

- *Primary Responsibility of the Security Council:* Article 24 entrusts the Security Council with primary responsibility for the maintenance of international peace and security. This responsibility encompasses identifying threats; taking appropriate actions to resolve disputes peacefully; and preventing and responding to any threat to the peace, breach of the peace, or act of aggression.
- *Duties of the Security Council:* Article 24 requires the Council to take prompt and effective action on behalf of the UN membership and, in discharging these duties, to "act in accordance with the Purposes and Principles of the United Nations."[4]
- *Powers and Authority of the Security Council:* The Charter grants the Security Council significant powers and authority to carry out its duties and responsibilities. The Council possesses the authority to examine any dispute or situation whose continuance is likely to threaten international peace and security. It can make recommendations or authorize peacekeeping operations under Chapter VI, impose sanctions or authorize military action under Chapter VII, or utilize regional security arrangements or agencies for preventive or enforcement actions under Chapter VIII of the UN Charter.

Power dynamics as well as the diversity of states' views and conflicting interests often hinder the effective functioning of the Security Council. One of the inherent challenges of an intergovernmental organization is the

[4] UN Charter art. 42.

tendency of its member states to prioritize their own national interests over collective security objectives—trapping themselves in a zero-sum dynamic rather than seeking a win-win scenario. This can deadlock negotiations in the Security Council, making it difficult to take decisive action in addressing threats to peace and security. Power dynamics among the permanent members of the Security Council also impede the Council's ability to fulfill its mandate. The veto power, as wielded by some of the permanent members, allows them to paralyze the Council even when a resolution enjoys widespread support from the rest of the UN member states.

The Security Council does not only have responsibility to respond to conflicts and other crises when they arise; perhaps more important, the Council has responsibility to prevent conflicts in the first place. The fifth Secretary-General of the UN, Javier Pérez de Cuéllar, on the occasion of the fortieth anniversary of the United Nations, stated:

> Crises have frequently been brought before the Council too late for preventive action; it would seem to follow that the Council might well establish a procedure to keep the world under continuing survey in order to detect nascent causes of tension.[5]

Nearly forty years later, the Council continues to face challenges in its ongoing efforts to streamline this process. Over time, Secretaries-General have occasionally assumed proactive and autonomous roles in identifying issues or possible risks to global peace and security. They would then informally communicate these concerns to Council members during consultations or at the monthly luncheons organized by the president of the Security Council. The Secretary-General or designated senior UN officials have also provided briefings on current or emerging security matters. To adapt to the evolving nature of global conflicts and geopolitical complexities, the Council must increasingly embrace proactive strategies and preventive diplomacy, and take preemptive measures, such as horizon scanning; initiating short, targeted missions; and dispatching envoys for specific peacekeeping or diplomatic endeavors.

Horizon scanning is a strategic approach to anticipate potential conflict. The Security Council employs horizon scanning to proactively identify and evaluate potential threats to international peace and security before

[5] UN SCOR, 2608th mtg. at para. 15, UN Doc. S/PV.2608 (Sept. 26, 1985).

they develop into full-scale conflicts. This process entails the meticulous gathering and analysis of intelligence, careful monitoring of global political trends, and utilization of early warning systems to pinpoint emerging risks. By adopting a proactive stance, the Council positions itself to better fulfill its mandate to prevent conflicts through timely diplomatic efforts and targeted interventions.

To enhance the efficacy of horizon scanning, the Council relies on regular briefings from the Secretary-General and senior officials, who provide insights into potential conflicts based on their recent visits to various regions or country teams on the ground. Additionally, maintaining an efficient flow of information between the Secretariat and the Council is vital for ensuring that the Council does not miss opportunities for action. The Council should employ a standardized format for these critical briefings to ensure consistency and coherence while maintaining conciseness and concreteness.

To remedy this, there should be a consistent practice of receiving regular political and security updates from the Secretary-General and the Secretariat as well as early warning briefings from the high commissioner for human rights. The broader UN membership ought to encourage and adopt these briefings as a routine aspect of the Council's operations, thereby reducing the likelihood of inaction in the face of emerging threats.

Short, targeted missions are another vital tool available to the Security Council to uphold its obligations under Article 24 of the Charter. Nimble and specific in nature, these missions provide the Council the means to rapidly engage with unfolding situations on the ground. They are meticulously designed to respond to particular crises or issues that pose a threat to international peace and security. Moreover, their limited duration ensures a concentrated and time-sensitive response, with clear objectives set to achieve measurable outcomes within a specified timeframe. Targeted missions may take various forms, including fact-finding missions to gather on-the-ground intelligence and assess the situation firsthand, or mediation endeavors aimed at deescalating tensions and fostering dialogue between parties to the conflict.

The Council's deployment of these short, targeted missions reflects its recognition of the need for a versatile and dynamic response mechanism. With the swift and effective insertion of the Council's presence in conflicts, targeted missions could potentially avert escalation and contribute to international peace and security. It is crucial to ensure that these missions do not lose their reactive edge and become solely information-gathering exercises.

One way to prevent this is through establishing a protocol for rapid deployment, ensuring that the necessary logistical, political, and strategic support is readily available. This would involve close coordination with UN member states, regional organizations,[6] and other stakeholders to mobilize resources and expertise quickly.

Similar to the Secretary-General's appointment of special envoys and special representatives, the Security Council, in its pursuit of more efficient and regionally informed decision-making processes, may appoint UN member states as representatives for specific files, with a preference for delegating roles to countries within the same geographic region. This approach would leverage the appointed member state's geographic proximity and deeper regional understanding. The designated representative would organize and conduct country visits to facilitate firsthand insight and engagement with the local situation. This would enhance the Security Council's effectiveness by incorporating more localized perspectives into its deliberations, ultimately contributing to a more nuanced and effective Council.

These strategies reflect the Security Council's recognition that maintaining international peace and security is not only about reacting to crises, but also about preventing them. However, these efforts are sometimes hampered by the challenges inherent within the Council's structure and the political will of its members. The effectiveness of these strategies is often contingent upon the unity and consensus among UN member states, particularly the permanent members with veto power.

Section III. Enforcing Global Decisions: The Role and Challenges of Article 25 of the UN Charter

In accordance with Article 25 of the UN Charter, member states are obliged to accept and carry out the decisions of the UN Security Council; moreover, they are expected to take any necessary measures to implement the Council's decisions within their national legal frameworks. Article 25 emphasizes the importance of collective action and the responsibility of member states to uphold the decisions adopted by the Council. It also confers a significant role upon the Security Council in the enforcement of decisions made under its authority.

[6] See further chapter 10, "Strengthening Regional Cooperation."

Article 25 is the cornerstone of the UN's collective security system, and crucial for the functioning and credibility of the United Nations and its Security Council. It ensures that the decisions taken by the Council are not mere recommendations (like those of the General Assembly), but binding obligations on member states. Article 25 underscores the commitments of UN member states—both to act collectively in carrying out the Council's decisions and to comply with those decisions themselves. This applies in particular to the Council's decisions adopted under Chapter VII of the Charter that impose measures, up to and including the use of force, to maintain or restore international peace and security, and to prevent or respond to threats to peace, breaches of the peace, or acts of aggression. By complying with the implied responsibilities of Article 25, member states uphold the principles of the UN Charter and international law, preserve the effectiveness and credibility of the Council, and contribute to the maintenance of international peace and security.

In theory, Article 25 should serve as a deterrent against state noncompliance with Security Council decisions; in practice, the deterrent effect has not materialized from the provisions of Article 25 alone. While Article 25 sets out state obligations, it does not explicitly outline the consequences for member states that fail to fulfill them.

Here, the Council's power to impose measures under Chapter VII plays a crucial role in ensuring member state compliance with their obligations pursuant to Article 25. In particular, sanctions are a key tool at the disposal of the Security Council to enforce its decisions. Sanctions can range from economic measures, such as trade embargoes and financial restrictions, to diplomatic and political sanctions. The Council may exercise these measures to put pressure on noncompliant states and encourage them to act in accordance with the Council's decisions. In cases where the Council has exhausted peaceful means and enforcement measures not involving the use of force, or where those means are deemed to be or have proven to be ineffective, it may authorize the use of force. It can authorize individual or collective military action by member states, enlist the assistance of regional arrangements, or resort to other collective security alternatives.

Beyond the duties that Article 25 imposes upon UN member states, the Responsibility to Protect (R2P) Doctrine emerged in the early 2000s as a normative framework underscoring the duty of states, and by extension the international community, to protect populations from mass atrocities. The first pillar of R2P recognizes that states have the primary responsibility to protect their populations. The second pillar confirms that the international community has a responsibility to assist when a state is unable to fulfill its responsibility. The third pillar confirms the international community's commitment to intervene, through the Security Council, when a state is either unwilling to fulfill its obligation to protect its population, or is itself committing the mass atrocities.

The Security Council has the power to authorize the necessary measures for collective intervention under R2P. This could lead to a range of options to encourage international peace and security and protect populations from mass atrocity crimes. The Council may employ a graduated response, beginning with diplomatic initiatives and culminating, as a last resort, in military intervention under Chapter VII.

One of the major critiques of the Security Council in particular and the United Nations in general is the issue of double standards or selective enforcement. Certain states consistently manage to evade the repercussions that others might face—some due to their P5 status and accompanying veto power, and others due to their alliance with the P5 states. Member states' trust in the UN as an institution is eroding due to the perceived and actual bias embedded within the UN's structure, further compounded by narrow political interests. Various agenda items under discussion in the Council often raise this point. Most recently, the agenda item on the situation in the Middle East and the Palestinian question have magnified the extraordinary humanitarian costs of selective enforcement.

Another dangerous development is the proposition by some members of the Security Council, including the permanent members, that they will not support resolutions on the grounds that the states in question might not enforce them. This stance poses a double challenge, venturing into precarious territory that could undermine both Article 25 and Chapter VII of the UN Charter, and undercutting the very foundation of the Council's authority. The Council would forfeit its authority and credibility should a practice emerge whereby the imposition of Council measures is subject to the consent of the noncompliant state.

In sum, the Security Council must discharge its duties in accordance with the UN's purposes and principles and all member states must accept and carry out the Council's decisions, especially those adopted under Chapter VII. The international community must call for and ensure equal application and consistent enforcement of the law. The Security Council must fulfill its role of ensuring member states are equally bound by the Charter and consistently held to account for any violations thereof. This would uphold the credibility and authority of the United Nations, the promises embedded within the UN Charter, and the protections afforded by international law.

Conclusion

The legitimacy and effectiveness of the Security Council relies on compliance with Articles 23, 24, and 25 of the UN Charter. The international community almost universally regards the Council's permanent membership, designed in the wake of World War II, as misaligned with the geopolitical realities of the twenty-first century. The anachronistic nature of the permanent membership, inequitable regional distribution of the nonpermanent seats, and P5 abuse of the veto power have led to calls for reform not only to expand the permanent membership but also to restrain the use of the veto.

The Security Council's credibility and capacity to maintain international peace and security have been compromised by the lack of responsibility of its permanent members and the lack of representativeness of its nonpermanent members. In essence, the uniquely paralyzing power of the unilateral veto betrays and defeats the principle of primary responsibility and the purpose of collective security that underpin the mandate of the Security Council at the heart of the UN Charter. To restore its legitimacy and effectiveness, the Security Council must embody and embrace a more equitable, representative, and accountable structure in accordance with Articles 23 and 24 of the UN Charter.

Reform must address not only the composition of the Council, but also the decision-making processes. Any reform should encourage greater responsibility of the P5, greater unity among the E10, and greater cooperation between the permanent and nonpermanent members. In particular, the unity of the E10 has great potential to challenge the status quo and catalyze meaningful change. By embodying the collective will of the broader UN membership, the E10 can assert the democratic ethos of the organization and press for a Security Council that is both responsive and responsible in its stewardship of global peace and security.

Looking ahead, the Security Council must enforce its decisions more proactively. This means ensuring respect for Article 25 by all member states, in particular when the Council is acting under Chapter VII. Upholding the collective security system is essential for the fulfillment of the UN's mission.

As the world continues to navigate complex international crises and shifts in the geopolitical balance of power, the need for a reformed Security Council has never been more pressing. It is imperative that the Council not only adapts to the changing landscape, but also upholds the founding principles of the UN Charter. Only through such reforms can the Security Council maintain its relevance and effectiveness, reflecting the aspirations of the international community for peace and security for all nations, and justice and human rights for all people.

2
Empowering the Elected Members

Syed Akbaruddin

Introduction

The United Nations Security Council (UNSC) is the second attempt of the twentieth century at a collective security mechanism to address international peace and security. In the aftermath of World War I, forty-one states launched the League of Nations. Nearly twenty years later, this first effort failed to prevent the outbreak of World War II. In 1945, fifty states met to draft the UN Charter and established the United Nations on October 24, 1945,[1] entrusting the Security Council with primary responsibility for the maintenance of international peace and security.

Designed to address the inadequacies of its predecessor and prevent another world war, the architects of the United Nations endowed the Council with authority that distinguishes it from other multilateral institutions. The UN Charter gave the UNSC the authority and responsibility for making legally binding decisions on behalf of all UN member states. The Council has powers to enforce its decisions through various measures, up to and including authorizing military force.[2] Enshrined in this unique collective security mechanism are the special rights and permanent roles of the victors of World War II. The Charter refers to the members the General Assembly elects as the nonpermanent members (NPMs), as they have two-year term limits. By design, some UN member states are more equal than others.

Article 27 of the Charter requires a specified majority of affirmative Council member votes to adopt UNSC resolutions, including the concurring vote of the five permanent members (P5).[3] Generally, UN member states

[1] Although representatives of fifty States met to draft the UN Charter at the San Francisco Conference, Poland signed the Charter shortly thereafter and became one of the founding UN members, bringing the total number to fifty-one.

[2] UN Charter; see especially arts. 1, 25, 41, 42.

[3] UN Charter art. 27.

Syed Akbaruddin, *Empowering the Elected Members* In: *Empowering the UN Security Council.* Edited by: Mona Ali Khalil and Floriane Lavaud, Oxford University Press. © Oxford University Press 2024.
DOI: 10.1093/oso/9780197780602.003.0003

interpret the P5 as concurring if they do not cast a negative vote, commonly called a veto.[4] The UNSC consisted of eleven members at its inception in 1945 (with a total UN membership of fifty-one), composed of the P5 and six NPMs. To pass a resolution, seven Council members needed to vote in its favor. In 1965, the NPMs increased from six to ten, and UNSC membership grew to fifteen. Still, the increase in UNSC membership did not change the sway of the permanent members in decision-making. It only changed the requisite majority to nine affirmative votes; all substantive resolutions are still subject to the P5 veto.[5]

The rationale for the lasting presence and privileges of the permanent members was threefold: the Great Powers would provide a measure of stability, prevent global conflagration, and use their military capabilities in enforcement actions when required. In short, with the UNSC, the UN architects envisioned the great powers of the time as a coalition of permanent members leading a liberal international organization notionally representing "We the Peoples."[6] The dominance of the P5 has led to the UNSC's depiction as a mechanism of "Five to Rule Them All."[7]

Efforts to address this inherent inequity through UNSC reform are almost as old as the institution itself. However, a perspicacious observer once remarked, "The history of reform seems like an ironic joke, a trap set by a malevolent deity.... The trickster laid the plans in 1945, inducing the victors of World War II to assign themselves veto power."[8] There is a very high bar for ringing in changes to the UN Charter. States disagree about the size and types of members eligible for prospective new permanent positions; they hold divergent views on the veto provisions; and they have expressed uncertainty about whether reform will lead to better representativeness and legitimacy, or instead undermine the Council's efficiency and efficacy. All of these concerns make substantive reform a daunting task.[9]

[4] Security Council Report, "The Veto," (Oct. 2015), accessed June 13, 2024, https://www.securitycouncilreport.org/atf/cf/%7B65BFCF9B-6D27-4E9C-8CD3-CF6E4FF96FF9%7D/research_report_3_the_veto_2015.pdf.

[5] See UN Charter art. 27(2)–(3).

[6] See UN Charter, preamble.

[7] See generally David Bosco, *Five to Rule Them All: The UN Security Council and the Making of the Modern World* (Oxford: Oxford University Press, 2009).

[8] Barry O'Neill, "Power and Satisfaction in the United Nations Security Council," *Journal of Conflict Resolution* 40, no. 2 (1996): 236.

[9] *See* Stewart Patrick et al., *UN Security Council Reform: What the World Thinks*, Carnegie Endowment for International Peace (2023), accessed June 13, 2024, https://carnegieendowment.org/2023/06/28/un-security-council-reform-what-world-thinks-pub-90032.

As structural reform efforts have not yielded dividends—except for the increase of NPMs in 1965—using gradual changes as an empowerment tool has been the only option. Adjusting processes and shaping procedures to enhance accountability, improve transparency, and incrementally expand the roles of NPMs has been the name of the game on the UNSC's uneven playing field. Procedural improvement of the UNSC's decision-making has become the narrow path on which reform has crawled ahead for decades.

Even when the UNSC was gridlocked during the Cold War, the consistent caucusing of the members of the non-aligned movement (NAM) in the Security Council to arrange a common position and derive strength from their numbers meant a NAM caucus room had to be set up within the precincts of the Council's antechamber. While the NAM caucus has since withered away, the room is a testimony to an unfulfilled desire of the elected members to carve out a distinctive role for themselves amidst the dominance of the P5.

This chapter explores the uneven playing field that is the Security Council. Section I tracks the evolution of the nonpermanent members from "birds of passage," elected for two-year terms, to more active actors focused on their elected status rather than their temporary incumbency. Section II describes the gradual change in the working methods of the Council by adjusting processes and shaping procedures to enhance accountability, improve transparency, and strengthen the role of the elected members. The chapter concludes that notwithstanding these modest improvements, the anachronistic concert of powers and the lack of representativeness continue to bedevil the Council.

Section I: Evolution of Players

The phase of post–Cold War activism witnessed several new initiatives that unlocked the UNSC's potential to contribute to resolving serious international peace and security issues.[10] These included setting up of ad-hoc international criminal tribunals, encouraging visiting missions of UNSC members to assess the ground situation, establishing multidimensional peacekeeping operations, authorizing non-UN operations, and the like.

[10] See *The UN Security Council in the 21st Century*, eds. Sebastian von Einseidel, David M. Malone, and Bruno Stagno Ugarte (Boulder: Lynne Rienner Publishers, 2015): 1–24.

The UNSC increased the scope of its competence to address a wide range of threats and developed a broad spectrum of diplomatic, legal, and operational tools.[11]

All UN member states contributed to this dynamic phase of the UNSC's evolution. Nonetheless, academic studies focusing on the formal status of members and voting requirements of the Council suggested that "a fair approximation as far as voting is concerned is that the Security Council has five members."[12] If power is the ability of an individual state to impact the outcome of a particular vote, each state without veto holds "almost no power."[13] Studies also concluded that since the voting power of an NPM is minuscule, adding more NPMs only further diminishes the already limited voting power of the NPMs.[14]

Accounts of many distinguished diplomatic practitioners who served on the UNSC in this activist phase confirm the academics' findings on P5 dominance. Some recorded that the role of the NPMs was relegated to rubber-stamping decisions reached among the P5 or choosing between contending positions staked out by the P5.[15] Others wrote of their stillborn efforts at reforming the working methods of the UNSC.[16] In short, the commonly held understanding of P5 dominance within the UNSC remains steadfast, despite the fact that the NPMs have leverage of their own should they have the will to use it; that is, denying the P5 the affirmative votes necessary to achieve the required majority.

As the post–Cold War era gives way to an uncertain global order, the activist phase of the UNSC has transitioned to one of fragmented UN diplomacy. In an increasingly polarized world, the permanent members are often divided into two opposing camps—one consisting of the United States, the United Kingdom, and France (together, the P3), and the other consisting of the People's Republic of China and the Russian Federation. The UNSC faces a crisis of relevance and representativeness. Its effectiveness is doubted, its

[11] See *United Nations Security Council Conflict Management Handbook*, eds. Haidi Willmot and Scott Sheeran (Abu Dhabi: Anwar Gargash Diplomatic Academy, 2023) co-authored by Adriana Abdenur, Renata Dwan, Richard Gowan, Ian Johnstone, Colin Keating, Mona Ali Khalil, and Paul Williams.

[12] Barry O'Neill, "Power and Satisfaction in the United Nations Security Council," *Journal of Conflict Resolution* 40, no. 2 (1996): 219–37.

[13] Ibid.

[14] Ibid.

[15] See Colin Keating, "Power Dynamics between Permanent and Elected Members," in *The UN Security Council in the 21st Century* (Boulder: Lynne Rienner Publishers, 2015).

[16] See Kishore Mahbubani, "Council Reform and the Emerging Powers," in *The UN Security Council in the 21st Century* (Boulder: Lynne Rienner Publishers, 2015).

credibility challenged, and its legitimacy questioned—even though there is no other effective global forum to address international peace and security matters. The deep divisions have further dimmed the already limited prospects of UNSC reform.

Nevertheless, visible changes in the practical functioning of the UNSC have been evident during the last two decades. The NPMs are playing more active roles than before, and now referred to collectively as the Elected 10 (E10) rather than the NPMs, the latter term being a holdover from UN Charter language. The new nomenclature has enhanced the elected members' provenance by focusing on their elected status rather than their temporary incumbency. The change in the name also signals the E10's keenness to evolve as a more cohesive construct.

Since 2017, the E10 has held monthly coordination meetings.[17] In 2018, they adopted "Ten Elements for Enhanced Coordination and Joint Action"[18] to enhance the E10's effectiveness on the Council. This entails agreement on procedural and substantive practices, such as the E10 permanent representatives having separate monthly luncheons with the UN Secretary-General, emulating the practice of the P5.[19] Greater engagement among the E10, such as having an E10 coordinator to convene regular monthly meetings of the E10, has strengthened their cooperation and coordination and led to improved coalition-building.[20]

The E10 have, at times, jointly worked to achieve significant outcomes. The adoption of Resolution 1904 (2009), which established the institution of the ombudsman for the Islamic State of Iraq and the Levant (ISIL, also known as Da'esh) and Al-Qaeda sanctions regime, was a seminal contribution to promoting the rule of law within the UNSC.[21] It was an initiative that began without the support of any P5 members. Initially, E10 members

[17] Arthur Boutellis, "Lessons from E10 Engagement on the Security Council," *International Peace Institute* 1 (Nov. 2022), accessed June 13, 2024, https://www.ipinst.org/wp-content/uploads/2022/11/Lessons-from-E10-Engagement-UNSC.pdf.

[18] UN Security Council, Letter from the E10 to the President of the Security Council, S/2018/1024 (Nov. 15, 2018). See also Ian Martin, "Elected Members Today: Overcoming the Handicaps," in *Elected Members of the Security Council: Lame Ducks or Key Players?*, eds. Nico Schrijver and Niels Blokker (Leiden: Martinus Nijhoff Publishers, 2020): 42–55.

[19] Arthur Boutellis, "Lessons from E10 Engagement on the Security Council," *International Peace Institute* 1 (Nov. 2022), accessed June 13, 2024, https://www.ipinst.org/wp-content/uploads/2022/11/Lessons-from-E10-Engagement-UNSC.pdf.

[20] Loraine Sievers and Sam Daws, *The Procedure of the UN Security Council* (Oxford: Oxford University Press, 2014).

[21] Alejandro Rodiles, "Non-Permanent Members of the United Nations Security Council and the Promotion of the International Rule of Law," *Goettingen Journal of International Law* 5, no. 2 (2013): 334–73.

such as Austria, Costa Rica, Mexico, and Libya worked together with several nonmembers of the Council and nongovernmental organizations to support the initiative.

European courts were critical of the UNSC's lack of due process and other human rights violations that arose in the course of the Council's designation of individuals as terrorists under its Chapter VII sanctions regime. These rulings helped forge a European approach that included France and the United Kingdom.[22] Once the United States aligned with the initiative, it led to greater fairness and transparency in the sanctions regimes, as well as the establishment of the ombudsman, despite reservations from Russia and China.

In the decade since the ombudsman's establishment, E10 members have also spearheaded efforts to refine the role of the ombudsman, including through Resolution 1989 (2011) that enabled the ombudsman to recommend to the sanctions committee either retention of a listing or to consider delisting. Such a recommendation can only be overturned by a consensual decision by the sanctions committee. The decisions of the ombudsman have played a key role in enhancing the legitimacy of designations pursuant to the UNSC's ISIL and Al-Qaeda sanctions regimes and in addressing litigation challenges from national courts.

Another interesting effort that has not attracted adequate attention was the innovative initiative and cross-regional coalition building by Saint Vincent and the Grenadines (SVG) during its UNSC membership in 2020–2021. SVG, elected from the Latin American and Caribbean region, is the smallest ever (in terms of population) member of the UNSC. The first-time member aligned with the three African elected members (A3) to launch the A3+1 alliance.[23] SVG coordinated with the A3 on specific African issues and some non-African ones when the A3 agreed on a joint stance.

The African heritage of a significant section of SVG's population grounded the rationale for this unusual arrangement.[24] In cases where the alliance members were on the same page, they worked together as a four-member group in the fifteen-member UNSC, increasing their collective bargaining

[22] See *Yassin Abdullah Kadi and Al Barakaat International Foundation v. Council and Comm'n*, European Court of Justice, Joined Cases C-402/05 P & C-415/05 P, ECLI: EU:C:2008:461 (Sep. 3, 2008); *Nada v. Switzerland*, European Court of Human Rights, App. No. 10593/08 (Sep. 12, 2012).

[23] Stéphanie Fillion, "The Smallest State to Ever Lead the UN Security Council: St. Vincent and the Grenadines," *Pass Blue* (Nov. 2 2020), accessed June 13, 2024, https://www.passblue.com/2020/11/02/the-smallest-state-to-ever-lead-the-un-security-council-st-vincent-and-the-grenadines/.

[24] Ibid.

power. However, this was not always so, as the A3 diverged on several issues, precluding SVG aligning with them. Nevertheless, when the A3+1 joined together—such as when the UNSC addressed the situation in Haiti following the assassination of President Jovenel Moïse in July 2021, and when Colombia requested in early 2021 to add to the mandate of the verification mission in Colombia—the African and Caribbean voices were amplified in the Council's deliberations.

These examples of differently placed elected members hailing from different regions, pursuing diverse individual objectives, and enhancing their impact through collaboration demonstrate the opportunities that innovative Council members have to chalk pathways to greater power. They also seize upon the UNSC's quest to arrive at broad-based decisions. Between 2000 and 2020, of the 1328 resolutions voted at the UNSC, 87% passed with the support of all fifteen members.[25] The UNSC members desire consensus to enhance the legitimacy of their decisions. This desire then creates greater space for coalitions of elected members to maneuver and influence outcomes.

In light of the fragmentation that plagues the UNSC, coalitions, even on a case-by-case basis, can empower an elected member to impact an outcome to a significantly greater degree than if it engages individually. Being part of a coalition naturally magnifies influence. Granted, one cannot overestimate the challenges of subsuming individual national interests to the dynamics of coalition-building—especially when working across regional divides. However, the possible benefits of collective bargaining in a fragmented UNSC far outweigh the perils of individual pursuits.

Another factor enhancing E10 power is the earlier elections by the General Assembly—since June 2016, six months earlier than in the past. The increased preparation time available to elected members before taking up their responsibilities in the UNSC has invariably benefitted incoming members. The "observation" period of the incoming elected members begins several months before they formally assume their seats on the Security Council. In order to better prepare for their responsibilities, members-elect are provided access to all communications of the Council for the five months immediately preceding their membership term (beginning August 1).[26] From October 1 on, they are invited to observe all informal consultations and meetings of the

[25] Jess Gifkins, "Beyond the Veto: Roles in UN Security Council Decision-Making," in *Global Governance: A Review of Multilateralism and International Organizations* 27, no. 1 (2021): 1–24.

[26] See UN Security Council, Note by the President of the Security Council, S/2021/645 (July 12, 2021).

UNSC and its subsidiary bodies for a period of three months.[27] Incoming members also have multiple opportunities to attend training workshops related to working methods. Finally, all incoming members also benefit from *The E10 Handbook: A Practical Guide For Elected Security Council Members* and a shared E10 database.[28]

Several practices have sprung up around E10 preparations for their term on the Council. Some incoming members deploy diplomats in missions of incumbent members so that they can gain experience. Others share locally hired staff. A few of the P5 offer training and invite incoming members for discussions in their capitals. Several incoming members use the observation period to lay down internal procedures and test their systemic readiness through dry runs.[29]

Section II: Evolution of Practices

Serious steps in capacity building by elected members can and do make a difference. An understanding of the E10's role on the Council and their value-added depends to an extent on their mastery of procedures and processes, as well as knowledge of the complex subjects on the agenda. The E10's willingness to "up their game," despite their limitations in terms of formal power, often manifests in the innovative plans of elected members to use the month-long presidency adeptly. In the past, they have sought to broaden the range of thematic issues the Council addresses, held signature events of a formal and informal nature, expanded the Council's interaction with regional and subregional organizations, and drawn upon civil society actors for support to develop initiatives for preventing or managing conflicts in specific situations. These are all elements that—while requiring planning, broad consultation, and careful implementation—also add to the influence of the elected members during their presidency of the UNSC.

On the other hand, the growth of the penholding practice has adversely impacted the functional roles of the elected members. According to the latest note by the president of the UNSC, penholding is "an informal arrangement

[27] See UN Security Council, Note by the President of the Security Council, S/2019/993 (Dec. 27, 2019).

[28] Arthur Boutellis, "Lessons from E-10 Engagement on the Security Council," International Peace Institute, 17 (Nov. 2022), accessed June 13, 2024, https://www.ipinst.org/wp-content/uploads/2022/11/Lessons-from-E10-Engagement-UNSC.pdf.

[29] Ibid., 3.

whereby one or more Council members initiate and facilitate the informal drafting process as well as timely initiatives, of the Council, among other and related tasks."[30] In practice, penholding entails extensive activities: taking the initiative on UNSC activities concerning the particular agenda item, such as requesting emergency meetings; organizing open debates at which the penholder speaks first; and initiating visiting missions, which the penholder usually leads or co-leads.[31] This system of continuous leadership on specific issues by individual Council members began in the first few years of this century. It gathered momentum around 2008–2009 and took firm root by 2010.[32]

In theory, any Council member can be a penholder or co-penholder. In reality, the P3 initially monopolized the penholder system. Even now, they maintain a near stranglehold over thematic and country-specific issues. The permanence of membership provides the P3 with an inside track for roles as penholders due to their institutional memory of UNSC decision-making. In contrast, the brevity of the two-year terms remains an impediment for the elected members. In 2019, out of thirty-nine agenda items that had penholders, P3 members held thirty (77%) penholderships or co-penholderships.[33] A recent analysis states that "P3 members independently hold the pen on 22 out of 33 country-specific files (including 11 out of 12 peacekeeping contexts); share the pen on an additional four country files; and lead on seven out of 12 Council thematic matters."[34]

The penholder system is a primary means of P3 influence within the UNSC and places elected members at a considerable disadvantage. It has engendered strong misgivings among the E10, supported by Russia and China, and led to repeated calls for diversifying the roster of penholders. The E10 pushback, as well as situations in which the P5 were at loggerheads, have led to the P3 becoming more open to sharing the pen with elected members, and occasionally allowing some elected members to wield the pen to break deadlocks among the P5.

[30] See UN Security Council, Note by the President of the Security Council, S/2023/945 (Dec. 1, 2023).

[31] Security Council Report , "The Penholder System," (Dec. 21, 2018), accessed June 14, 2024, https://www.securitycouncilreport.org/research-reports/the-penholder-system.php.

[32] Ibid.

[33] Jess Gifkins, "Beyond the Veto: Roles in UN Security Council Decision-Making," in *Global Governance: A Review of Multilateralism and International Organizations* 27, no. 1 (2021): 10.

[34] Julie Gregory, "Sharing the Pen in the UN Security Council: A Win for Inclusive Multilateralism?" IPI Global Observatory (Apr. 7, 2023), accessed June 14, 2024, https://theglobalobservatory.org/2023/04/sharing-the-pen-un-security-council-inclusive-multilateralism/.

A recent review of elected members sharing the pen concluded that the number of such instances has increased from one in 2014 to six as of the end of 2023.[35] Ecuador shared the pen with the United States on UN peace support efforts in Haiti, and with France on Ukraine's humanitarian issues in 2023 in the context of Russia's invasion. Albania continued to be the copenholder with the United States on Ukraine's peace and security issues, including political initiatives that are distinct from humanitarian assistance matters. France briefly shared the pen with the United Arab Emirates on the Mali sanctions relating to asset freezes and travel bans on specific individuals prior to the dissolution of the sanctions regime, on account of Russia vetoing extension of the sanctions regime in August 2023. Japan and the United Arab Emirates led on Afghanistan, with Brazil and Switzerland on the Syria humanitarian file, and Ghana and Switzerland on the UN Office in West Africa and the Sahel.[36]

An interesting example is the Syrian humanitarian file, where the copenholders have been E10 members since 2013 due to cleavages among the P5. After the term of the first co-penholders, Australia and Luxembourg, the pen was passed to incoming elected members, with Brazil and Switzerland leading in 2023. On many occasions, the elected members as co-penholders navigated the divisions in the Council to achieve outcomes that may not have been achieved if it was left to the P5. It represents a model of E10 members building bridges amidst the fissures that bedevil the P5. Sharing of the pen by the elected members has helped address perceptions of partiality and facilitated more inclusive working methods, contributing in some measure toward more balanced, collaborative, and credible outcomes on the Syria humanitarian file.

Further improvements in E10 status will lead to greater opportunities for their holding the pen. Thus far, progress has been limited due to the reluctance of the P3 to cede space. This is especially so in the case of the United Kingdom and France, who no longer rely on the veto as a tool to achieve desirable outcomes; they instead wield the pen creatively, ensuring a level of power in deliberations far in excess of their current geopolitical standing.

The blossoming of sanctions as a favored tool of diplomacy has meant an exponential increase in their use by UNSC subsidiary bodies in the form

35 Ibid.

36 Security Council Report, "In Hindsight: The Security Council in 2023," (Jan. 1, 2024), accessed June 14, 2024, https://www.securitycouncilreport.org/monthly-forecast/2024-01/in-hindsight-the-security-council-in-2023.php.

of sanctions committees. Article 41 of the UN Charter grants the Council the authority to impose enforcement measures. Possible measures include sanctions, ranging from comprehensive sanctions used previously in Iraq that resulted in severe humanitarian consequences, to the more targeted or smart sanctions now prevalent. The latter includes travel bans and asset freezes, as well as arms embargoes and other measures.

The purposes behind sanctions have also expanded. Sanctions now address a range of issues. Stopping hostilities, improving governance, deterring nuclear proliferation, combatting terrorism, and stopping the use of child soldiers and sexual violence in armed conflict all fall within sanctions' purview.[37] There are presently fourteen sanctions committees.[38] Each sanctions regime is established through a UNSC resolution. All sanctions regimes are chaired by E10 members and not by the P5. This enhances the profiles of individual elected members, but it also adds to their workload. The enhanced workload has led the E10 to call for better burden-sharing by the P5 and a more equal distribution of work.

The unwillingness of the E10 to take on a higher workload stems from the lack of a structured link between the chair of the subsidiary bodies and penholders on the same agenda. It therefore limits the ability of elected members to contribute substantively to an issue where they may have knowledge, expertise, and interest. Essentially, the E10 have the tiresome responsibility of chairing the sanctions committee, while the P5 retain the ultimate authority to lead on substantive aspects as the penholders.

Twice in recent years, the E10 have become penholders on issues where they serve as chair of the same sanctions file. The first enhancement shift came in 2019 when Germany, as chair of the Libya sanctions committee, was invited by the United Kingdom to share the pen on the Libya sanctions file.[39] And as recalled above, in 2023, France briefly shared the pen with the United Arab Emirates on the Mali sanctions file prior to the

[37] *See* Joanna Weschler, "The Evolution of Security Council Innovations in Sanctions," *International Journal: Canada's Journal of Global Policy Analysis* 65, no. 1 (Winter 2009–10).

[38] Paul Romita, Erik Ramberg, and Karin Landgren, "The United Nations in Hindsight: UN Security Council Sanctions," *Just Security* (Dec. 1, 2023), accessed June 14, 2024, https://www.justsecurity.org/90394/the-united-nations-in-hindsight-un-security-council-sanctions/.

[39] Security Council Report, "Lead Roles within the Council in 2019: Penholders and Chairs of Subsidiary Bodies," (Jan. 31, 2019), accessed June 14, 2024, https://www.securitycouncilreport.org/monthly-forecast/2019-02/lead-roles-within-the-council-in-2019-penholders-and-chairs-of-subsidiary-bodies.php.

dissolution of the sanctions regime.[40] These are the exceptions rather than the rule. Strengthening the linkage and making the chairpersons of sanctions committees (usually diplomats of E10) co-penholders (usually P5 states) of substantive files on the same agenda item would enhance the attractiveness of chairing these subsidiary bodies and strengthen the roles of the elected members.

Currently, the P5 play a key role in selecting the chairpersons of subsidiary bodies. Before 2016, the P5 allocated the chairs of subsidiary bodies. Since then, a facilitator from the P5 and the chair of the Security Council's Informal Working Group on Documentation and Other Procedural Questions (IWG) have worked together to agree on the selections. Despite this arrangement, an objection from any of the P5 prevails—even in the face of the E10 proposing an agreed-upon candidate.[41] The collective will of the E10 matters less than the objections of any one of the P5, even in the little-known subterranean world of subsidiary bodies of the UNSC. Removing this effective veto by the P5 on what is a procedural matter is an overdue baby step toward normalcy.

All these disparate examples indicate that individual voting power is not the sole determinant of success at the UNSC. The considerable evolution of practices has provided elected members with creative options that they can pursue to enhance influence and leave an impact that, prior to this time, was rarely possible. These changes have not only become the established practice, but have been recorded in individual notes by the president of the UNSC. At the initiative of Japan in 2006, as chair of the IWG, these notes on various individual or specific issues were codified for the first time into Note 507, which consolidates all previous notes into a single compendium. Updated versions of Note 507 followed in 2010 and 2017 when Japan chaired the IWG during its subsequent term on the UNSC. Since then, the compendium has not been updated. However, in its position as chair of the IWG, Kuwait adopted eight specific presidential notes amending various procedures. SVG added five, and Albania made three more additions.

Codification of practices provides institutional source material for those without institutional memory of UNSC procedures. The presidential notes also prove that the Council's established practice is no longer limited by the

[40] Security Council Report, "In Hindsight: The Security Council in 2023," (Jan. 1, 2024), accessed June 14, 2024, https://www.securitycouncilreport.org/monthly-forecast/2024-01/in-hindsight-the-security-council-in-2023.php.

[41] Interviews with two permanent representatives, November 20, 2023 (referring to a P5 member objecting to India as chair of the ISIL/Al-Qaeda Sanctions Committee in 2021 as a case in point).

explicit provisions of the UN Charter and the Provisional Rules of Procedure (PRP). For example, the PRP refers only to public and private meetings of the Council. The notes list several other formats of meetings that remain absent in the more formal documents.[42] This process of codification is yet another initiative by the elected members that now benefits all. Codification has dissipated the earlier heated debates that the PRP have remained "provisional," despite more than seven decades having passed since the initial promulgation of the PRP. It demonstrates the concerted efforts of elected members to use available tools to systematically improve UNSC working methods and, in turn, to try to shape better outcomes through more inclusive practices and processes.

By their will, determination, ingenuity, and innovativeness, elected members have institutionally enhanced their roles to some degree. History shows that E10 members can seize opportunities to bring about change. In multilateral affairs, incremental changes of procedures can potentially have longer-term impacts on enhancing the roles of stakeholders who initially may have been playing much smaller parts in a large group. Incremental change can influence the work of the Council in ways that are not yet fully captured or tangibly documented. We have seen especially fruitful results where the E10 have developed strategic alliances, strengthened cooperation among themselves, and taken initiative to develop greater diplomatic capacities and competencies. It is clear, however, that the E10 have achieved both a sense of empowerment as well as a measure of institutional evolution.

Conclusion: Limits of Change

The work of the "birds of passage" (as the E10 are often referred to on account of their short terms) in the UNSC has not been able to address the inequitable power dynamics enjoyed by the P5 on account of the permanence of their membership and their veto. Even proposals that seek to restrain the use of the veto have not made any headway with the P5. Liechtenstein's proposal on behalf of the Accountability, Coherence and Transparency (ACT) Group for adherence to a voluntary "code of conduct" that commits

[42] Alejandro Rodiles, "Non-Permanent Members of the United Nations Security Council and the Promotion of the International Rule of Law," *Goettingen Journal of International Law* 5, no. 2 (2013): 334–73.

UNSC members to not vote against a credible draft resolution against genocide, crimes against humanity, or war crimes has not found support from the United States, Russia, or China.[43] Similarly, a French-Mexican initiative for a "Political Declaration on Suspension of Veto Powers on Cases of Mass Atrocity" did not gain traction with the same permanent members.[44]

Improving UNSC processes is necessary. It provides opportunities for the elected members to play a greater role and to gain a stronger status. However, this comparably limited empowerment will never correct the inherent inequality of the UNSC between permanent and nonpermanent members. Moreover, we cannot ignore the need for a Security Council that more equitably represents the geographical and developmental diversity of the United Nations—especially from Africa, Latin America, and the Asia-Pacific—and more accurately reflects contemporary geopolitical realities. The power differential between an anachronistic concert of powers with critical authority, which they are loath to relinquish, and the rest of the elected members is a foundational divide embedded in the UN Charter that states cannot bridge by tinkering at the fringes.

No improvement in procedure or deliberative process can eliminate the inequality between the permanent and elected members. Refinements and enhancements can at best improve the inclusivity of the Council's deliberations, the fairness of its designations, and the transparency of its negotiations. Ultimately, the veto still holds the UNSC's decision-making hostage. For example, the adoption by the General Assembly in April 2022 of Resolution 76/262 makes it mandatory for the president of the General Assembly "to convene a formal meeting within 10 working days of the casting of a veto by one or more permanent members of the Security Council, to hold a debate on the situation as to which the veto was cast, provided that the Assembly does not meet in an emergency special session on the same situation." The much-lauded initiative recognizes the role of the wider UN membership in complex situations, allowing non-Council members to fulfil their responsibilities on matters relating to international peace and security beyond the UNSC's "primary responsibility." However, it has not deterred the continued and repeated use of the veto, even in the face of aggression and

[43] UN Security Council, Letter from the Permanent Representative of Liechtenstein to the United Nations addressed to the Secretary-General, A/70/621–S/2015/978 (Dec. 14, 2015).

[44] Political Statement on the Suspension of the Veto in Case of Mass Atrocities Presented by France and Mexico, 70th General Assembly of the United Nations (Sep. 2015), accessed June 14, 2024, https://onu.delegfrance.org/IMG/pdf/2015_08_07_veto_political_declaration_en.pdf.

mass atrocity crimes. At the time of writing, the P5 have exercised their veto sixteen times since the adoption of Resolution 76/262, blocking the adoption of thirteen UNSC resolutions.

The quest for UNSC reform is a long-standing pastime for UN diplomats. In the same breath, few global issues have generated more talk and less action than UNSC reform. The inability of UN member states to address core issues, such as the expansion of UNSC membership and the veto, means that peripheral innovations, like modest enhancement of the roles of elected members and the wider membership, have moved to center stage. The deeper illness is left untreated.

The emergence of a new E10 culture in New York is little comfort in the face of a veto by one or more permanent members rendering the UNSC unable to fulfil its primary responsibility to prevent and respond to the many conflicts across the globe. Since amendments to the UN Charter altering the veto or the dispensation of power enjoyed by the P5 are essentially off the table, we are left meandering around, passing off technical readjustments trying to make the UNSC fit for purpose for the twenty-first century.

It is the equivalent of a present-day version of an old nursery rhyme where "all the king's horses and all the king's men" are trying to put Humpty Dumpty together again. The harsh truth is that Humpty Dumpty had his great fall when the P5 pushed him off the wall. It will take more than remedial measures to put Humpty Dumpty together again. It is time to think bigger and build back better.

PART II

FULFILLING THE RESPONSIBILITY

3

Improving the UN Response to Aggression and Mass Atrocities

Axel Marschik[*]

Introduction

Most of humanity seeks stability, predictability, and order. Over the centuries, we have cushioned ourselves in comforting layers of ethical and social codes of conduct, increasingly complex repetitive procedures, and institutional systems—from family rituals to global governance. Rules give us structure; repetition gives us comfort.

Since the founding of the United Nations after World War II, our quest for regulation and ritualistic repetition has significantly increased in the international realm. We now possess complex international and regional institutions, organizations, and procedures. These mechanisms reassure us, provide stability, and allow international actors to address almost all issues. The result is a highly professional, multipronged, multilateral system issuing resolutions and conventions designed to regulate the behavior of and relations between states. Whether in trade, finance, labor, health, climate, or human rights—there is no lack of institutions that elaborate informal guidelines, aspirational resolutions, and primary norms of international law. We have empowered ourselves with options: the choice of mechanisms allows us to decide whether to establish a regulation of a more aspirational and political nature, or a binding rule enforceable using the tools of international law.

While the establishment of primary regulation—norms, principles, "rules"—has been fairly straightforward, implementation of and compliance

[*] The views expressed in this chapter are exclusively the author's views in his personal capacity and do not reflect any opinion of or attribution to the Republic of Austria's Federal Ministry for European and International Affairs.

Axel Marschik, *Improving the UN Response to Aggression and Mass Atrocities* In: *Empowering the UN Security Council*. Edited by: Mona Ali Khalil and Floriane Lavaud, Oxford University Press. © Oxford University Press 2024.
DOI: 10.1093/oso/9780197780602.003.0004

with these norms is more problematic. Whether the reason is the vast proliferation of new primary norms, or a change in attitude toward international commitments, international law has gradually been treated more like a set of recommendations than a strict code of rules. Because enforcement of international law is to a large degree inconsistent and decentralized, and because of the current trend of recourse to alternative realities and disinformation, it is easier than ever for states to flout rules and get away with it.

As a result, the binding, normative character of international law is increasingly under pressure. We are in jeopardy of losing a very useful instrument to regulate international relations, an instrument based on good faith and goodwill that fosters stability, predictability, and reassurance—a cornerstone for sustainable peace. That is especially tough on smaller states who rely on international law and principles of the UN Charter for their security. Small states base their buy-in to the UN system on the promise of security, stability, and legality that the Charter's system of collective security supposedly offers. If that promise no longer holds, smaller states will look elsewhere for security. We recently observed this precise development in Europe as a reaction to the aggression of the Russian Federation against Ukraine in 2022. States clamored to accede to regional security alliances like NATO out of fear for their own borders—even those like Finland and Sweden which, prior to Russia's invasion, famously prided themselves on their policy of military neutrality.

Clearly, the United Nations is not solely a security organization. It fulfills many functions: a stage for nations to speak their mind, a forum to discuss and develop international standards, and an international mechanism to support states in need. But the UN's main purpose, as its architects envisioned in 1945, is very clear: to prevent future wars and to ensure that the "rule of law" replaces the "rule of the strong."

This chapter seeks a more efficient and effective response to the most serious violations of international law, including aggression and mass atrocity crimes. Section I discusses the multiple tools provided for in Chapters VI and VII of the UN Charter to empower the Security Council to prevent or address these violations. Section II describes the effect that the veto has on the rule of law and the UN's ability to respond to aggression and mass atrocity crimes. Section III outlines a number of reforms and initiatives by member states to address the shortcomings of the current system. The chapter concludes with proposals for additional measures, including a preauthorized sanctions mechanism to achieve greater automaticity and to ensure efficient response and effective accountability.

Section I: It's the Law until It's Not

By definition, "law" is no mere recommendation. Law contains an accepted normative, obligatory element to distinguish it from mere declarations of intent. While some perceive international law as less binding or "hard" than national law due to the lack of a global enforcer, the UN Charter is, as the International Court of Justice (ICJ) confirmed,[1] a multilateral treaty and a binding norm of international law. The secondary rules compiled by the International Law Commission on state responsibility[2] and reflecting customary law contain clear normative elements that enable coercive (albeit individual) decentralized enforcement.

For treaties, the binding character of law is their very essence, their raison d'être. The principle of *pacta sunt servanda* as enshrined in Article 26 of the Vienna Convention on the Law of Treaties stipulates that treaties must be binding upon their parties and must be performed by them in good faith. That is, of course, also true for the UN Charter.[3] To remove any doubt, the drafters of the Charter stressed in Article 2(2) not only that all UN member states must fulfill the obligations of the Charter, but that they have the duty to fulfill them in good faith.

Nevertheless, states have committed Charter violations on many occasions. While some violations are minor, like the nonpayment of annual dues under Article 17, states have also committed grave violations of major principles, such as the prohibition on the use or threat of force against another state set forth in Article 2(4). Iraq clearly violated the latter Charter provision in its invasion of Kuwait in 1990; so did the United States, United Kingdom, and others in their invasion of Iraq in 2003; and so did the Russian Federation in its invasions and occupation of parts of Ukraine in 2014 and 2022—just to name a few examples. This practice of noncompliance does not diminish the norm that was violated. No state claimed to act as a persistent

[1] Conditions of Admission of a State to Membership in the United Nations (Article 4 of the Charter), Advisory Opinion, 1948 ICJ. 57 (May 28).

[2] Int'l Law Comm'n, Rep. on the Work of Its Fifty-Third session, A/56/10 (2001).

[3] Vienna Convention on the Law of Treaties art. 26, May 23, 1969, 1155 UNTS 331.

objector, and the reactions by other UN states make clear that there is no tacit consent or evolving subsequent practice permitting deviation from the rules.

In response to Iraq's aggression and attempted annexation of Kuwait in 1990, the Security Council, acting under Chapter VII, authorized a multinational force to liberate Kuwait and required Iraq to assume state responsibility for the loss of life and property. However, such robust response to a Charter violation is more of an exception than the rule. In many cases, great power politics prevents the restorative or response measures outlined within the Charter. The maintenance of international peace and security requires prompt and effective action by the Security Council as provided in Article 24(1) of the UN Charter.

The Charter itself provides multiple tools to empower the Security Council to prevent or address violations of the Charter in its Chapters VI and VII.

A. Chapter VI

Chapter VI gives the Security Council the authority to support and encourage states in preventing or peacefully settling a dispute. Pursuant to Article 33, the Council can call upon states to seek a solution by negotiation, enquiry, mediation, conciliation, arbitration, judicial settlement, resort to regional agencies or arrangements, or other peaceful means of their own choice. Article 34 specifically mentions the right of the Council to investigate any dispute, either through fact-finding missions or commissions of inquiry. Article 36 enables the Council to recommend appropriate procedures, in particular to use dispute settlement by transitional justice mechanisms and courts. This includes recourse to the ICJ, either through principal UN organs' requests for advisory opinions or parties instituting contentious cases before the Court. The established practice of the Council has also introduced new tools, ranging from good offices and confidence-building measures, to humanitarian relief operations that include both special political missions and peacekeeping.

B. Chapter VII

Chapter VII empowers the Security Council to impose provisional measures and enforcement measures involving or authorizing the use of force where the Council finds either a threat to the peace, a breach of the peace, or an act of aggression under Article 39 of the Charter. In addition to the provisional measures set forth in Article 40, the Council can establish sanctions regimes ranging from comprehensive sanctions to the more targeted, more modern option often called "smart sanctions." Promulgated under Article 41 of the Charter, smart sanctions include arms embargoes, travel bans, and asset freezes. Under Chapter VII, the Council can also authorize very robust measures, including inspection of sea vessels carrying weapons or other prohibited items. Article 42 permits the Council to authorize the use of armed force beyond self-defense, including for targeted peace enforcement actions or full-scale military operations by individual states, coalitions of states, or regional and other organizations.

The power to impose binding measures on member states as well as nonmember states in cases of serious violations of the Charter constitutes the core element of the UN system of collective security. As stated in Article 1(1) of the Charter, one of the primary purposes of the United Nations is "to maintain international peace and security, and to that end: to take effective collective measures for the prevention and removal of threats to the peace, and for the suppression of acts of aggression or other breaches of the peace."

Together with the inherent right of self-defense enshrined in Article 51 of the Charter, an elaborate system enables the UN to enforce its own fundamental principles and obligations to ensure that any violation of these core principles and prohibitions will not be tolerated. Where aggression or other breaches of the peace or threats to the peace cannot be prevented, the system foresees a counteraction intended to reestablish the peace and remedy the wrong. As such, the primary norms of the Charter—and other norms of international law whose violations can trigger recourse to Chapter VII—are, in theory, well-protected by a strong enforcement mechanism of Security Council rights and responsibilities, provided the Council is willing and able to act.

Section II: Words Alone Are Not Enough

Due to difficult relations among the great powers throughout the more than seventy-five-year history of the United Nations and, more specifically, the use of the veto by its five permanent members (P5), the Security Council has not always reliably fulfilled its role as guardian of the UN Charter. As a result, norm violations often do not lead to any systemic reaction at all. Sometimes the Council can only adopt a presidential statement indicating its expectations or its displeasure; sometimes, it cannot take any action at all. In these instances, the General Assembly may convene to adopt a nonbinding resolution.

In reaction to the Russian Federation's aggression against Ukraine in 2022, more than 140 states voted in the General Assembly in favor of a resolution that determined Russian actions were illegal and a violation of the UN Charter. Russia's full-scale invasion was only the culmination of its persistent violations of basic principles of the UN Charter in the preceding years—not only the earlier invasion of Ukraine in 2014 and the subsequent illegal annexation of Crimea, but also the Russian incursion and subsequent occupation of South Ossetia in Georgia in 2008, and Russia's involvement in Moldova in the region of Transnistria. This is a clear pattern of disregard for the territorial integrity and sovereignty of smaller states in Russia's neighborhood. Russia's ability to act with impunity in these situations is due to its veto preventing the Council from holding it to account. In general, the lack of a global power to enforce international law and the UN Charter is somewhat counterbalanced by the far-reaching powers vested in the Security Council; but in the case of a permanent member violating the Charter, any P5 state can shield itself from repercussions unfolding from its own violations of the Charter and international law.

The veto-wielding permanent members not only shield themselves but also their allies. In reaction to the United States' veto of Security Council resolutions addressing Israel's response to the Hamas terrorist attack on October 7, 2023, more than 150 member states voted in favor of a resolution in the General Assembly demanding an immediate humanitarian ceasefire in Gaza and the release of all hostages. Despite UN member states' consistent condemnation of the horrific events of October 7, 2023, and notwithstanding their recognition of Israel's inherent right of self-defense, most regarded Israel's response in the densely populated civilian areas in Gaza as contrary to international humanitarian law.

While some states and regional organizations may adopt unilateral or regional sanctions in the absence of Security Council action, in practice, there are too often no meaningful consequences for even the most egregious Charter violations. As a result, potential violators are not deterred from breaking the law; they will violate the Charter when they believe they can get away with it. And for the most part, they do get away with it. Perhaps understandably, other states are reluctant to endanger their bilateral relations with repeat offenders or their powerful allies out of concern for their own security.

The weak response to such aggression and mass atrocities undermines the primacy of international legal norms and erodes confidence in the collective security system of the United Nations. If states do not respect peremptory norms, the norms appear to be no more than aspirational resolutions. This creates insecurity and uncertainty and contributes to the trend of undermining the system of customary international law as binding and universal—not overnight, but gradually. Since the UN Charter and international law are the foundation of all areas of international relations, weakening or eroding the concept of hard law or binding obligations profoundly threatens our international order.

Section III: Initiatives Abound

To address the shortcomings of the current system, the past years have seen a number of reform efforts devoted to different organs of the United Nations. The following section highlights states' and UN bodies' main initiatives.

A. The Security Council

The key target of international dissatisfaction is the UN Security Council. Many have called for a reform of the Council, especially diversifying its composition; expanding the number and categories of membership; and limiting the use of the veto. The Intergovernmental Negotiations on Security Council Reform (which morphed out of the prior open-ended working group on the same subject) has been trying to identify reform options since 2009. As Charter amendments require the consent of the five permanent members as stipulated in Article 108 of the Charter, any major reform is difficult and unlikely. That said, due to increasing pressure from many states—especially those in the Global South—expectations of Security Council reform have risen over the past years that some reforms must be implemented to ensure reliable and sustainable buy-in to the UN system.

Several initiatives aim to restrict the veto in certain situations.

In February 2015, the Elders—an independent advisory group of world leaders for the UN system—adopted a statement which, inter alia, called on the permanent members of the Security Council "to pledge 'not to use, or threaten to use, their veto' in crises in which genocide or other mass atrocities are committed or threatened 'without explaining, clearly and in public, what alternative course of action they propose, as a credible and efficient way to protect populations in question.' "[4]

In July 2015, a cross-regional group—the Accountability, Coherence, and Transparency Group (ACT)—announced a code of conduct for member states which calls upon all members of the Security Council (both permanent and elected) to not vote against any credible draft resolution intended to prevent or end the commission of genocide, crimes against humanity, and war crimes.[5]

In August 2015, France and Mexico launched the "Political Declaration on Suspension of Veto Powers in Cases of Mass Atrocities," proposing a collective and voluntary agreement among the permanent members of the Security Council to the effect that the permanent members would refrain from using the veto in case of mass atrocities.[6]

The Council's working methods are another area that clearly could be the focus of reform. These do not require Charter amendments. Under Article 30 of the Charter, the Council is free to adopt its own rules of procedure. One particular point of criticism is the current application (or rather, disregard) of Article 27(3), which provides that a party to a dispute should abstain from voting on a decision under Chapter VI. In theory, that should prevent a veto on resolutions in reaction to disputes that include one or more of the P5. In practice, after an initial period in which Article 27(3) was applied, the P5 have used their veto in such situations without much contestation by other states. To rectify this practice, some suggest an advisory opinion from the ICJ or a resolution by the General Assembly recommending a new practice—one that fully respects Article 27(3).

[4] The Elders, "Strengthening the United Nations," Feb. 7, 2015, accessed June 16, 2024, https://theelders.org/sites/default/files/2015-04-22_elders-statement-strengthening-the-un.pdf.

[5] Global Centre for the Responsibility to Protect, "List of Signatories to the ACT Code of Conduct," last modified June 8, 2022, accessed June 16, 2024,https://www.globalr2p.org/resources/list-of-signatories-to-the-act-code-of-conduct/.

[6] Political Statement on the Suspension of the Veto in Case of Mass Atrocities presented by France and Mexico, 70th General Assembly of the United Nations, Sep. 2015, accessed June 16, 2024, https://onu.delegfrance.org/IMG/pdf/2015_08_07_veto_political_declaration_en.pdf.

Much of the criticism of the Security Council is warranted, especially in cases when there is a veto blocking a resolution in reaction to an act of aggression or a fundamental violation of the Charter. But even in times of extreme tension among the great powers, the Council has not been completely paralyzed. In 2022—the year of Russia's aggression against Ukraine—it held 419 meetings and consultations on 49 agenda items, making it one of the busiest years in UN history. (Only 2017 had more—the year the UN warned that the world was facing the largest humanitarian crisis since World War II.) The Council invited 445 outside experts under Rule 39 of its rules of procedure, making it the most open to outside experts ever. It adopted fifty-four resolutions, seven presidential statements, and sixty-seven press statements. Compared to 1959 when the Council had only five meetings and adopted one resolution all year, the Security Council was actually very active. The problem is that it devotes its time primarily to administrating and discussing international affairs rather than taking action to enforce the Charter.

B. The General Assembly

In view of the Council's unreliability, some argue for a stronger role for the General Assembly. There have been incremental steps. In April 2022, the General Assembly, "[a]mid growing criticism of inaction by the Security Council on the war in Ukraine," adopted what it called a landmark resolution "aimed at holding the five permanent Council members accountable for their use of veto."[7] The resolution, entitled "Standing Mandate for a General Assembly Debate When a Veto Is Cast in the Security Council," seeks to increase the political cost of using the veto.

Now generally referred to as the "veto initiative," Liechtenstein launched the project with eighty-three co-sponsoring member states, including three P5 members—France, the United Kingdom, and the United States. Russia and China did not oppose the draft resolution, which was adopted without a vote as UN General Assembly Resolution 76/262 of April 28, 2022. The resolution provides that the president of the General Assembly must convene a mandatory meeting of the General Assembly within ten days of a veto being cast in the Council, "provided that the Assembly does not meet in an emergency special session on the same situation."

[7] UN General Assembly, Resolution 76/262, A/RES/76/262 (Apr. 26, 2022).

In some instances, the General Assembly has invoked the "Uniting for Peace" resolution and convened an emergency special session (EES).[8] Eleven such sessions have been convened since 1950, with two currently ongoing. The General Assembly first convened the tenth EES in 1997 on the situation in the Occupied Palestinian Territories; it is still active. The Security Council convened the eleventh and most recent EES in 2022 in response to the Russian invasion of Ukraine; this constituted the first invocation of an EES by the Security Council in forty years. The last time the Security Council convened an EES was in 1982 in response to Israel's annexation of the Syrian Golan Heights.[9]

Clearly, the General Assembly could do more: it is the most representative body of the UN, where every member state is present and equal with one vote. Since resolutions of the Assembly are not binding, any measures it recommends would need to be implemented voluntarily by states themselves, and often against much more powerful states—something most are only likely to do in larger organized groups.

In the context of the General Assembly's discussions on Security Council reform, several ideas have been informally mentioned, such as expanding the veto initiative from merely holding a meeting to also adopting resolutions (albeit with unclear legal effects), or enabling the General Assembly to effectively overrule a veto by a qualified majority. While such proposals have garnered increasing political support fueled by frustration, the legality and possible consequences of such actions are not clear. Even as a political matter, it is questionable what the effect of a resolution by the Assembly purporting to override the veto of a permanent member would achieve in practical terms. The measure would thus presumably primarily serve to chastise the veto-casting State, a procedure that already exists today thanks to the veto initiative codified in the standing mandate under Resolution 76/262.

C. The Secretary-General

Some advocate for a stronger role of the Secretary-General. However, as the situations in Ukraine and in Israel and Palestine demonstrate, the Secretary-General has little room to maneuver if a permanent member of the Security

[8] UN General Assembly, Resolution 377 (V), A/RES/377 (V) (Nov. 3, 1950).

[9] See General Assembly of the United Nations, "Emergency Special Sessions," accessed June 16, 2024, https://www.un.org/en/ga/sessions/emergency.shtml.

Council is directly or indirectly involved. At the same time, the current Secretary-General António Guterres has successfully brokered humanitarian agreements of prisoner exchanges and the Black Sea Grain Initiative in the Russia/Ukraine context.

Most recently, Secretary-General Guterres invoked Article 99 of the Charter to call for a humanitarian ceasefire in the face of the UN's collapsing humanitarian system in Gaza. In doing so, the Secretary-General exercised what had been a historically neglected article of the Charter that allows the Secretary-General to bring to the attention of the Council any matter which they believe may threaten international peace and security. Interestingly, criticism as a consequence of this action mainly focused on the fact that Article 99 had to date only been invoked extremely rarely—so far regarding only the Congo in 1960, Iran in 1979, and Lebanon in 1989. In light of its underuse, Israel and its allies considered the use of Article 99 unnecessary and unfair.

The reticence of consecutive office holders to make recourse to Article 99 has been explained with reference to the fact that it was unnecessary; the Secretary-General has ample opportunities to interact with Council members and thus does not need to make a formal interjection. This is hardly convincing—even less so in today's world where the public expects fast reaction by the United Nations to crises and there are high expectations regarding transparency. Clearly, the Secretary-General should make more use of this competence proactively in the future. This will also serve to protect the independence of the Secretariat, one of the principal organs of the United Nations.

D. International courts and tribunals

There is wide interest in increasing resort to judicial recourse and accountability for serious violations of the UN Charter and international law. We see this in the establishment of new mechanisms on accountability and discussion of new tribunals, as well as in the growing workload facing existing institutions. This includes the increasing resort to the ICJ where we have seen recent requests for advisory opinions on the Chagos Archipelago and climate change, as well as cases under the Genocide Convention in respect of alleged acts of genocide in Myanmar, Ukraine, and Palestine.

Key problems, however, include the lack of compulsory jurisdiction, as well as the stagnation of declarations under Article 36 of the Statute of the

ICJ, the length of proceedings, and lack of implementation of decisions in contentious cases. Another historically neglected article of the UN Charter is Article 94(2), which entitles any party to have recourse to the Security Council if the other party fails to perform the obligations incumbent upon it under a judgment rendered by the Court. To enforce the ICJ judgment, the Security Council may, if it deems necessary, make recommendations or decide upon measures to be taken to give effect to judgment.

Conclusion: So What Else Can Be Done?

In view of the UN Summit of the Future in September 2024, more innovative ideas are being sought with greater urgency and attention than usual. One idea proposed by this author is to focus on mechanisms that incorporate an automaticity of response to norm violations. The idea is simple: humans break the law when they think they can get away with it—take speeding, illegal parking, or exceeding a credit limit as simple examples. What works best to ensure compliance in such cases is automaticity of penalty: a speed radar that automatically sends a ticket if it is triggered by a speeding vehicle; an automatic block of a credit card if limits are exceeded. Automaticity has a deterrent impact on behavior. We know we can't argue our way out, no matter how important we are. We know we'll get the ticket, so we slow down.

Creating automaticity is more difficult in international law, but it exists, even in the UN Charter. For example, Article 19 stipulates that if member states fall into arrears in the payment of UN membership dues, they automatically lose their right to vote in the General Assembly. One could envision a system with similar automaticity in response to serious violations of the Charter, including but not limited to acts of aggression as defined in General Assembly Resolution 3314. The General Assembly could agree *ex ante* in a resolution that whenever it decides that a state has gravely violated the Charter, certain consequences automatically arise: financial assistance from international organizations is withheld, the violator is deemed ineligible for election to functions or subsidiary organs of the General Assembly, member states are automatically authorized to take certain measures, diplomatic or financial sanctions may be imposed, or bilateral assistance may be withheld. As long as the appropriate organs of the UN system are included in the mechanism well ahead of time, even more drastic measures could be envisioned: automatic suspension from international travel could leave flights grounded, access to the internet could be limited or wholly denied, energy sources and their carrier systems (such as gas pipelines) could be reduced or cut off entirely, and the use of international satellites could be suspended. The UN could encourage individual member states to adopt specific punitive sanctions (also agreed upon in advance), such as asset freezes and travel bans.

Since measures would be agreed upon in advance, there would be no reason to assume measures were haphazardly taken in a "biased" or "unfair" manner and reflecting "double standards," as often claimed by those subjected to *ex post* sanctions. The act of the norm violation alone would trigger the automatic response; just like a driver of a speeding car triggers the fine, the aggressor would trigger the sanction and would alone be responsible for the consequences—consequences that are well known at the time the state commits the transgressive act.

Such an idea is not completely new. Article 16 of the Covenant of the League of Nations provided for automaticity in the event of war:

> Should any Member of the League resort to war in disregard of its covenants under Articles 12, 13 or 15, it shall ipso facto be deemed to have committed an act of war against all other Members of the League, which hereby undertake immediately to subject it to the severance of all trade or financial relations, the prohibition of all intercourse between their nationals and the nationals of the covenant-breaking State, and the prevention of all financial, commercial or personal intercourse between the nationals of the covenant-breaking State and the nationals of any other State, whether a Member of the League or not.[10]

The League of Nations is clearly not the best precedent to emulate. However, the mechanism set forth in Article 16 is different in one crucial way from the idea proposed in this chapter: under Article 16, a war triggers measures that UN member states have to individually adopt. As explained above, this is difficult in practice for small states against their powerful neighbors. Conversely, the proposal presented here envisions measures that are automatically implemented by the UN itself. States and other international officials merely receive the authority to act if they so wish, thereby ensuring a fixed and predetermined set of consequences—and possibly more, should

[10] League of Nations Covenant art. 16.

member states decide to implement additional sanctions on an individual basis.

In spite of its shortcomings, Article 16 of the Covenant is interesting for another reason: it shows that 100 years ago, international lawyers were also thinking about how best to deter states from violating their most important commitments. Today, we should be able to establish a more refined and reliable automatic mechanism that is effective enough for states to think twice before violating the Charter.

International law can be the path to international peace and security. But at the moment, it is itself in peril and facing threats in all regions of the world. States must work together in cooperation and compliance with their international legal obligations. To this end, states must restore trust in each other's respect for international law and in the equal application of the law. With its universal membership, the United Nations should be the central forum to undertake these efforts to strengthen the rule of law and better contribute to the maintenance of international peace and security.

4
Ensuring Criminal Accountability

Adama Dieng

Introduction

The UN Security Council has increasingly sought to ensure accountability and enforce the rule of law in response to mass atrocities and serious human rights violations. For example, in the face of mass atrocities, the UN Security Council has established ad hoc international criminal tribunals, sanctions regimes, and peacekeeping missions to ensure justice and restore the rule of law. This chapter contends that the Security Council should employ these tools to not only respond but also prevent serious violations of international humanitarian and human rights law. In addition to these tools, the UN Security Council and member states can also resort to the International Court of Justice (ICJ) to prevent genocide and to the International Criminal Court (ICC) to ensure accountability for perpetrators, up to and including heads of state, in order to deter further atrocities and violations.

The use of these tools for preventative—not only reactive—purposes will contribute to the peaceful settlement of disputes as well as to the protection of civilians and international peace and security. The preventive approach applies not only at the international level, but also at the regional and national levels. UN member states must implement their international and regional obligations in good faith. As recognized by the concept of complementarity in the Rome Statute of the ICC, states must make genuine efforts to hold perpetrators of serious violations of international humanitarian and human rights law accountable; when states are either unable or unwilling to do so, then it is for the international community to step up to ensure justice.

To undertake the preventive approach at the national level, member states should nurture and respect rule of law institutions; ensure that such institutions are capable of adjudicating differences impartially and efficiently among citizens; and empower them to hold all perpetrators accountable, regardless of positions of power. Member states should also respect the

Adama Dieng, *Ensuring Criminal Accountability* In: *Empowering the UN Security Council*. Edited by: Mona Ali Khalil and Floriane Lavaud, Oxford University Press.
DOI: 10.1093/oso/9780197780602.003.0005

independence of the judiciary, ensure access to justice, comply with courts' decisions, and fulfill their human rights and other legal obligations.

This chapter explores how the UN Security Council can prioritize the rule of law to respond to and prevent violations of international humanitarian and human rights law. Section I discusses the importance of a preventive and human rights–based approach to prevent conflict and protect civilians. Section II considers how the failure of a UN member state to respect and promote the rule of law may itself constitute a threat to international peace and security, even insofar as to warrant remedial action from the Security Council. Section III discusses the intersection of accountability for mass atrocity crimes and other human rights violations with the rule of law, focusing on post-conflict contexts. Section IV considers the specific challenges states face in promoting the rule of law and advancing justice and accountability. The chapter concludes with proposals of practical actions that the Council may undertake to promote the rule of law and prevent mass atrocity crimes.

Section I: Commitment to the Rule of Law

A preventive and human rights–based approach is the best option to prevent conflict and protect civilians.[1] States must pursue the prevention of conflict and protection of populations from large-scale human rights violations in furtherance of justice and the rule of law. Multilateralism—based on trust and pursued in good faith—and responsive rule-of-law institutions are key to maintain peace and security in any society. They are critical to ensuring accountability and ending impunity. Strong rule-of-law institutions—whether at the national, regional, or international level—safeguard against possible abuses of power, enhance confidence in the administration of justice, promote equality and accountability, and help ensure respect for human rights. The development of strong rule-of-law institutions is a central pillar in the prevention of mass atrocities and other serious violations of human rights.

The international community cannot undertake meaningful prevention without commitment to the rule of law and respect for human rights

[1] See generally Adama Dieng, "The Maintenance of International Peace and Security through Prevention of Atrocity Crimes: The Question of Cooperation between the UN and Regional Arrangements," in *Arcs of Global Justice: Essays in Honour of William Schabas*, eds. Margaret M. deGuzman and Diane Marie Amann (Oxford: Oxford University Press, 2018).

and fundamental freedoms. Such rights are universally recognized and guaranteed by the International Bill of Human Rights, itself composed of the Universal Declaration of Human Rights (UDHR); the International Covenant on Civil and Political Rights; and the International Covenant on Economic, Social, and Cultural Rights, along with other international and regional instruments.[2] If states are to achieve sustainable peace, they must reaffirm their commitment to the primacy of justice and fundamental human rights, an obligation they undertook in their ratification of the UN Charter.

The erosion of the rule of law significantly contributes to gross violations of human rights. When a state abdicates its responsibility to protect its citizens and fails to apply the law to all equally and without discrimination, this failure may devolve into violence. In other words, to safeguard justice and the rule of law, a government—just like its citizens—must be bound by laws which are publicly promulgated and independently adjudicated. Additionally, citizens must be able to seek protection of their rights and have recourse when their rights are violated through the political, legal, and judicial channels at national, regional, and international levels.

Effective prevention demonstrates the ability of all states to protect their borders, ensure their citizens' confidence in their judicial institutions, ensure accountability for violations of legal norms and universal values, and cooperate to address global challenges. These include armed conflicts, climate change, refugee and migration crises, hunger, poverty, and failures in social justice, among others. Above all, the ability and willingness of states to pursue their social, economic, and political interests while respecting their obligations in accordance with the UN Charter and other universally accepted values will demonstrate their responsibility to protect their people at home and contribute to peace and the rule of law around the world.

Section II: Rule of Law within the UN Institutional Setting

The UN Charter does not assign the Security Council the primary responsibility for promoting the rule of law. Rather, the primary responsibility of the Security Council set forth in the Charter is to maintain international peace and security.[3] The pertinent question is: Can the failure or inability of a UN

[2] See Christopher N. J. Roberts, *The Contentious History of the International Bill of Human Rights* (Cambridge: Cambridge University Press, 2015).
[3] UN Charter art. 24.

member state to respect and promote the rule of law constitute a threat to international peace and security of such a nature as to warrant the intervention of the Security Council?

To answer this question, one must examine the aims and purposes of the UN Charter. According to the preamble of the Charter, the United Nations aims, inter alia, to save future generations from the scourge of war, reaffirm faith in fundamental human rights, establish conditions under which justice and respect for the obligations arising from treaties and other sources of international law can be maintained, and promote social progress and better standards of life. Article 1 of the Charter sets out the purposes of the United Nations, including to maintain international peace and security; develop friendly relations among nations based on respect for the principle of equal rights and self-determination of peoples; achieve international cooperation in solving international problems of an economic, social, cultural or humanitarian character; promote and encourage respect for human rights and fundamental freedoms for all without distinction as to race, sex, language, or religion; and harmonize the actions of nations in the attainment of its common aims.[4] The Charter imposes an obligation upon all member states to assist the United Nations in carrying out its functions in accordance with the Charter.[5]

The preamble to the UDHR expressly provides that the rule of law is necessary for the advancement and realization of human rights. Although the UDHR does not define the "rule of law," this preambular provision suggests that the rule of law is a formal and procedural safeguard for advancing and realizing human rights. To the drafters, all human rights and freedoms enshrined in the UDHR could only be fully guaranteed through the rule of law.[6] The inclusion of "rule of law" in a landmark document like the UDHR is significant precisely because it provides a foundational basis for the crucial role of the United Nations and its various agencies in promoting human rights to this day.

Increasingly, the UN Security Council considers the rule of law as an essential tool for preventing and resolving conflicts. From the Council's perspective, the international community can attain a global order–based

[4] UN Charter art. 1(3).
[5] UN Charter art. 2(5).
[6] William A. Schabas, *The Universal Declaration of Human Rights: The Travaux Préparatoires*, vol. I: October 1946 to November 1947 (Cambridge: Cambridge University Press, 2013). See also Johannes Morsink, *The Universal Declaration of Human Rights: Origins, Drafting, and Intent* (Philadelphia: University of Pennsylvania Press, 1999).

peace and security, as well as justice and the international rule of law. The Security Council contributes to the promotion of the international rule of law through its encouragement of UN member states to settle their disputes peacefully; its establishment of peacekeeping missions with human rights and protection of civilians in their mandates; its introduction of measures for violations of international humanitarian and human rights law in its Chapter VII sanctions regimes; its establishment of ad hoc international criminal tribunals to hold to account perpetrators of mass atrocities; and its referral of situations to the ICC.

In 2005, UN member states unanimously recognized the need "for universal adherence to implementation of the rule of law both at the national and international level" and reaffirmed their commitment to an "international order based on the rule of law and international law" in the World Summit Outcome Document.[7] The rule of law at national and international levels generally connotes "reliance on law as opposed to arbitrary power in international relations"; the settlement of disputes by law over force; and the realization that States can—and should—use law as an instrument to advance international cooperation, and to address social and economic justice to preserve "values of freedom and human dignity."[8]

To go from theory to reality, international commitments require effective national implementation to strengthen the rule of law at the national level. The strength of a country's adherence to and fulfillment of its international obligations, including its human rights obligations to its own people, contributes to upholding the UN Charter and the international rule of law. The ability and willingness of states to implement their international commitments differs from one country to another. International assistance to enhance national capacity, as well as other forms of bilateral and international cooperation to promote human rights globally, are essential to the international rule of law, as recognized by the Vienna Conference on Human Rights in 1993. The Vienna Conference was the first UN conference on human rights since the end of the Cold War and marked the first time that the international community made an express undertaking, both bilateral and multilateral, to collaborate and support each other in promoting human rights and advancing the rule of law.

[7] UN General Assembly, Resolution 60/1, A/RES/60/1 (Oct. 24, 2005).
[8] William W. Bishop, "The International Rule of Law," *Michigan Law Review* 59, no. 4 (1961): 553.

Section III: The United Nations, Accountability, and Rule of Law

Adherence to the rule of law requires accountability for atrocity crimes and other violations of human rights. Peace and justice are like identical twins joined at the hip. It is difficult to separate them and still achieve sustainable peace in post-conflict situations, or any other society. A credible peace process pays attention to the whole spectrum of justice and reconciliation. Those who have committed serious crimes of genocide, war crimes, and crimes against humanity must be held to account. There can be no amnesty for such serious crimes.[9] Truth-seeking mechanisms, which are of utmost importance for victims, must also accompany criminal accountability. It is only when the truth has been established that actual healing can take place and the victims are able to forgive or seek reparations.

Local judicial systems are often ill-equipped and inadequately resourced to sufficiently respond to the demands for justice and accountability. Throughout the world, certain justice systems have been deprived of appropriate training and financial resources; justice systems whose officers have been bribed, harassed, intimidated, and even killed; and justice systems that have been de facto stripped of their very raison d'être. These complex challenges facing judicial institutions in most countries have made peace, justice, and reconciliation elusive in many post-conflict situations. When serious violations are taking place, there should be no room for complacency. While states seem to understand this today, action is still necessary to achieve justice and accountability.

Traditionally, the UN Security Council viewed justice and accountability as a tool to respond to mass atrocities, rather than as a tool to prevent large-scale human rights violations. For example, on November 8, 1994, the Security Council passed Resolution 955, which established the International Criminal Tribunal for Rwanda (ICTR).[10] The ICTR's mandate was to investigate and prosecute those alleged to have planned and executed the acts of genocide and other serious violations of international humanitarian and human rights law. As most of the high-ranking military and government

[9] See Sarah Williams, "Amnesties in International Law: The Experience of the Special Court for Sierra Leone," *Human Rights Law Review* 5, no. 2 (2005).

[10] UN Security Council, Resolution 955, S/RES/955 (Nov. 8, 1994). This resolution was passed with thirteen votes in favor, one against (Rwanda), and one abstaining (China). UN SCOR, 3453rd mtg. at 3, UN Doc. S/PV.3453 (Nov. 8, 1994).

officials had fled Rwanda, they could only be captured and brought to justice with the help of the international community.

Similarly, with Resolution 827,[11] the Security Council established the International Criminal Tribunal for the Former Yugoslavia (ICTY) in 1993, which exercised accountability over those accused of masterminding the mass atrocities committed in the former Yugoslavia. To the extent that the ICC had not yet been established, it was necessary for the international community to establish the ICTR and ICTY as ad hoc international criminal tribunals to hold perpetrators accountable, while also contributing to the restoration of sustainable peace.

In any post-conflict context, transitional justice can significantly contribute to the restoration of the rule of law and consolidation of peace. Transitional justice processes must demonstrate that no matter who the perpetrators may be, the law applies to all equally. Accountability mechanisms should also provide an opportunity for victim recognition, while allowing victims to claim their voice by ensuring their tormentors are brought to justice.[12]

The ICTR played a central role in investigating and prosecuting key figures that planned and executed the genocide in Rwanda. This aspect is crucial. Rwanda was unable to undertake such a complex endeavor due to the lack of institutional and human capacity. In the wake of genocide, most government officials—including judicial officers—were killed in the conflict, an aspect that made it difficult for the state to prosecute those accused of crimes. The trial of the most senior officials at the ICTR (most notably, the prime minister) demonstrated that nobody is above the law. Similarly, the ICTY "provided victims an opportunity to voice the horrors they witnessed and experienced, and proved that those suspected of bearing the greatest responsibility for atrocities committed during armed conflicts can be called to account."[13]

The positive impact of the work of ad hoc tribunals like the ICTR and ICTY laid the foundations for individual accountability up to and including heads of state and government officials, and "changed the landscape of international humanitarian law."[14] A mere twenty years ago, prosecution of these former heads of state would have been simply unimaginable. ICTR

[11] UN Security Council, Resolution 827, S/RES/827 (May 25, 1993).

[12] For a comprehensive coverage on this subject, see M. Cherif Bassiouni, "International Recognition of Victims' Rights," *Human Rights Law Review* 6, no. 2, (Jan. 2006).

[13] United Nations International Residual Mechanism for Criminal Tribunals, "International Criminal Tribunal for the Former Yugoslavia," accessed June 16, 2024, https://www.icty.org/.

[14] Ibid.

and ICTY jurisprudence have seriously challenged the prevailing norms and reaffirmed that absolute immunity for heads of state and other high-level officials is neither legally nor morally acceptable. Building on the work of these tribunals, states negotiated the Rome Statute, leading to the establishment of the ICC.

In the two decades since the birth of the ICC, we have witnessed tremendous efforts in holding perpetrators of atrocity crimes accountable.[15] The ICC has built on the legacy of the ICTR and ICTY with its indictments of two heads of state: first, Omar Al Bashir,[16] who is being investigated in relation to crimes allegedly committed in Darfur. The Security Council referred the situation in Darfur to the ICC with Resolution 1593 in 2005.[17] Second, Muammar al-Gaddafi,[18] who was investigated in relation to crimes allegedly committed in Libya. The Council referred the situation in Libya to the ICC with Resolution 1970 in 2011.[19] Neither indictment would have been possible if the Security Council had not referred the situations in Sudan and Libya to the ICC for investigation and prosecution pursuant to Chapter VII of the UN Charter.[20]

Beyond its authority to refer situations involving mass atrocity crimes to the ICC, the Security Council has expanded the scope of its preventive measures, including the sanctions regimes under Chapter VII of the UN Charter. Many of the current sanctions regimes include measures against "planning, directing, or committing acts that constitute human rights violations or abuses or violations of international humanitarian law, as applicable, including those acts involving the targeting of civilians, including killing and maiming, rape and other sexual violence, abduction, forced displacement, and attacks on schools and hospitals."[21] The Chapter VII sanctions regimes of the Security Council are largely recognized as "preventive measures,

[15] See International Criminal Court, "Cases," accessed June 16, 2024, https://www.icc-cpi.int/cases.

[16] See International Criminal Court, "Al Bashir Case," accessed June 16, 2024, https://www.icc-cpi.int/darfur/albashir.

[17] UN Security Council, Resolution 1593, S/RES/1593 (Mar. 31, 2005).

[18] See International Criminal Court, "Muammar Gaddafi," accessed June 16, 2024, https://www.icc-cpi.int/defendant/muammar-gaddafi.

[19] UN Security Council, Resolution 1970, S/RES/1970 (Feb. 26, 2011).

[20] For the case against Bashir, see the *Prosecutor v. Omar Hassan Ahmad Al Bashir*, ICC-02/05-01/09. See also Reed Brody, "Bringing a dictator to Justice: The Case of Hissène Habré," *Journal of International Criminal Justice* 13, no. 2 (May 2015).

[21] See UN Security Council, Resolutions 2293, S/RES/2293, para. 7 (June 23, 2016); 2521, S/RES/2521, para. 15 (May 29, 2020); 2174, S/RES/2174, para. 4 (Aug. 27, 2014); 2213, S/RES/2213, para. 11(a) (Mar. 27, 2015); among others.

including with the aim of facilitating the peaceful resolution of conflict and the cessation of hostilities, humanitarian efforts, non-proliferation, compliance with international human rights law, and more."[22] The sanctions regimes impose penalties such as travel bans and freezing of assets on designated individuals and entities to prevent further violations of international humanitarian and human rights law.

The Council has also employed peacekeeping missions as another means of securing international peace and security.[23] The practice of using peacekeepers to monitor ceasefires, oversee foreign troops' withdrawals, or provide a buffer zone between belligerents began in 1956 with the establishment of the first peacekeeping mission by the UN General Assembly.[24] But there is a major difference between the peacekeeping forces authorized before 1999, and those established after the failures of UN peacekeeping in the former Yugoslavia and Rwanda. Prior to 1999, peacekeepers were simply meant to create a buffer zone between the parties and "keep the peace" by providing an environment conducive to achieving a peaceful settlement of the conflict..[25] Such UN peacekeeping missions enjoyed the inherent right of self-defense. After 1999, because peacekeeping forces were increasingly operating in hostile environments with active armed conflicts, the Security Council began to mandate UN peacekeeping operations to protect civilians and authorized the use of force beyond self-defense for the protection of civilians under Chapter VII. For example, various UN-led peacekeeping missions have had to engage in combat to defend themselves as well as civilians and humanitarian personnel.[26] The peacekeeping missions' experiences in the Democratic Republic of the Congo, Ivory Coast, Mali,

[22] See Fionnuala Ní Aoláin, "The Impact of Counter-Terrorism Targeted Sanctions on Human Rights," UN Human Rights Office of the High Commissioner (2021): 3 accessed June 16, 2024, https://www.ohchr.org/sites/default/files/2021-11/position-paper-unsrct-on-unsc-use-of-ct-targeted-sanctions.pdf.

[23] See Norrie MacQueen, *United Nations Peacekeeping in Africa Since 1960* (New York: Longman, 2002).

[24] The first mission explicitly labeled "peacekeeping" was the UN Emergency Force (UNEF) dispatched to the Sinai Peninsula following the Suez Crisis of 1956. The UN General Assembly established the UNEF during its first emergency special session. UN General Assembly, Resolution 1001 (ES-I), A/RES/1001(ES-I) (Nov. 7, 1956). See William J. Durch, ed., *The Evolution of UN Peacekeeping: Case Studies and Comparative Analysis* (New York: St. Martin's Press, 1993), 7.

[25] See Richard K. Betts, "The Delusion of Impartial Intervention," *Foreign Affairs* 73, no. 6 (Nov.–Dec. 1994).

[26] See Jackson Nyamuya Maogoto, "Yesterday's Mistakes Still Today's News: The Persisting Cloud of Humanitarian Violations over United Nations Peacekeeping: A New Agenda for Accountability," *African Yearbook of International Law* 16, no. 1 (2008).

and South Sudan against attacks by parties to the respective conflicts highlight this new reality.

Since the early 1990s, Security Council resolutions on peacekeeping have explicitly authorized peacekeepers to engage in core rule of law activities.[27] These missions have been involved in implementing peace agreements, disarmament, demobilization, reintegration of former combatants, and strengthening of judicial and state institutions. Peacekeeping functions are performed in the wider framework of promoting human rights, enhancing socioeconomic development, and supporting state institutions central for the advancement of the rule of law. Through such mandates, the Council seeks to help countries torn apart by conflicts to create conditions for sustainable peace and sustainable development. Alleviating the root causes of conflict and promoting justice as well as the dignity and worth of human beings contributes to international peace and stability, which in the process guarantees the realization of global order based on the international rule of law.

Since 1999, the Security Council has also sought to protect civilians and to prevent mass atrocities in the mandates it entrusts to the UN peacekeeping missions and operations including, inter alia, "to prevent the outbreak of conflict or the spill-over of conflict across borders; to stabilize conflict situations after a ceasefire, to create an environment for the parties to reach a lasting peace agreement"; to protect and promote human rights; and to promote social and economic recovery and development.[28] The Security Council has also established thematic mandates, including those for the protection of women and children in armed conflict, and for the protection of civilians.[29]

Section IV: Challenges to Justice and Rule of Law as a Prevention Tool

The rule of law—both at national and international levels—can hardly advance when individuals commit mass atrocity crimes with impunity, or

[27] See generally Robert A. Blair, "UN Peacekeeping and the Rule of Law" *American Political Science Review* 115, no. 1 (2021).

[28] See United Nations Peacekeeping, "Mandates and the Legal Basis for Peacekeeping," accessed June 16, 2024, https://peacekeeping.un.org/en/mandates-and-legal-basis-peacekeeping.

[29] See UN Security Council Resolutions 1325 Resolution on Women, Peace and Security, S/RES/1325 (Oct. 31, 2000); 1612 Resolution on Children and Armed Conflict, S/RES/1612 (Jul. 26, 2005); 1674 Resolution on Protection of Civilians in Armed Conflict, S/RES/1674 (Apr. 28, 2006).

when states fail to implement their international treaty obligations in good faith, whether by prosecuting the perpetrators in their courts or by referral to international courts or tribunals.[30] Indeed, events in Rwanda and the Balkans are reminders that the international community has an obligation to work together to prevent and punish these crimes—not only as a tribute to victims, but as a deterrent for future crimes and a mechanism to strengthen global order based on justice and equal rights. Provided that its member states have the requisite political will, the Security Council can prevent mass atrocity crimes and bring perpetrators to justice. By ensuring accountability and ending impunity, the Council can send a clear message to perpetrators and those who aid and abet them.

Through multilateralism, states can successfully and collectively address myriad obstacles facing the international community. Indeed, states *must* tackle certain challenges by working together through the multilateral framework, including existential threats such as climate change and nuclear proliferation, as well as other global threats like pandemics, terrorism, and transnational crime, among others. However, there is evidence to show that some powerful states are selective in how they uphold their international responsibilities and implement decisions of international bodies.[31] These developments do not inspire confidence in the legitimacy and application of the international rule of law. When states selectively implement decisions of international bodies, or selectively fulfill their international legal obligations, they willfully undermine the very institutions at the heart of prevention efforts and forestall the peaceful resolution of conflicts and amicable settlement of disputes.[32]

Often, the Security Council has failed to agree on how to address the wide range of violent and nonviolent threats to international peace and security, like climate change, that face our common humanity. The permanent members of the UN Security Council, by virtue of their privileged

[30] On state challenges to uphold their treaty obligations, see Divyanshu Kumar and Rudransh, "Frail International Obligation and Imperiled Global Peace: The Myth of Pacta Sunt Servanda," *International Journal of Law Management & Humanities* 5, no. 3 (May 2020): 868.

[31] For example, see Legal Consequences of the Separation of the Chagos Archipelago from Mauritius in 1965, Advisory Opinion, 2019 ICJ 95 (Feb. 25). See also UN General Assembly, Resolution 73/295, para. 3, Advisory Opinion of the International Court of Justice on the Legal Consequences of the Separation of the Chagos Archipelago from Mauritius in 1965, A/RES/73/295 (May 22, 2019).

[32] On selective or unequal application of international law among states, see generally Gerry Simpson, *Great Powers and Outlaw States: Unequal Sovereigns in the International Legal Order* (Cambridge: Cambridge University Press, 2004).

positions and veto power, should always look above their national interest by reaffirming the Council's primary responsibility and affirmative duty to prevent aggression, genocide, and other mass atrocity crimes in the collective interests of the global human family. The UN Charter envisions a multilateral approach and collective response to such global challenges. The permanent members must demonstrate their commitment to the Charter's vision and principles in order to enhance confidence among both developing and developed countries, and to restore the credibility of the Security Council as a legitimate and effective actor in the face of modern threats to the peace and security of the world.

Only through legitimacy and legality of Council decisions may global citizens have confidence in its actions. Yet ongoing crises in Ukraine, Palestine, and Sudan, and lingering conflicts in Haiti, Myanmar, Syria, Ethiopia, and elsewhere do not inspire confidence in the ability of the Council to look beyond the geopolitical interests of its permanent members. Further, the inability of some powerful member states to implement in good faith the decisions of the ICJ and the warrants of the ICC demonstrates the unequal application of international law and inconsistent enforcement of Council resolutions. This is especially true for those powerful states that consider themselves beacons of upholding an international order based on the rule of law.[33]

Mindful that the United Nations cannot address all global challenges because of its limited resources and reach, there is a strong need to encourage and support regional and national efforts to enhance the rule of law as a prevention tool. The United Nations can complement rather than supplant these efforts. As foreseen in Chapter VII of the UN Charter, regional arrangements and other organizations can also play a relevant and consequential role. It is critical that the international community in general, and the Security Council in particular, support these regional efforts, both bilaterally and multilaterally through the United Nations.

The peacekeeping deployments of the African Union and the Economic Community of West African States and the jurisprudence of the African Court on Human and Peoples' Rights have made a significant contribution, both as powerful prevention tools and accountability mechanisms. The Organization of American States and the Inter-American Court of Human Rights have also made important contributions to preventive diplomacy,

[33] See Chagos Archipelago, Advisory Opinion, 2019 ICJ 95; A/RES/73/295, para. 3.

peacekeeping, and criminal accountability. The North Atlantic Treaty Organization and the League of Arab States have been important partners to the Security Council in Afghanistan, Kosovo, Libya, and Syria. The effective exercise of the powers of these organizations at the regional level will not only bolster international efforts but will also encourage states to address their disputes amicably, while warning perpetrators of international crimes that they will be held to account for their actions.

The rule of law is critical both within countries—especially those emerging from conflicts—as well as among the nations of the world. Efforts to advance the rule of law are necessary in every country and every region, within the UN and throughout the actions and activities of the organization of its member states. The Summit of the Future, to be held in September 2024, can form a partnership to advance the universal values and principles of the UN Charter and give effect to the commitments already made but yet to be fulfilled in the 1993 Vienna Declaration and Programme of Action, which called upon states to collaborate on aspects of common interest on the basis of those very same shared values to advance the rule of law and human rights.

Conclusion and Way Forward

As we approach the twentieth anniversary of the Responsibility to Protect, I recall my words on the occasion of its tenth anniversary:

> We are . . . witnessing an alarming decline in the protection of human rights and respect for international humanitarian law . . . [and of] the legal framework for the prevention and punishment of atrocity crimes, including the Convention on the Prevention and Punishment of the Crime of Genocide, the Geneva Conventions, and the Rome Statute of the International Criminal Court . . . We must do better, not simply because atrocity crimes present a deep affront to our common humanity, but also as a matter of pragmatic policy. As today's headlines demonstrate so clearly, atrocity crimes exacerbate protection needs, turn existing crises into more severe humanitarian emergencies, and generating lasting instability, both within and across borders. . . . It is thus imperative that we accelerate

implementation of the Responsibility to Protect and invest new resources in atrocity prevention.[34]

If supported and strengthened, accountability and the rule of law can immensely contribute to prevent international human rights violations and mass atrocities. Justice and the rule of law are also tools to promote development and social justice. Ensuring that states can implement their international and regional legal obligations in good faith will contribute to creating an international order based on justice and equal rights.

It is equally true that while states continue to create international and regional frameworks and institutions to prevent conflicts, some very powerful states have and continue to undermine these multilateral institutions and systems by selectively implementing, or worse yet, violating their obligations. This situation has challenged not only the legitimacy of such institutions, but also the very trust in the fairness and efficacy of the multilateral system, especially by those who are economically and politically less powerful in the Global South. Multilateralism can only succeed when based on equal application of the law, mutual trust, and good faith. While the UN Charter reaffirms the sovereign equality of states in international affairs, some powerful states continue to flout these basic norms, especially when they are acting based on narrowly defined national interests. This selective application of supposedly universal norms undermines the basic trust in the workings of the international system and its multilateral institutions.

The UN Security Council has increasingly relied on accountability and the rule of law to strengthen international efforts to prevent conflicts. The Security Council can do more to respect the jurisdiction of the ICJ and ICC, to ensure compliance with their decisions, and to encourage cooperation with and support for their work. International law must apply equally to large and small nations alike, to powerful and not-so-powerful states alike. Indeed, while the ICJ and ICC are critical to the advancement of accountability and the rule of law, their inability to hold everyone accountable and ensure all states implement their decisions in good faith leaves them susceptible to criticism of selective justice. This wholly undermines their raison d'être as impartial guarantors of the international legal order.

[34] Adama Dieng, "Ten Years of the Responsibility to Protect," (keynote address, Law, Justice and Development Week, Washington, DC, Nov. 16, 2015), accessed June 16, 2024, https://pubdocs.worldbank.org/en/515491448037451017/AdamaDieng-Keynote-LJDWeek2015.pdf.

Ultimately, if the Security Council succeeds in preventing and seeking accountability for mass atrocity crimes, it should encourage the building of preventive capabilities and institutions at the national level, promote cooperation with security arrangements at the regional level, and strengthen its preventive diplomacy and early deployments at the international level. The United Nations and its member states must ensure greater commitment to and investment in national and international institutions that are responsible for the protection of civilians, to ensure the dignity and worth of every human being. Ensuring human rights and respect for the rule of law eliminates the root causes of conflict and threats to national, regional, and international peace and security.

Overall, for accountability and the rule of law to succeed as a preventive tool, the Security Council should cooperate with member states, regional organizations, and international courts to fulfill the vision and promise of the UN Charter and other international and regional human rights frameworks. The UN's success is dependent upon its member states' willingness to respect the human rights of their own people; to commit to multilateralism that is grounded in mutual respect and good faith; to accept equal application of the law where all states are equally bound to fulfill their treaty obligations; and to carry out the decisions of the Council and the national, regional, and international courts even when they do not fully align with states' national interests. Such accountability for the obligations of the most powerful and such respect for the rights of the less powerful will realize the aspirations of our collective humanity as expressed by "We the Peoples" in the UN Charter.

PART III

RESTRAINING THE VETO

5

Restoring the Legitimacy of the Security Council

Ian Johnstone

Introduction

In the heady days at the end of the Cold War, the UN Security Council unleashed itself from tight constraints on its ability to act brought about by superpower rivalry. It adopted unprecedented measures to drive Iraq out of Kuwait and dismantle its weapons of mass destruction. The Council also established international criminal tribunals for the former Yugoslavia and for Rwanda; deployed "robust" peacekeeping missions where there was no real peace to keep and authorized them to use force beyond self-defense and for the protection of civilians; mandated transitional administrations in East Timor and in Kosovo; and adopted far-reaching resolutions to suppress terrorism and the proliferation of weapons of mass destruction. The worry then was about a Council inclined to overreach. Those days are gone.

Today, the worry is about an underachieving Council, one that is failing in its primary responsibility for the maintenance of international peace and security. Recent uses of the veto by Russia, China, and the United States have contributed to this concern, but the looming dysfunctionality extends beyond those cases. Geopolitical tensions among the Great Powers, combined with the nationalist, inward-looking brand of populism that has taken hold in many countries, makes one wonder whether the Council will soon become incapable of doing anything to prevent, contain, manage, or resolve conflicts.

To what extent is the Council's failure to act damaging its legitimacy? What can be done, short of reforms that require UN Charter amendment, to restore that legitimacy? Those are the questions this chapter explores. Employing a sociological conception of legitimacy, it focuses on perceptions or beliefs about the Council's right to exercise authority and posits that those

Ian Johnstone, *Restoring the Legitimacy of the Security Council* In: *Empowering the UN Security Council*. Edited by: Mona Ali Khalil and Floriane Lavaud, Oxford University Press. © Oxford University Press 2024. DOI: 10.1093/oso/9780197780602.003.0006

perceptions depend at least in part on the Security Council's performance—or lack thereof—in maintaining international peace and security. Drawing on the theory of deliberative democracy, the chapter treats the quality of the Council's deliberations as a measure of its legitimacy. Though far from an ideal setting for principled deliberation, certain features of the Council make such deliberations possible.

Finally, the chapter offers a set of proposals designed to generate greater pressure on Council members—the permanent five (P5) in particular—to live up to their responsibilities more fully. These measures alone cannot redeem the Council in the eyes of those who see it as a fundamentally flawed institution, but they can help to address the Council's legitimacy deficit. In so doing, the measures may help pave the way to the more far-reaching reforms to the composition and P5 veto power that can only be achieved by amending the Charter.

Section I: The Legitimacy of the UN Security Council

A. Sources of legitimacy: a sociological perspective

Legitimacy is a notoriously elusive concept, but it is an important feature of good governance. Governments or institutions that lack legitimacy rule primarily through fear and coercion. "Police states" do not have inherent legitimacy and for that reason must rely heavily on coercive power to rule their subjects. All legal systems depend on coercion to an extent (the threat of litigation or incarceration), but well-functioning societies do not operate on the basis of fear and the threat of punishment alone. The citizenry "buys into" the system and follows the rules voluntarily.

Allen Buchanan and Robert O. Keohane define political (or institutional) legitimacy simply as "the right to rule."[1] In other words, an entity that exercises authority is legitimate if it has the right to exercise that authority. The authors draw a distinction between "normative" and "sociological" conceptions of legitimacy.

A normative approach tries to identify objective criteria against which any institution's authority can be measured. In other words, it asks what features

[1] Allen Buchanan and Robert O. Keohane, "The Legitimacy of Global Governance Institutions," *Ethics and International Affairs* 20, no. 4 (December 2006): 405.

of the governing institution give it the right to rule. Conversely, a "sociological" or "subjective" approach does not search for objective criteria that apply universally, but focuses instead on the beliefs of those who are subject to the authority. According to Jonas Tallberg, legitimacy is "the perception or belief within a given audience that an institution's authority is appropriately exercised."[2] Does that audience believe the institution has the right to rule?

Adopting a sociological approach does not mean it is pointless to speak about legitimacy criteria, but simply that the inquiry is empirical, not theoretical. Those who are deciding whether an institution is worthy of their support might well apply criteria that look much like what normative theorists have identified. (Is the institution representative? Does it have the consent of the governed? Does it produce good outcomes?) But those criteria are not "objective" standards that apply universally, but rather the standards that tend to be applied in a particular community at a particular moment in time.

From a subjective, sociological perspective, the question is, "What are the sources of legitimacy in a particular context or society?" The list of potential sources is long and varies from society to society. They could be *procedural*, for example, whether a government is elected. They could be tied to *performance*, for example, how well the authorities deliver basic services, such as security, health, or education. The source of legitimacy might stem from tradition, religion, identity, or ideology. For most institutions in most places, the relevant sources of legitimacy are a combination of the above. A governing authority may benefit from multiple sources of legitimacy and may seek to legitimize its authority through different techniques.

Transposing this to the UN Security Council (UNSC), the question is whether states and other stakeholders perceive the institution to be legitimate. And if so, on what basis? The standard critique of the Council relates to its structure: the five permanent members with veto power no longer reflect the distribution of power in the world, nor do they "represent" all states, let alone peoples. That critique is true, but it is not the whole story. How the Council goes about fulfilling its mission (process legitimacy) and what it achieves (performance legitimacy) are also part of the story.

[2] Jonas Tallberg, "Legitimacy and Modes of Global Governance" in *Global Governance in a World of Change*, ed. Michael Barnett, Jon Pevehouse, and Kal Raustiala (Cambridge: Cambridge University Press, 2021), 311.

B. The Security Council's failure to act

Questions about the UNSC's performance legitimacy arise in two ways: when it acts and when it fails to act. The first has been the subject of a large body of literature, including scholarship on whether the International Court of Justice has the power of judicial review.[3] A strong case can be made that, when the UNSC chooses to act in response to a threat to the peace, it is not entirely unconstrained in the actions it may take. These constraints have legal roots in Article 24(2) of the UN Charter, which states the UNSC must act in accordance with the purposes and principles of the UN Charter. There is also a body of opinion suggesting that, while binding Security Council decisions may supersede any other international *agreements* (Article 103), they cannot conflict with *jus cogens* obligations.[4] Under pressure from the E10, the UNSC amended the procedures in its targeted sanctions regimes to ensure greater fairness, transparency, and due process—suggesting that at least some members acknowledged implicitly there were limitations on the Council's powers.[5]

As noted in the introduction, however, current questions about the UNSC's performance relate more to its inaction than to what it does when it chooses to act. While members of the UNSC do not have a legal obligation to respond to every threat to the peace, there are institutional, political, and maybe even ethical constraints on their discretion to do nothing.[6] These constraints also have roots in the UN Charter. For example, Article 24(1) imposes a responsibility to act on behalf of the membership as a whole and to do so promptly and effectively. Jennifer Trahan claims that, in certain circumstances, use of the veto would be a violation not only of the UN

[3] José Alvarez, "Judging the Security Council," *American Journal of International Law* 90 (1996): 28; Ian Johnstone, "Legislation and Adjudication in the UN Security Council: Bringing Down the Deliberative Deficit," *American Journal of International Law* 102 (2008): 275; Erica de Wet, *The Chapter VII Powers of the United Nations Security Council* (Oxford: Hart Publishing, 2004).

[4] *See* Michael Wood and Eran Shtoeger, *The UN Security Council and International Law* (Cambridge: Cambridge University Press, 2022); Joined Cases C-402/05 P & C-415/05 P, *Yassin Abdullah Kadi and Al Barakaat International Foundation v. Council and Comm'n*, ECLI:EU:C:2008:461 (Sep. 3, 2008).

[5] See, e.g., UN Security Council, Resolution 1904, S/RES/1904 (Dec. 17, 2009) (establishing the Office of the Ombudsperson to the ISIL (Da'esh) and Al-Qaida Sanctions Committee); UN Security Council, Resolution 2664, S/RES/2664 (Dec. 9, 2022) (approving humanitarian exemption to asset-freeze measures imposed by UN sanctions regimes).

[6] Ian Johnstone, "The UN Security Council's Responsibility to Act," (background paper, "Peace as a Global Public Good" Experts Roundtable, Mar. 11, 2022), accessed June 8, 2024, https://highleveladvisoryboard.org/download/the-un-security-councils-responsibility-to-act/.

Charter but also of the Genocide Convention and Geneva Conventions.[7] Her argument, in effect, is that the five permanent members have a legal obligation *not* to veto a resolution when states violate the prohibition of genocide and other *jus cogens* norms.[8]

This is an interesting (albeit contestable) position. Even if one accepts that there is a "duty to act" in certain circumstances, converting that into an actionable legal obligation is difficult. A theory has been advanced that an "unreasonable use of the veto" opens the door to forcible action by a state or group of states that would otherwise be illegal.[9] Indeed, at the UN's founding San Francisco conference, France and other states proposed that UN member states should have the right to act "in the interest of peace, right, and justice" in the face of Security Council paralysis.[10]

Beyond the right of self-defense, states did not accept this view when the Charter was drafted. However, the suggestion did resonate during the Cold War when the Security Council found it difficult to act on any threat to the peace. It also served a rhetorical purpose in the post-Cold War era after the UNSC was criticized for doing too little in Bosnia and in Rwanda. In the context of the Kosovo crisis, Sir Christopher Greenwood testified to the UK House of Commons Foreign Affairs Committee that "interpretation of international law which would forbid intervention to prevent something as terrible as the Holocaust, unless a permanent member could be persuaded to lift its veto, would be contrary to the principles on which modern

[7] Jennifer Trahan, *Existing Legal Limits to the Security Council Veto Power in the Face of Atrocity Crimes* (Cambridge: Cambridge University Press, 2020), 142–259.

[8] Jennifer Trahan, "Legal Issues Surrounding Veto Use and Aggression," *Case Western Reserve General of International Law* 55, no. 1 (2023). Louise Arbour, former Canadian Supreme Court judge, UN high commissioner for human rights, and ICTY prosecutor, considers the possibility that the Genocide Convention, as interpreted by the ICJ in the Bosnia case, imposes an obligation on the five permanent members of the Security Council not to exercise their veto to prevent an end to genocide. Louise Arbour, "The Responsibility to Protect as a Duty of Care in International Law and Practice," *Review of International Studies* 34, no. 3 (2008): 453. For a contrary view, see André Nollkamper, "'Failures to Protect' in International Law," in *The Oxford Handbook on the Use of Force in International Law*, ed. Marc Weller (Oxford: Oxford University Press 2015), 448–52. See also Anne Peters, "The Responsibility to Protect: Spelling Out the Hard Legal Consequences for the UN Security Council and Its Members," in *From Bilaterialism to Community Interest: Essays in Honour of Bruno Simma*, eds. Ulrich Fastenrath et al. (Oxford: Oxford University Press, 2011), 320.

[9] For an analysis (and rejection) of the theory, see Ian Johnstone, "When the Security Council Is Divided: Imprecise Authorizations, Implied Mandates, and the 'Unreasonable Veto,'" in Marc Weller, ed., *Oxford Handbook on the Law on the Use of Force* (Oxford: Oxford University Press, 2015), 246–48.

[10] France and Australia, for example. Ruth B. Russell, *A History of the United Nations Charter: The Role of the United States, 1940–1945* (Washington, DC: Brookings Institution, 1958); Carsten Stahn, "Enforcement of the Collective Will after Iraq," *American Journal of International Law* 97, no. 4 (Oct. 2003): 810.

international law is based as well as flying in the face of the developments of the last 50 years."[11]

The problem with the unreasonable use of the veto argument is that there are no criteria for determining when a veto is "unreasonable." That might have been addressed by the International Commission on Intervention and State Sovereignty's (ICISS's) six principles on when intervention would (and would not be) appropriate, ideally with UNSC authorization but if necessary without it.[12] But the World Summit of 2005, in endorsing the idea of a "responsibility to protect," did not endorse intervention without UNSC authorization, nor did it adopt the ICISS criteria. Moreover, the World Summit outcome document was carefully drafted to preclude an interpretation that R2P imposed a positive legal duty on the UNSC to end or prevent mass atrocities.[13] Nevertheless, these normative considerations do have a political effect. Even if a member of the Council cannot be held accountable in a court for failing to live up to a "duty to act," political pressure can be brought to bear, even on the P5. Despite appearances, none of the P5 want a completely dysfunctional Council. They all have some interest in preserving its credibility for varying and diverging reasons.

Someday, maybe soon, one or more of the P5 could cease to see the Council that way, but that day has not yet come. Until it does, they understand that, if the Council develops the reputation for being a mere vessel for manipulation by the most powerful states, it would lose all influence.[14] That understanding will never be enough to force the Council to act in a manner that one of the P5 sees as contrary to its fundamental security interests. It may, however, provide enough of an incentive to stop the Council from fading into irrelevance because it has lost all legitimacy.

[11] Christopher Greenwood, "International Law and the NATO Intervention in Kosovo," *International and Comparative Law Quarterly* 49, no. 4 (Oct. 2000): 930.

[12] International Commission on Intervention and State Sovereignty, *The Responsibility to Protect* (Ottawa: International Development Research Centre, Dec. 2001), xi–xiii, accessed June 8, 2024, https://www.globalr2p.org/wp-content/uploads/2019/10/2001-ICISS-Report.pdf.

[13] UN General Assembly, Resolution 60/1, A/RES/60/1, paras. 138–39 (Oct. 24, 2005). On the negotiations leading to the wording, see Ian Johnstone, *The Power of Deliberation: International Law, Politics and Organizations* (New York: Oxford University Press, 2011): 71–72.

[14] Jeremy Farall et al., "Elected Member Influence in the United Nations Security Council," *Leiden Journal of International Law* 33 (2020): 112.

Section II: Deliberative Legitimacy in the UN Security Council

A. Theory of deliberative democracy

Calls for reform of the UN Security Council are often couched in terms of democracy, a touchstone of legitimacy.[15] However, "democratizing" the Council is a tall order not only from a practical political point of view, but also as a matter of democratic theory. After all, neither the principle of "one state, one vote" nor that of "one person, one vote" can apply unproblematically to an international organization. The first in effect gives each citizen of Bahrain (population about 1.5 million in 2023) nearly a thousand times more voting power than a citizen of India (population more than 1.4 billion). One could argue that sovereign equality in voting power is the appropriate decision-making formula in an international organization, but it is not "democratic" if by democracy we mean rule by the people. One person, one vote, on the other hand, is more democratic by that measure, and it can be operationalized through weighted voting based on population. But the normative foundation for majority rule by population assumes there is some demos—some sense of peoplehood, some community—within which the minority is prepared to accept and live by the decisions of the majority. There is room for debate about whether a demos exists at the European level, but it does not exist at the global level.

Yet looking only at voting power reflects an overly narrow conception of democracy. The theory of deliberative democracy rests on the principle that, in addition to voting arrangements, the quality of deliberations that precede and follow votes is a measure of legitimacy. In other words, democratic legitimacy stems not simply from the aggregation of preferences of the citizenry, but from the collection of reasoned arguments and viewpoints. According to one useful definition, deliberation occurs when "participants exchange views in order to arrive at well-informed individual positions or group decisions, justify their conclusions to others who are affected by them, and reveal the process by which the group reached those conclusions."[16] The idea has a long pedigree that dates back to Immanuel Kant, since shaped by the

[15] See Allen Buchanan and Robert O. Keohane, "The Legitimacy of Global Governance Institutions," *Ethics & International Affairs* 20, no. 4 (Dec. 2006).

[16] Chad Raphael and Christopher Karpowitz, "Good Publicity: The Legitimacy of Public Communication of Deliberation," *Political Communication* 30 (2013): 18.

philosophies of Jürgen Habermas and John Rawls. Reduced to its simplest formulation, deliberation means that good arguments should underpin public policy decisions.

What counts as a good argument varies with context. Nevertheless, Amy Gutmann and Dennis Thompson suggest it is possible to generalize about what constitutes a good argument in any public policy setting. Public policy disagreements, they argue, are settled through the exchange of "reciprocal reasons." "You make your claims on terms that I can accept in principle . . . I make my claims on terms that you can accept in principle."[17] More concretely, good arguments on matters of public policy are impartial (i.e., not purely self-serving), are cast in terms that are understood as being relevant to the purpose of the enterprise, and at least notionally account for the interests of all those affected.[18] Obviously, consensus is not always possible in a pluralistic society, which is why legislatures vote. Political actors often trade those votes in a bargaining process where power and self-interest matter a great deal, but the bargains struck and the outcome of votes are influenced by the arguments and reasons exchanged in public debate.

Importantly, the theory is both descriptive and prescriptive. It is meant to describe not only what *should* happen in public debates about matters of policy, but what *actually does* happen. Of course, participants sometimes explain their positions based purely on self-interest, and there is value in that. (It is useful to know how one's interlocutors understand their interests.) But if the goal is to persuade others to support your position, then you are more likely to use arguments that serve not only your interests, but also the interests of those you are trying to persuade.

Consider a hypothetical. Suppose an ambassador to the UN Security Council from State X is seeking to win support for a resolution authorizing military action against State Y, a country that is amassing a large quantity of weapons, contrary to an arms embargo that the Council has imposed. Suppose also that large reserves of valuable natural resources exist in State Y. It would do the ambassador little good to say to the other members of the Council, "I seek your support for this resolution because my country has an interest in acquiring those natural resources and would like to install a regime that will guarantee our exclusive access to it." That argument is entirely

[17] Amy Gutmann and Dennis Thompson, *Democracy and Disagreement* (Cambridge, MA: Belknap Press, 1996), 55.

[18] *See* Ian Johnstone, *The Power of Deliberation: International Law, Politics, and Organizations* (Oxford: Oxford University Press, 2011): 14–16.

self-serving and not based on any mutually acceptable understanding of the purpose the Security Council serves. The ambassador would be wiser to say, "I seek your support for this resolution because State Y is in violation of the arms embargo imposed by this Council, which was designed to eliminate the threat to regional and international security those weapons pose." The second argument is also self-serving (State X has an interest in regional and international security), but it is not purely so because it appeals to a collective interest. Moreover, it is based on a reasoning that reflects a shared understanding of the UNSC's purpose. Even if State X's principal motivation is to get its hands on the natural resources of State Y, it will not argue that in a public meeting of the UN Security Council. Doing so would not help but rather hurt its chances of getting the support it seeks. As applied to international relations, deliberative theory does not suggest states ever argue against their national interests (or that we should expect them to), but rather that to win support for their position, they would do better to frame those interests in terms of some principle or purpose that the speaker and listener share.

B. Deliberation in the Security Council

To assess the legitimacy of the UNSC, it is useful to think of its deliberations in terms of four concentric circles: the P5 are at the center, surrounded by the ten elected members (E10), who in turn are surrounded by the rest of the UN membership. These three circles are situated within a broad constellation of nonstate actors (nongovernmental organizations, think tanks and academics, the private sector, philanthropies, and the like) that are affected by and pay attention to what the Council does. The P5, in other words, are embedded in the Council as a whole. The Council is embedded in the broader UN membership. And the broader UN membership—that is, the governments of the world—are embedded in or at least influenced by their own publics and transnational civil society. Most of these actors have only limited ability to participate directly in Council meetings, although various mechanisms have been developed to allow Council members to hear from nonmembers and nonstate actors, as discussed further below. But just as important as participation is the principle of "publicity": the idea that the need to justify one's position in public is a check on taking positions that others would view as unjustifiable.

There is, however, a problem with transposing deliberative democracy principles to the international level, similar to the problem with transposing majority rule by population beyond the level of the nation-state. While a demos in the sense of "peoplehood" may not be necessary for principled deliberation, the theory is premised on there being a repository of shared experiences, assumptions, and understandings that makes it possible for people to speak *to* rather than *past* each other. Some scholars who write on the European Union see such a repository at the European level.[19] To varying degrees, it may exist in other regions or subregions or among groups of like-minded states. It is a stretch to suggest it exists at the global level.

If one moves beyond abstractions, however, it is worth asking whether the UN Security Council inhabits what Jürgen Habermas has called a "common lifeworld" and others have described in terms of "background knowledge."[20] The UNSC is a highly pluralistic body where the distribution of power and national security interests vary widely. Members of the Council may profess a commitment to the principles embodied in the UN Charter, but do they share, as a result of their membership, a repository of experiences, assumptions, and understandings about their role? Arguably not, especially at moments of great geopolitical tension when the divisions are not only about competing interests, but also different ideologies.

Yet the P5 have been meeting with each other on a daily basis for close to eighty years. In discussing and debating how to respond to crises, they have in effect been deliberating about what the maintenance of international peace and security means, with the UN Charter serving as a frame of reference. These debates are often in private, but informed by the expectations and understandings of the broader UN membership. Whatever disagreements they may have on how to manage conflicts, the states have come to acquire certain shared understandings about the purpose of the joint enterprise in which they are mutually engaged.

One or another member of the Council may try to push the boundaries from time to time. That may generate opposition, but the opposition is typically framed in terms of the appropriate role for the UNSC. For example, do nonviolent threats such as to the environment and to public health fall

[19] Jürgen Habermas, "Why Europe Needs a Constitution," *New Left Review* 11 (2001): 5-26; Michael Zurn, "Democratic Governance Beyond the Nation State: The EU and Other International Institutions," *European Journal of International Relations* 6 (2000): 183-221.

[20] John Searle, *Expression and Meaning: Studies in the Theory of Speech Acts* (Cambridge: Cambridge University Press, 2011), 1, 4.

within the UNSC's competence or not? Those involved in the debate may disagree, but they are speaking to rather than past each other. That in itself is important. Deliberation does not always lead to agreement, even in the most cohesive polities. If anything, the more important outcome of democratic deliberation is to make it easier to live peacefully with disagreement.

It is certainly possible that the Council has become so divided, and the world so polarized, that the conditions for reasoned deliberation no longer exist. A body of writing on "comparative international law" posits that there is no single international law, but rather there are multiple, fundamentally different approaches—an American approach, a Chinese approach, a European approach, a Russian approach, and so on.[21] In the view of this author, that literature overstates the degree of divergence, but it is not hard to see how the current geopolitical fissures and nationalistic impulses may slowly erode whatever shared norms existed in the heady post–Cold War days. Perhaps the body at the epicenter of these fissures—the UN Security Council—can help to stave that off.

Section III: Addressing the Security Council's Legitimacy Deficit

If one reason the Security Council is facing a legitimacy crisis is its failure to act in response to security threats, then one way of addressing that crisis is by generating a greater sense of responsibility to act, and to act responsibly. Improving the quality of deliberation in the Council can do that. Below are a set of proposals to achieve this goal, underpinned by the twin principles of participation and publicity. Participation does not simply mean a seat at the UNSC table. As noted above, there are multiple formats for consultation between UNSC members, non-UNSC members, and nonstate actors. Where once the UNSC only had open and closed meetings, it now has "informal interactive dialogues," Arria formula meetings, meetings with troop- and police-contributing countries, and Security Council visiting missions, to name but a few of the wide-ranging, interactive consultative formats.[22]

[21] See Anthea Roberts et al., eds., *Comparative International Law* (Oxford: Oxford University press, 2018).

[22] See Loraine Sievers and Sam Daws, *The Procedure of the UN Security Council*, 4th ed. (Oxford: Oxford University Press, 2014); Permanent Mission of Japan to the United Nations, *Handbook on the Working Methods of the Security Council* (Jan. 2021), accessed June 8, 2024, https://www.un.org/securitycouncil/sites/www.un.org.securitycouncil/files/handbook_on_the_working_methods_of_the_security_council.pdf.

Similarly, publicity is not simply about publicizing the work of the Council. It is about leveraging the audience effect; shining a spotlight on Council members and requiring them to justify their action or inaction, as does the recent General Assembly resolution creating a standing mandate for a General Assembly debate when a veto is cast in the Security Council.[23] Some of the proposals below are new; most are not. Some are aimed at generating restraint in the exercise of the veto; others are about enhancing the sense of responsibility among all UNSC members.

A. Empower the E10

Each of the E10 has an *individual* voice in the Council. They also, potentially, have a *collective* voice, either as the entire group or some subset of it. As individual states, they participate directly in the UNSC debates and, in principle, speak for the UN membership as a whole (Article 24[1]). The E10 are likely to feel that responsibility more directly than the P5 for two reasons. First, they have an interest in getting reelected to the Council someday. Second, their influence vis-à-vis the P5 depends in part on the extent to which they are seen to be speaking for a broader constituency. Much of what the UNSC does—from sanctions regimes, to nonproliferation and counterterrorism measures, to peacekeeping missions—requires buy-in from member states who are not on the Council. Each of the E10 can leverage that in trying to wield influence with the P5 and with other members of the E10.

In addition to participation, the E10 play a dual role in giving effect to the publicity principle—the idea that having to justify oneself in public generates pressure not to speak or act in a way that other actors will be view as "unjustifiable." On one hand, they are the first and most important audience to which the P5 must appeal in order to garner the nine affirmative votes required to pass a resolution. On the other hand, the E10 must think about their own audience—whether a particular region or constituency or the UN membership as a whole. Not being able to explain their action—or inaction—in terms their own audience finds acceptable undermines their credibility and future electability.

Of course, the E10 are as diverse as the wider UN membership, and each has bilateral relationships with P5 states. Reaching agreement among all E10

[23] UN General Assembly, Resolution 76/262, A/RES/76/262 (Apr. 26, 2002).

members, especially agreement on a matter that runs counter to the position taken by one of the P5, is difficult. It may be more realistic to forge unity among a like-minded subset of the E10, working together not just on one file but on all files throughout their two-year terms. A collective negative vote or abstention by seven E10 members of the UNSC can block Council action; equally, a collective positive vote of nine E10 members can be a call for action. As is pointed out in the *UN Security Council Conflict Management Handbook*,[24] the P5 sometimes threaten to use the veto in private because they do not want to have to do so in public.[25] When an initiative has enough support among the elected members to muster nine affirmative votes, these circumstances can influence permanent members to join with the majority rather than using the veto.

Moreover, an "E10 identity" is starting to emerge, which may restrain the inclination of each elected member to engage bilaterally or in transactional relations with one of the P5.[26] The E10 can cultivate this inclination by, for example, holding regular informal gatherings among their permanent representatives. For years, the Secretary-General has held monthly luncheons with P5 ambassadors, a tradition that Secretary-General António Guterres extended to the E10 ambassadors.[27] In 2019, the permanent representative of Indonesia initiated "sofa talks" among all members of the Council: unscripted "chats" with no set agenda or expected outcomes.[28] "Sofa talks" among the E10 could complement those of the Council as a whole and encourage cultivation of an E10 identity.

B. Engage with regional and other informal groupings of states

The E10 can leverage their influence with the P5 not only by working together, but also by working with their regional groups. Consider the so-called

[24] Haidi Willmot and Scott Sheeran, eds., *United Nations Security Council Conflict Management Handbook* (Abu Dhabi: Anwar Gargash Diplomatic Academy, 2023), 466, accessed June 8, 2024 , https://www.agda.ac.ae/docs/default-source/2023/unsc-conflict-management-handbook.pdf.

[25] Ibid.

[26] Arthur Boutellis, "Lessons from E10 Engagement on the Security Council," International Peace Institute (November 2022): 11.

[27] Ibid., 1.

[28] Loraine Sievers and Sam Daws, "Chapter 2, Section 13," update website of *The Procedure of the UN Security Council*, 4th ed,, Nov. 30, 2019, accessed May 21, 2024, https://www.scprocedure.org/chapter-2-section-13b. The idea originally came from Ambassador Karen Pierce of the UK. Indonesia picked up on it because the chairs of the Association of Southeast Asian Nations (ASEAN) had been holding similar meetings to good effect for many years.

A3 (the three African members of the UNSC). Increasingly, the A3 have been trying to speak on behalf of the entire Africa group through structured cooperation with the African Union (AU) Peace and Security Council and the AU Commission. One can imagine other E10 members doing the same: a Southeast Asian member, for example, coordinating with ASEAN states, or a Latin American member engaging with countries across Latin America and the Caribbean to forge collective positions. This need not be restricted to regional groups. The Group of Seven Plus (g7+) is a group of twenty states from Asia, Africa, and the Caribbean affected by conflict and fragility who formed as they were negotiating the sustainable development goals and who pushed for language about peace and justice in response to the challenges they faced in meeting the millennium development goals. Speaking on behalf of such a group could carry weight in stimulating UNSC action in fragile states. The same is true of small island developing states (SIDS) and least-developed countries (LDCs).

More structured engagement with regional and other groupings serves both participation and publicity goals. If the positions UNSC members take are informed by consultations with a broader group, they carry greater weight with the P5. It also ratchets up the audience effect. If nonpermanent members make it their business to keep their constituencies informed, it may cause the P5 to think harder about unpopular positions. While it may not stop them from using the veto when they perceive their core interests to be at stake, it could stop them from blocking initiatives where they have less at stake, such as the extension of a peacekeeping mandate in another part of the world.

C. Open up the informal processes

Much of the work of the Council takes place in informal processes. Stakeholders need opportunities to engage more fully with these informal processes, some of which have become rather pro forma, despite their informal nature.[29] Doing so would be consistent with the spirit of Articles 12, 15, 31, and 32, which require the UNGA to be kept informed and call

[29] Haidi Willmot and Scott Sheeran, eds., *United Nations Security Council Conflict Management Handbook* (Abu Dhabi: Anwar Gargash Diplomatic Academy,2023), 466, accessed June 8, 2024, https://www.agda.ac.ae/docs/default-source/2023/unsc-conflict-management-handbook.pdf.

for the participation of nonmembers in situations that specially affect them. Some positive developments have occurred in the use of informal interactive dialogues for that purpose. They began as private, open-ended UNSC consultations with the membership at large, but became stilted when the Council Members presented a united front rather than engaging participants to help resolve differences. They are now used more effectively for off-the-record meetings of the Council with representatives of one or more non-UNSC members facing a crisis, sometimes including other relevant stakeholders such as representatives of regional organizations. A more institutionalized way of doing this could be modeled on the Peacebuilding Commission configuration—composed according to the needs of the situation, bringing in non-UNSC members and international organizations on a regular basis.[30]

The presidency of the Council could also be used more robustly to augment both participation and publicity. For many years, the Council has organized formal "wrap-up" sessions at the end of each month, when the president provides an account to the wider membership of the activities for that month.[31] In 2015, Spain introduced "Toledo-style" meetings, in which a group of Council representatives "respond to questions and comments from the membership about what has and has not been achieved during the month."[32]

These informal wrap-ups not only provide greater transparency; they also "have the added benefit of allowing interactivity and allowing all General Assembly colleagues to ask us questions."[33] After four years of Toledo-style meetings, Council members felt they could be improved. To that end, a 2019 note on working methods encourages Council presidents "to forgo detailed summaries of the Council's activities during the month in favor of a more analytical discussion with non-Council members and utilize more time to hear their feedback."[34] The above-mentioned UNSC *Conflict Management Handbook* recommends using these wrap-up sessions not only to report on

[30] Ibid., 484.

[31] President of the Security Council, Note by the President of the Security Council, para. 7, UN Doc. S/2017/507 (Aug. 30, 2017).

[32] UN Security Council, 71st Sess., 7740th mtg. at 7, UN Doc. S/PV.7740 (July 19, 2016).

[33] UN Security Council, 71st Sess., 7616th mtg. at 10, UN Doc. S/PV.7616 (Jan. 29, 2016).

[34] President of the Security Council, Note by the President of the Security Council, para. c, UN Doc. S/2019/1994. On these wrap-ups, see generally Loraine Sievers and Sam Daws, "Chapter 2, Section 7," update website of *The Procedure of the UN Security Council*, 4th ed., Jan. 30, 2020, accessed June 8, 2024, https://www.scprocedure.org/chapter-2-section-7-changes.

and answer questions about the Council's work but also to stimulate action on "unfinished business."[35]

D. Magnify the audience effect

The recent UNGA Resolution 76/262 requiring Security Council members who exercise the veto to explain their rationale for doing so to the General Assembly was a major breakthrough for a number of reasons.[36] One of those is that it institutionalizes the principle that important decisions of policy should be subject to public scrutiny, inducing the decision-makers to take into account the interests of those who will be affected by compelling them to explain their actions to those stakeholders.

The France-Mexico initiative calling for restraint in exercising the veto in cases of mass atrocities would augment the impact of Resolution 76/262. P5 members who make the pledge would be in the spotlight if they break it, or if they offer unpersuasive reasons as to why it does not apply in a particular situation. Some scholars have suggested that a duty to give reasons should be extended to all Council members on all votes.[37] We should not assume the E10 are any less inclined to act in their narrow national interests than the P5. Why not create mechanisms that put the same kind of pressure on them to "do the right thing"?

E10 engagement with regional groups and wrap-up meetings also give effect to the publicity principle, generating the need to argue for the positions one has taken or intends to take. Arria-formula meetings can serve a similar purpose, especially when they are webcast to a large audience.[38] To enhance the role of transnational civil society, the General Assembly could establish an "advisory committee" of rotating members dedicated to keeping an eye on the Council and engaging with it through informal mechanisms (such as Arria-formula meetings). Even if the actual provision of advice is limited, the committee would impact Council deliberations through the audience effect.

[35] Haidi Willmot and Scott Sheeran, eds., *United Nations Security Council Conflict Management Handbook* (Abu Dhabi: Anwar Gargash Diplomatic Academy, 2023), 466, accessed June 8, 2024, https://www.agda.ac.ae/docs/default-source/2023/unsc-conflict-management-handbook.pdf.

[36] UN General Assembly, Resolution 76/262, A/RES/76/262 (Apr. 28, 2022).

[37] This could be done by amending the rules of procedure.

[38] On the pros and cons of webcasting Arria-formula meetings, see Loraine Sievers and Sam Daws, "Chapter 2, Section 11," update website of *The Procedure of the UN Security Council*, 4th ed., July 5, 2023, accessed June 8, 2024, https://www.scprocedure.org/chapter-2-section-11-changes.

Conclusion

Seeking to improve the quality of deliberations is not a substitute for structural reforms, but rather an interim albeit necessary step in that direction. Changing the composition of the Council may seem like an impossible task, but it is not, for some of the reasons addressed in this chapter. The P5 do not want a completely dysfunctional Council, emerging powers and coalitions have increasing leverage, and the world is facing multiple intersecting crises that may shift the political dynamics in favor of Charter amendment. Moreover, if and when structural reform does happen, the quality of deliberations will be no less important. In the meantime, states can preserve the legitimacy and utility of the Council through incremental steps to stem the current drift into inefficacy and irrelevance.

6

Restraining the Use of the Veto

Juan Manuel Gómez-Robledo and Pablo Arrocha Olabuenaga

Introduction

Much has been said and written over the past seven decades about the veto power of the five permanent members of the Security Council (P5). The debates go back to the very origins of the veto at the Yalta conference in February 1945,[1] at the Chapultepec conference in Mexico later that month,[2] and at the San Francisco conference in the spring of that same year. The architects of the United Nations sought to ensure that the new international organization would avoid the failures of the League of Nations and that the Allied powers of World War II would remain committed to the United Nations and the pursuit of international peace and security. To that end, the UN Charter accorded the five Great Powers—the United States, the United Kingdom, the Russian Federation (then, the Union of Soviet Socialist Republics), China, and France—permanent membership and veto power, and it entrusted the Security Council with primary responsibility for the maintenance of international peace and security.

At the same time, the vast majority of the founding members of the United Nations were aware of the danger of the P5 abusing the veto power, paralyzing the Security Council, and jeopardizing its ability to fulfill its primary responsibility. Nonetheless, the veto was the sine qua non condition for the creation of the United Nations with the participation of the five Great Powers—four of which had defeated the Axis powers of Germany, Italy, and

[1] For more details on the drafting history of Article 27 and on the Yalta formula on the veto, see Bruno Simma et al., eds., *The Charter of the United Nations: A Commentary*, 2nd ed., vol. 1 (Oxford: Oxford University Press, 2002), 581–82.

[2] For conference documents, see Office of the Historian, "The Inter-American Conference on Problems of War and Peace, held at Mexico City, February 21–March 8, 1945 (The Chapultepec Conference)—Foreign Relations of the United States: Diplomatic Papers, 1945, The American Republics, Volume IX," accessed June 11, 2024, https://history.state.gov/historicaldocuments/frus1945v09/ch1.

Juan Manuel Gómez-Robledo and Pablo Arrocha Olabuenaga, *Restraining the Use of the Veto* In: *Empowering the UN Security Council*. Edited by: Mona Ali Khalil and Floriane Lavaud, Oxford University Press. © Oxford University Press 2024. DOI: 10.1093/oso/9780197780602.003.0007

Japan. This is why China, the Soviet Union, the United Kingdom, and the United States issued a joint declaration on June 7, 1945, at the San Francisco conference, where they stated:

> In view of the primary responsibilities of the permanent members, they could not be expected, in the present condition of the world, to assume the obligation to act in so serious a matter as the maintenance of international peace and security in consequence of a decision in which they had not concurred. Therefore, if a majority voting in the Security Council is to be made possible, the only practicable method is to provide, in respect of nonprocedural decisions, for unanimity of the permanent members plus the concurring votes of at least two of the nonpermanent members.[3]

The four permanent members further stated: "It is not to be assumed, however, that the permanent members, any more than the nonpermanent members, would use their 'veto' power willfully to obstruct the operation of the Council."[4] The four permanent members were also conscious of the risks of frequent invocation or potential abuse of the veto, and sought to discipline the use of the veto and to ensure that the P5 regarded it as a responsibility—not as a privilege.

In spite of this noble intention, the reality has been a radically different one. While the introduction of the veto did away with the unanimity rule that led to the failure of the League of Nations,[5] it also planted the seed for the paralysis of the Security Council and its inability to discharge its primary responsibility under the UN Charter.

This chapter will not delve into the limits of what the Security Council can do; rather, it will explore what the P5 can prevent the Council from doing. Section I sets forth the legal limits on the use of the veto found in the purposes and principles of the UN Charter and under customary international law. Section II discusses initiatives to restrain the use of the veto in situations involving mass atrocity crimes like genocide, crimes against

[3] *See* Bruno Simma et al., eds., *The Charter of the United Nations: A Commentary*, 2nd ed., vol. 1 (Oxford: Oxford University Press, 2002), 521–23.

[4] See "Statement by the Delegations of the Four Sponsoring Governments on Voting Procedure in the Security Council," UNCIO 11 (1945), 713. Cited in Anthony Mango and Jan Osmanczyk, eds., *Encyclopedia of the United Nations and International Agreements*, 3rd ed., vol. 4 (New York: Routledge, 2003), 2587.

[5] League of Nations Covenant art. 5. See also Stephen C. Schlesinger, *Act of Creation*, (Colorado: Westview Press, 2003), 26–27.

humanity, and war crimes. Section III presents other efforts to enhance accountability and improve the effectiveness of the Security Council.

Section I: Legal Limits on the Use of the Veto

The veto enjoyed by the five permanent members of the Security Council derives from Article 27 of the UN Charter, which establishes the required majority and other procedural modalities and working methods of the Council. In particular, Article 27(3) provides that decisions on all matters other than procedural matters "shall be made by an affirmative vote of nine members including the concurring votes of the permanent members."[6] And so, if the veto applies to substantive decisions, it is necessary to consider which legal limits would apply to its use.

Beyond the general obligation to fulfill its mandate under the UN Charter, the Security Council has a primary responsibility to take prompt and effective action to restore or maintain international peace and security. This obligation derives from Article 24 of the Charter, which states that the Members of the United Nations confer on the Security Council the "primary responsibility for the maintenance of international peace and security."[7] In carrying out its duties, the Security Council acts on all UN member states' behalf.

On one hand, this means that the exercise of the veto prevents the Security Council from effectively fulfilling its responsibility to maintain peace and security through decisive action. On the other hand, it means that the exercise of the veto by one or more permanent members stops action of the entire UN membership on whose behalf the Council is intended to act.

Under certain circumstances, the veto is contrary to customary international law. It is generally acknowledged that decisions of the Security Council should not breach the *jus cogens* rules or peremptory norms and the *erga omnes* obligations of states under customary international law.[8] This is without prejudice to Article 103 of the Charter, which provides that in the

[6] It is worth noting, however, that on occasions it is difficult to make a clear-cut distinction between what the Security Council considers a substantive decision as opposed to a procedural one. For example, the established practice is that the veto does not apply to decisions related to the election of judges of the International Court of Justice (ICJ), as per Articles 415 of the statute of the ICJ, but it does apply to the decisions by which the Security Council recommends to the General Assembly the appointment of the Secretary-General in accordance with Article 97 of the Charter.

[7] UN Charter art. 24.

[8] See Jennifer Trahan, *Existing Legal Limits to Security Council Veto Power in the Face of Atrocity Crimes* (Cambridge: Cambridge University Press, 2020).

event of a conflict between the obligations of UN member states under the Charter and their obligations under any other international agreement, their obligations under the Charter shall prevail.[9]

The underlying premise for this discussion is that legal limits to the Security Council's authority exist. It is undeniable that the Council has an enormous discretion and margin of flexibility to act;[10] however, its powers are not unlimited.[11] In particular, there are two legal bases that set forth legal limits on the use of the P5's veto power. The first basis for setting a legal limit on the use of the veto is found in Article 24(2), which states that, in fulfilling its mandate, the Security Council "shall act in accordance with the Purposes and Principles of the United Nations."[12] This limit stems from a holistic and coherent treaty interpretation of the Charter as a whole. Violations of the prohibition on the use of force in Article 2(4) of the Charter offer the clearest example. If a state uses force against another state without the authorization of the Security Council and acts beyond the limits of the inherent right to individual or collective self-defense under Article 51 of the Charter, this would constitute a grave violation of Article 2(4), a breach of the peace within the meaning of Article 39, and potentially an act of aggression, also in violation of Article 39.[13]

In these circumstances, a veto exercised by one or more permanent members preventing the Security Council from taking the necessary action would de facto allow the unlawful act to continue in clear violation of the purposes and principles of the United Nations. States cannot condone the use of the veto in this context. The whole UN membership should condemn use of the veto in these circumstances as an abuse of Article 27(3) and a violation of the letter and spirit of the UN Charter. There is almost certainly no legally sound argument that a state could invoke a procedural modality such as the veto with that objective. Moreover, it would be near impossible to argue that Article 27(3) was purposefully drafted to allow for this eventuality.

[9] UN Charter art. 103.

[10] For a wider analysis of the way in which the Security Council has interpreted its role when acting under Chapter VII of the Charter, see Juan Manuel Gómez-Robledo, *La práctica del Consejo de Seguridad después de la Guerra Fría y la interpretación de la Carta de las Naciones Unidas* (Valencia: Tirant lo blanch, 2018).

[11] See Geert-Jan Knoops, *The Prosecution and Defense of Peacekeepers under International Criminal Law* (Ardsley, NY: Transnational Publishers, 2004), 46.

[12] UN Charter art. 24.

[13] Reference to "aggression" as defined by General Assembly Resolution 3314 (XXIX), with the definition of aggression annexed to it, adopted on December 14, 1974.

Article 31(1) of the Vienna Conventions on the Law of Treaties (VCLT) establishes that "a treaty shall be interpreted in good faith in accordance with the ordinary meaning to be given to the terms of the treaty in their context and in the light of its object and purpose."[14] Under a holistic reading of the UN Charter, interpreted in good faith and in light of its object and purpose, use of the veto is contrary to the Charter in at least two respects. First, states' use of the veto permits breaches of the UN's purposes and principles. Second, wielding the veto impedes the Security Council's ability to prevent or respond to those breaches to maintain or restore international peace and security.

A second source of limitation on the Council's powers arises from violations of the *jus cogens* rules (or "peremptory norms") and *erga omnes* obligations of states under customary international law. According to Article 53 of the VCLT, *jus cogens* rules are norms "accepted and recognized by the international community of States as a whole as a norm from which no derogation is permitted and which can be modified only by a subsequent norm of general international law having the same character."[15] Further, as mentioned by the International Law Commission (ILC) in its draft conclusions on "Identification of Peremptory Norms of General International Law," adopted in 2022, "[P]eremptory norms of general international law (*jus cogens*) reflect and protect fundamental values of the international community. They are universally applicable and are hierarchically superior to other rules of international law."[16] In its "Conclusion 19" regarding particular consequences of serious breaches of *jus cogens* norms, the ILC indicated that "States shall cooperate to bring to an end through lawful means any serious breach by a State of an obligation arising under a peremptory norm of general international law (*jus cogens*)"[17] and that "no State shall recognize as lawful a situation created by a serious breach by a State of an obligation arising under a peremptory norm of general international law (*jus cogens*), nor render aid or assistance in maintaining that situation."[18] Article 41 of the Articles

[14] Vienna Convention on the Law of Treaties art. 31 para. 1, May 23, 1969, 1155 UNTS 331.
[15] Ibid.
[16] International Law Commission, "Draft Conclusions on Identification and Legal Consequences of Peremptory Norms of General International Law (*jus cogens*), with Commentaries," UN Doc. A/77/10 (2022), 18.
[17] Ibid., 70.
[18] Ibid.

on Responsibility of States for Internationally Wrongful Acts confirms this principle.[19]

There is no consensus on a definitive list of *jus cogens* norms. However, the ILC included in its draft conclusions a nonexhaustive list of norms that it had previously referred to as having that status. The Commission's list includes the prohibition of aggression, the prohibition of genocide, and the prohibition of crimes against humanity.[20]

It follows that the exercise of the veto by a member of the P5 that would prevent the Security Council from taking action in order to respond to a breach of a *jus cogens* norm—for example, to stop an act of aggression, or the commission of genocide, or crimes against humanity—would be contrary to its obligations vis-à-vis said norm, violate its individual obligation to cooperate in order to bring that breach to an end, and violate its obligation to not recognize the situation as lawful. Even worse, exercising the veto would arguably assist the aggressing or violating state in contravention of the P5 member's *erga omnes* obligations under customary international law, including those codified in the Geneva Conventions (the core treaties of international humanitarian law) and the Genocide Convention.

Allowing such use of the veto would not only place the procedural requirements of Article 27(3) above the *jus cogens* norms of customary international law, but it would also aid and abet the violations of such norms.

Section II: Initiatives to Limit the Use of the Veto

The General Assembly has always been concerned with the use and abuse of the veto. As early as 1949, the Assembly adopted Resolution 267 (III) on "the problem of voting in the Security Council," in which it recommended that the P5 "exercise the veto only when they consider the question of vital importance, taking into account the interest of the United Nations as a whole, and to state upon what ground they consider this condition to be present."[21] That same year, United States delegate Warren R. Austin declared: "To insist on the exercise of the veto regardless of its effects on the organized international community and to reject any efforts to regulate its application under

[19] *Article 41*, 2 2021 Yearbook of the International Law Commission vol. 2, part 2, 113-16, UN Doc. A/CN.4/SER.A/2001/Add.1.

[20] UN Doc. A/77/10 (2022), 89.

[21] UN General Assembly, Resolution 267(III), A/Res/267(III), para. 3(c) (Apr. 14, 1949).

the Charter, in the light of experience, is to stand in the way of effective progress by the United Nations."[22]

Eliminating the veto entails a reform to the UN Charter which, per Article 108, not only requires a two-thirds majority agreement of the General Assembly, but also needs ratification by "two-thirds of the Members of the United Nations, including all the permanent members of the Security Council."[23] The conclusion is simple: unless there is a political will of all of the P5—which seems very unlikely in the foreseeable future—the P5 will continue to hold the Security Council hostage with their use, or threat of use, of the veto.

Notably, states did adopt one successful Charter amendment in 1963. General Assembly Resolution 1991(XVIII) A on the "Question of equitable representation on the Security Council and the Economic and Social Council" expanded the membership of the Council from eleven members to its current fifteen.[24] Although the P5 did not support this resolution in the General Assembly,[25] all five states ultimately ratified the amendment, which came into force in 1965. The P5 may have assessed that failing to ratify the amendment would entail too high a political cost for a structural change that largely did not affect their supremacy. Unlike an amendment that would eliminate or restrict the use of the veto, the expansion of the nonpermanent membership of the Council did little to alter the status quo.

In 1979, the General Assembly's agenda included the item "Question of equitable representation on and increase in the membership of the Security Council and related matters."[26] In 1993, the Assembly established an open-ended working group to continue discussing the issue.[27] Neither effort made any progress. In 2008, an informal process of intergovernmental negotiations (IGN) replaced the working group. To this day, the IGN is the only negotiating venue wherein states may address equitable representation

[22] Cited in Bardo Fassbender, *UN Security Council Reform and the Right of Veto* (The Hague: Kluwer Law International, 1998), 340.

[23] UN Charter art. 108.

[24] UN General Assembly, Resolution 1991(XVIII)A, A/Res/1991(XVIII)A, para. 1 (Dec. 17, 1963).

[25] Resolution 1991(XVIII)A was adopted with ninety-seven votes in favor, eleven against, and four abstentions. The states who cast votes against were Bulgaria, Belarus, Cuba, Czechoslovakia, France, Hungary, Mongolia, Poland, Romania, Ukraine, and the USSR. The four abstentions came from the United States, Portugal, the United Kingdom of Great Britain and Northern Ireland, and South Africa.

[26] UN General Assembly, Decision 34/431, A/DEC/34/431 (Dec. 14, 1979).

[27] UN General Assembly, Resolution 48/26, A/Res/48/26 (Dec. 3, 1993).

and expansion of Council membership as part of a comprehensive Council reform. This is not for want of trying.

Throughout the years, states have put forward several proposals for Council reform. None have yet yielded a successful outcome. In 1993, Ukraine suggested giving the General Assembly the power to annul a veto if one of the P5 had cast it exclusively.[28] In 1996, the Non Aligned Movement suggested that the P5 should limit their use of the veto to decisions adopted under Chapter VII of the Charter, seeking to exempt all measures for the pacific settlement of disputes available in Chapter VI from possible vetoes.[29] In 1996, Mexico made a similar proposal,[30] suggesting amendments of Articles 4, 5, 6, 27, 97, 108, and 109 of the Charter to limit the veto to Chapter VII–related issues. Under this framework, the P5 could not exercise the veto on the admission of new members to the United Nations; the suspension of rights and privileges of a member state; expulsions from the organization; any resolution arising under Chapters VI, VIII, or XII;[31] the recommendation on the appointment of the Secretary-General; or the entry into force of Charter amendments. In January 2023, Mexico presented a new proposal to the IGN for its consideration which, inter alia, calls for expansion of the Security Council and restraint in the use of the veto.[32]

Notwithstanding these proposals, the reality is that no amendment of the Charter involving reform of the Security Council is within reach—let alone one that purports to eliminate the use of the veto. As a result, member states have resorted to various creative initiatives, all of a political nature, aimed at limiting the exercise of the veto—or, at the very least, increasing the political cost of its use. The two most active initiatives that states continue to invoke, and which delegations increasingly promote in UN debates are, first, the Accountability, Coherence and Transparency Group (ACT) code of

[28] UN General Assembly, 48th Sess., 64th plen. mtg. at 16, UN Doc. A/48/PV.64 (Dec. 7, 1993).

[29] Permanent Mission of Egypt to the United Nations, Question of the Veto: Working Paper by Egypt on Behalf of the Movement of Non-Aligned Countries, para. 11, UN Doc. A/AC.247/1996/CRP.9 (May 20, 1996).

[30] Permanent Mission of Mexico to the United Nations, Mexico: Working Paper on the Veto, UN Doc. A/AC.247/1996/CRP.7 (May 13, 1996).

[31] These chapters refer to pacific settlement of disputes, regional arrangements, and the trusteeship system, respectively.

[32] Permanent Rep. of Mexico to the UN, Letter dated Jan. 25, 2023, from the Permanent Rep. of Mexico to the United Nations addressed to the Secretary General, UN Doc. A/77/717 (Jan. 27, 2023). For a comprehensive explanation of Mexico's initiative, see Juan Ramón de la Fuente et al., "Mexico's Participation in the United Nations Security Council and Mexican Foreign Policy," *Apuntes de Política Exterior*, Núm. 22 (junio 2023), accessed June 11, 2024, https://www.gob.mx/cms/uploads/attachment/file/831713/Interiores_APE22-bilingual.pdf.

conduct regarding Security Council action against genocide, crimes against humanity, or war crimes; and second, the French-Mexican initiative on the voluntary restriction of the veto. The international community should continue to focus efforts on these two initiatives, which have gathered the most support among UN member states.[33]

In 2013, a cross-regional group of twenty-seven small and mid-sized states came together to form the ACT Group, with the purpose of "address[ing] both the Council's internal functioning as well as its relations to the broader UN Membership."[34] The same year, the ACT Group drafted a code of conduct with the objective of improving the working methods of the Security Council. In 2015, the group submitted its proposed code of conduct to the Secretary-General, calling upon all Security Council members—both the P5 and the ten elected members (E10)—not to vote against any draft resolution that aims to prevent or stop mass atrocities like genocide, crimes against humanity, or war crimes.[35] To date, 130 states have subscribed to the code of conduct, which contains five provisions addressed to current and future members of the Council:

i. *Pledge* to support timely and decisive action by the Security Council aimed at preventing or ending the commission of genocide, crimes against humanity, or war crimes;
ii. *Pledge in particular* to not vote against a credible draft resolution before the Security Council on timely and decisive action to end the commission of genocide, crimes against humanity, or war crimes, or to prevent such crimes;
iii. *Invite* the Secretary-General, making full use of the expertise and early-warning capacities of the United Nations system, in particular the Office of the United Nations High Commissioner for Human Rights and the United Nations Office on Genocide Prevention and the Responsibility to Protect, to continue to bring to the attention of the Council situations that, in her or his assessment, involve or are likely to lead to genocide, crimes against humanity, or war crimes;

[33] Trahan, *Existing Legal Limits to Security Council Veto Power*, 139–40.

[34] Mission of Switzerland to the United Nations in New York, "Accountability, Coherence and Transparency Group," last updated Feb. 5, 2024, accessed June 11, 2024, https://www.eda.admin.ch/missions/mission-new-york/en/home/act-statements.html.

[35] Permanent Rep. of Liechtenstein to the UN, Letter dated Dec. 14, 2015, from the Permanent Rep. of Liechtenstein to the United Nations addressed to the Secretary-General, UN Doc. A/70/621–S/2015/978 (Dec. 14, 2015).

iv. *Pledge* to fully and promptly take into account such an assessment by the Secretary-General; [and]

v. *Also invite* all other Member States of the United Nations to express their commitment to this Code of Conduct.[36]

In line with its objectives, the ACT Group remains active in submitting letters to the Security Council on various issues regarding its working methods, including beyond the issue of the veto.

In August 2015, France and Mexico launched the "Political Declaration on Suspension of Veto Powers in Cases of Mass Atrocities," an initiative that calls for voluntary restraint in the P5's use of the veto. The political declaration states:

> We, the undersigned, Member States of the United Nations, reaffirm that the United Nations were created to save succeeding generations from the scourge of war and to protect the dignity and worth of the human person as well as the fundamental human rights. We further reaffirm that the Security Council was given the primary responsibility to maintain international peace and security by the United Nations Charter.
>
> We consider that situations of mass atrocities, when crimes of genocide, crimes against humanity, and war crimes on a large scale are committed, may constitute a threat to international peace and security and require action by the international community. In that regard, we recall that the Heads of State and Government of the United Nations expressed their readiness to "take collective action, in a timely and decisive manner, through the Security Council, in accordance with the Charter" when national authorities fail to protect their populations from genocide, crimes against humanity, or war crimes (World Summit Outcome Document of 2005).
>
> We therefore consider that the Security Council should not be prevented by the use of veto from taking action with the aim of preventing or bringing an end to situations involving the commission of mass atrocities. We underscore that the veto is not a privilege, but an international responsibility.
>
> In that respect, we welcome and support the initiative by France, jointly presented with Mexico, to propose a collective and voluntary agreement among the permanent members of the Security Council to the effect that

[36] Ibid.

the permanent members would refrain from using the veto in case of mass atrocities. We express our strong resolve to continue our efforts to prevent and end the commission of mass atrocities.[37]

The key aspects of this initiative are, first, that the veto is not a privilege but a responsibility; and second, that states cannot use a procedural mechanism to contravene the purposes and principles of the UN Charter, or the peremptory norms of customary international law.[38] As of January 1, 2023, 106 states had endorsed the French-Mexican initiative.[39]

At first glance, it may seem that these two initiatives are duplicative at best and competitive at worst. However, a closer look shows that they are complementary and mutually reinforcing. The code of conduct appeals to all member states that have a seat on the Council and goes beyond the exercise of the veto, while the French-Mexican initiative is a direct appeal to the P5 to voluntarily refrain from using the veto. France, which has only used the veto eighteen times since 1945 and not once in the last thirty years, is the only member of the P5 who has joined both initiatives. The United Kingdom has signed the code of conduct but has not yet endorsed the French-Mexican initiative. No other P5 member has subscribed to either initiative.

As evidenced by states' frequent invocation of these initiatives in Security Council and General Assembly debates, they are pragmatic proposals. Rather than focusing on amendments to the UN Charter and the imposition of formal limits on the use of the veto (or even its total elimination), the initiatives take a different tack: namely, restraining the use of the veto on a voluntary basis and increasing the political cost of its use in cases involving mass atrocities.

Recent statements by the United States inspired optimism that it may consider joining these initiatives. On September 8, 2022, during the meeting held in San Francisco on the future of the United Nations, Ambassador Linda Thomas-Greenfield, permanent representative of the United States to the United Nations, announced that "the United States will subscribe to six

37 Political Statement on the Suspension of the Veto in Case of Mass Atrocities presented by France and Mexico, 70th General Assembly of the United Nations, Sep. 2015, accessed June 11, 2024, https://onu.delegfrance.org/IMG/pdf/2015_08_07_veto_political_declaration_en.pdf.

38 See Joel Hérnandez Garcia, "El Consejo de Seguridad y la iniciativa franco-mexicana para la restricción del uso del veto en caso de atrocidades en masa," *Revista Mexicana de Política Exterior* 110, (mayo-agosto de 2017): 45–59.

39 "Support to the French Mexican Initiative on Veto Restraint in Case of Mass Atrocities (as of 1st January 2023)," French Ministry for Europe and Foreign Affairs, accessed June 11, 2024, https://www.diplomatie.gouv.fr/IMG/pdf/veto_-_carte_des_106_soutiens_en_-05-06-23_cle01d6c9.pdf.

clear principles for responsible behavior for Security Council Members."[40] As a third principle, she said,

> [W]e will refrain from the use of the veto except in rare, extraordinary situations. In particular, any Permanent Member that exercises the veto to defend its own acts of aggression loses moral authority and should be held accountable. And I will note that since 2009, Russia has cast 26 vetoes, 12 of which were joined by China—while the U.S. has only used the veto four times.[41]

Later that month at the opening debate of the Seventy-Seventh UN General Assembly, President Joe Biden stated that "members of the UN Security Council, including the United States, should consistently uphold and defend the UN Charter and . . . refrain from the use of the veto, except in rare, extraordinary situations, to ensure that the Council remains credible and effective."[42]

It seemed then that the United States could consider joining these initiatives. However, the ongoing crisis in Gaza, in response to which the United States has repeatedly resorted to the veto, appears to have pushed this possibility farther away. In any case, the international community should continue to hold the United States accountable to its own principles and standards—as well as to the UN Charter and international law.

Section III: Other Efforts toward Accountability and Effectiveness

Current crises test the credibility and effectiveness of the Security Council, and there is an escalating international concern about the use of the veto. The E10 and broad UN membership share a desire to ensure a greater measure of accountability for, and political cost of, the use and abuse of the

[40] United States Mission to the United Nations ," Remarks by Ambassador Linda Thomas-Greenfield on the Future of the United Nations," (Sept. 8, 2022), accessed June 11, 2024, https://usun.usmission.gov/remarks-by-ambassador-linda-thomas-greenfield-on-the-future-of-the-united-nations/.

[41] Ibid.

[42] The White House , "Remarks by President Biden before the 77th Session of the United Nations General Assembly," (Sept. 21, 2022), accessed June 11, 2024, https://www.whitehouse.gov/briefing-room/speeches-remarks/2022/09/21/remarks-by-president-biden-before-the-77th-session-of-the-united-nations-general-assembly/.

veto—especially in cases involving aggression and mass atrocities. This goal has led to new initiatives that focus primarily on those issues, rather than on more general Security Council reform or limits to the veto.

The best example is "the veto initiative," originally put forward by Liechtenstein.[43] On April 26, 2022, the General Assembly adopted Resolution 76/262 on a "Standing mandate for a General Assembly debate when a veto is cast in the Security Council."[44] Under Resolution 76/262, when one or more of the P5 cast a veto, the president of the General Assembly has ten days to convene a meeting to address said veto, unless the General Assembly meets in an emergency special session in accordance with the Uniting for Peace Resolution—a mechanism through which the General Assembly may circumvent the Security Council "because of lack of unanimity of the permanent members."[45] Resolution 76/262 gives precedence in the list of speakers to the P5 member or members that cast a veto. In practice, this prompts the P5 member in question to provide the General Assembly with a justification for exercising its veto. The resolution also invites the Security Council to submit a report on any P5 member's use of the veto at least seventy-two hours before the debate in the General Assembly. The Assembly adopted the resolution by consensus, without a vote, and with the co-sponsorship of eighty-three UN member states, including France, the United States, and the United Kingdom. China and Russia joined the consensus.

Since the adoption of Resolution 76/262, through the beginning of 2024, the P5 cast more than a dozen vetoes in the Security Council blocking the adoption of at least ten resolutions, triggering corresponding General Assembly debates. Some debates occurred in the Assembly's regular session; others took place in the tenth and eleventh emergency special sessions, which focused exclusively on the Israel-Palestinian conflict and Russia's invasion of Ukraine, respectively.

The veto initiative has ushered in a new era of transparency and accountability in the United Nations. It has resurrected the General Assembly's authority to request reports from the Security Council and reinforced the principle enshrined in Article 24(1) that the Council is acting on behalf of

[43] See also Pablo Arrocha Olabuenaga, "GA Res. 76/262 on a Standing Mandate for a General Assembly Debate When a Veto Is Cast in the Security Council (UN)," *International Legal Materials* 62, no. 2 (Apr. 2023): 284–288.

[44] UN General Assembly, Resolution 76/262, A/Res/76/262 (Apr. 26, 2022).

[45] UN General Assembly, Resolution 377 (V), A/Res/377 (V) (Nov. 3, 1950).

the entire UN membership. Mexico emphasized these principles in its statement in the General Assembly upon the adoption of Resolution 76/262:

> [T]oday we have also strengthened the mandate derived from Article 24 (1) of the Charter, by indicating that the Security Council acts on behalf of all the Member States of the Organization. If this is so, how could it be justified that the permanent member or members that have decided to resort to the veto do not explain to the rest of the Member States the reasons that led them to stop the Security Council from carrying out the primary responsibility entrusted to it by the Charter of the United Nations?[46]

Mexico's representative went on to explain that when a P5 member exercises the veto, it prevents the Security Council from taking the necessary action and from fulfilling its primary responsibility under the UN Charter, and also obstructs the will of the entire membership of the United Nations.

Resolution 76/262 has also opened the door to explore other ways the General Assembly can contribute to the transparency and effectiveness of the Security Council. The ongoing conflicts in Ukraine and Gaza have highlighted the importance and urgency of fully observing Article 27(3) of the Charter—in particular, the obligation of a party to a dispute to abstain from voting in decisions under Chapter VI and Article 52(3) of the Charter.

It is a generally accepted principle of international law, recognized in the jurisprudence of the Permanent Court of International Justice,[47] that no party can act as judge in their own case: *nemo debet esse judex in propria sua causa*.[48] During the General Assembly debate marking the first anniversary of the adoption of Resolution 76/262, several delegations emphasized the need to enforce this principle.[49] A large majority of delegations also voiced their support for the French-Mexican initiative and the ACT code of

[46] Misión Permanente de México ante la Organización de las Naciones Unidas, "Statement by Mexico during the Adoption of the Resolution on the Veto Initiative," (Apr. 26, 2022), accessed June 11, 2024,https://mision.sre.gob.mx/onu/images/2022/CSONU/Intervenciones/260422_Intervencin_Veto_ingls.pdf.

[47] Permanent Court of International Justice, Article 3, para. 2, of the Treaty of Lausanne (Frontier between Turkey and Iraq), Advisory Opinion of 21 November 1925 (Series B, No. 12), The Hague, Publications of the Permanent Court of International Justice, 1925, p. 32.

[48] Article 3, para. 2, of the Treaty of Lausanne (Frontier between Turkey and Iraq), Advisory Opinion, 1925 PCIJ (ser. B) No. 12, at 32 (Nov. 21).

[49] See Meetings Coverage, General Assembly, General Assembly Holds First-Ever Debate on Historic Veto Resolution, Adopts Texts on Infrastructure, National Reviews, Council of Europe Cooperation, UN Meetings Coverage GA/12500 (Apr. 26, 2023), accessed June 11, 2024, https://press.un.org/en/2023/ga12500.doc.htm.

conduct, inviting those states who have not yet done so to join and support both initiatives.

Conclusion

The debate on the legal limits on the use of the veto in the Security Council has existed as long as the veto itself. It is even more pronounced when the Council is prevented from responding to aggression, genocide, and other mass atrocity crimes. The current global crises and the activism of member states at large present a fork in the road. The P5 can continue down the path they are on, further eroding the rule of law and the multilateral system built to sustain it—or, ideally, they will change course, charting the path foreseen in Article 24 of the Charter by regaining their sense of responsibility and recommitting to the UN's purposes and principles. For a better future, there is only one option. The P5 must exercise restraint in the use of their veto power. If they do so, the Security Council will be better able to fulfill its primary responsibility for the maintenance of international peace and security and to discharge its duties in the face of aggression and mass atrocity crimes.

PART IV
REIMAGINING THE PARTNERS

7

Tapping the Full Potential of the General Assembly

Mona Ali Khalil

Introduction

The twenty-first century started with the tragic terrorist attacks of September 11, 2001. The world was united in condemnation, and the Security Council responded promptly and unanimously, imposing sanctions against Al-Qaeda and the Taliban.[1] On March 19, 2003, the United States and the United Kingdom invaded Iraq, thereby destroying the unity of purpose of the Security Council. Thus began a slow but steady unraveling of the credibility and efficacy of the post–World War II multilateral system. Russia's invasions of Ukraine in 2014 and 2022 dealt yet another major blow, leaving three of the five permanent members (P5) responsible for aggression in the twenty-first century.[2] Aggression, according to the Nuremburg military tribunals, is "the supreme international crime differing only from other war crimes in that it contains within itself the accumulated evil of the whole."[3]

Contrary to the vision of the architects of the United Nations, the P5 have emerged, not as the intended guardians, but rather as the most consequential threats to international peace and security. They have abused their veto—not only to shield themselves from accountability, but also to bestow their allies with the same impunity.

[1] See UN Security Council, Resolution 1368 (2001) (12 September 2001) and Resolution 1373 (2001) (28 September 2001).

[2] While the United States and United Kingdom as well as Russia have invoked the right of self-defense, the weight of international legal opinion and an overwhelming majority of states regard the invasions of Iraq and Ukraine as unlawful.

[3] *US, France, UK, and USSR v. Herman Wilhelm Goring, et al.*, Judgment, Oct. 1, 1946, *The Trial of Major War Criminals: Proceedings of the International Military Tribunal Sitting at Nuremberg, Germany* 22, 421.

Mona Ali Khalil, *Tapping the Full Potential of the General Assembly* In: *Empowering the UN Security Council.*
Edited by: Mona Ali Khalil and Floriane Lavaud, Oxford University Press. © Oxford University Press 2024.
DOI: 10.1093/oso/9780197780602.003.0008

Article 24(1) of the Charter entrusts the Council and its members with primary albeit not exclusive responsibility to take prompt and effective action against threats to international peace and security. Article 24(2) of the Charter requires the Council—and by extension, its members—to discharge these duties in accordance with the purposes and principles of the United Nations. The Charter foresees the possibility of the Council's failure and vests the General Assembly with residual authority to maintain international peace and security. General Assembly Resolution 377 (V), also known as the "Uniting for Peace" resolution,[4] codifies the Assembly's residual authority and its emergency special sessions operationalize its subsidiary responsibility.

When the Security Council fails to fulfill its primary responsibility, the General Assembly can and should step up to uphold the UN Charter, including by availing itself of the full powers of the Uniting for Peace resolution. While the General Assembly cannot impose binding obligations on member states who do not wish to act, it can and should provide a legal basis for action by the member states who are willing and able to give effect to the will of the international community. The General Assembly can tap the full potential of the Uniting for Peace resolution to respond to aggression and mass atrocity crimes.

There are many words that are quintessentially associated with the United Nations, words that do not actually appear in the UN Charter. None are more consequential than the word veto, which has often impeded the UN Security Council from fulfilling its primary responsibility for the maintenance of international peace and security.[5]

Article 27 of the UN Charter requires "the concurring votes of the permanent members" for all nonprocedural matters before the Security Council. As such, the P5—namely, China, France, Russia, the United States, and the United Kingdom—enjoy a direct veto over all nonprocedural matters before the Security Council. Article 27 also requires "an affirmative vote of nine members." As such, the ten elected members enjoy an indirect veto on all matters procedural and substantive. The difference between the two vetoes, however, lies in the difference between the whim of one or more states and the will of the majority of nations.

[4] See UN General Assembly, Resolution 377 (V), A/RES/377 (V) (Nov. 3, 1950).

[5] See Mona Ali Khalil, "The UN Must Be Impartial to the Parties but Not Neutral to the Law," *UN Today*, Nov. 1, 2022, accessed June 16, 2024, https://untoday.org/the-un-must-be-impartial-to-the-parties-but-not-neutral-to-the-law/.

When a permanent member invokes a veto, the state in question effectively blocks action that is otherwise desired by the majority of the international community. When the majority of the members of the Council vote against a proposed resolution, it signifies that the international community is opposed to the action in question. The latter was visibly demonstrated when, for example, the United States and United Kingdom failed to obtain the required majority of nine affirmative votes for their draft resolution authorizing the use of force against Iraq in 2003 before they launched their unlawful invasion.

Exercising the veto in certain situations contravenes the spirit and aims of the UN Charter and impedes the fulfillment of the purposes and principles of the United Nations as set out in Articles 1 and 2 thereof. A veto that blocks the will of the international community to prevent or reverse aggression; to prevent or punish genocide; or to prevent or respond to other situations requiring the protection of civilians from war crimes, crimes against humanity, and ethnic cleansing not only defeats the spirit but also defies the letter of the Charter. It also potentially violates *erga omnes* obligations under customary international law including the Genocide Convention and the Geneva Conventions. A veto in these situations erodes the rule of law and paralyzes the Council's ability to fulfil its responsibility to maintain international peace and security. Various efforts to restrain the use of the veto have thus far failed to alter the behavior of at least three of the five permanent members: China, Russia, and the United States.[6]

Between January 1, 2000, and December 31, 2023, these three members of the P5 vetoed forty-nine resolutions including fifteen resolutions vetoed by China and Russia together, eighteen by Russia alone, and sixteen by the

[6] The first initiative was in May 2012 by the governments of Costa Rica, Jordan, Liechtenstein, Singapore, and Switzerland (see UN General Assembly, Draft Resolution A/66/L.42/Rev.2 (May 15, 2012)). In February 2015, the Elders adopted a statement which, inter alia, called on the P5 "to pledge 'not to use, or threaten to use, their veto' in crises in which genocide or other mass atrocities are committed or threatened. . . ." (See statement by the Elders (Feb. 7, 2015), accessed June 16, 2024,https://theelders.org/sites/default/files/2015-04-22_elders-statement-strengthening-the-un.pdf). In July 2015, a cross-regional group calling itself Accountability, Coherence and Transparency announced a code of conduct which calls upon all members of the Security Council not to vote against any credible draft resolution intended to prevent or end the commission of genocide, crimes against humanity and war crimes. (See UN General Assembly, UN Doc. A/70/621 (Dec. 14, 2015)). In August 2015, the governments of France and Mexico launched the "Political Declaration on Suspension of Veto Powers in Cases of Mass Atrocities." accessed June 16, 2024,https://onu.delegfrance.org/IMG/pdf/2015_08_07_veto_political_declaration_en.pdf.) In April 2022, at the initiative of Liechtenstein, the General Assembly adopted Resolution 76/262 entitled "Standing Mandate for a General Assembly Debate When a Veto Is Cast in the Security Council" (see UN General Assembly, Resolution 76/262, A/RES/76/262 (Apr. 28, 2022)).

United States alone.[7] Of the fifteen resolutions China and Russia vetoed together, ten blocked Council action on the mass atrocities being committed in Syria. Of the sixteen vetoes by Russia alone, eight concerned Syria, and four concerned Russia's own invasions of Ukraine in 2014 and 2022.[8] Fourteen of the United States' sixteen vetoes prevented the Council from responding to Israel's grave violations in the Occupied Palestinian Territory.[9] These vetoes not only blocked action against states; they also blocked action against nonstate actors who have also committed serious violations of international humanitarian law, including the Wagner Group in Ukraine and Hamas in the Occupied Palestinian Territory. The use of the veto thus allows both state and nonstate perpetrators to operate with impunity.[10] Thus far in 2024, there have been six vetoes blocking five resolutions: three vetoes by Russia, two by the United States and one by China.

This chapter seeks to tap the full potential of the Uniting for Peace" resolution.[11] Section I examines the legal bases for the evolution of the General Assembly's powers in respect of the maintenance of international peace and security. Section II discusses the practice of the emergency special sessions from 1950 to the present, by which the Assembly codified its residual authority and operationalized its subsidiary responsibility demonstrating its ability to act when the Security Council is unable to fulfill its primary responsibility for international peace and security. Section III describes the untapped potential of Uniting for Peace using the ongoing tenth and eleventh emergency special sessions on the situations in Palestine and Ukraine as case studies.[12] The chapter concludes that, when the Security Council is paralyzed by the veto, the General Assembly can and should act to maintain international peace and security, especially in situations involving aggression and mass atrocity crimes.

[7] See "UN Security Council Meetings & Outcomes Tables: Veto List," United Nations Dag Hammarskjöld Library, accessed June 16, 2024, https://research.un.org/en/docs/sc/quick.

[8] This chapter only deals with the UN response to the Russian invasion of Ukraine in 2022; it does not address the response to the Russian invasion of Ukraine in 2014.

[9] See "UN Security Council Meetings & Outcomes Tables."

[10] The non-state actors in Syria, including the so-called Islamic State of Syria and the Levant (ISIL), are dealt with separately in the series of Security Council resolutions imposing sanctions and other measures on ISIL and foreign terrorist fighters including UN Security Council, Resolutions 2170, S/RES/2170 (Aug. 15, 2014) through 2610, S/RES/2610 (Dec. 17, 2021).

[11] A/RES/377 (V).

[12] The situation in Syria has been addressed in regular sessions of the General Assembly including Resolution 71/248 establishing the International, Impartial, and Independent Mechanism (IIIM) to Assist in the Investigation and Prosecution of Persons Responsible for the Most Serious Crimes under International Law Committed in the Syrian Arab Republic since March 2011. UN General Assembly Resolution 71/248 (Dec. 21, 2016).

Section I: The Legal Bases for the General Assembly's Evolving Powers

The General Assembly has established and evolved a long-standing practice that has effectively enhanced its powers under two legal bases. The first rests on Articles 10 and 11 of the Charter, under which the Assembly has explicit powers to, inter alia, consider, discuss, and make recommendations on international peace and security. These powers are subject to the limitation in Article 12(1) of the Charter which provides, "While the Security Council is exercising in respect of any dispute or situation . . ., the General Assembly shall not make any recommendation with regard to that dispute or situation unless the Security Council so requests." Despite this limitation, the Assembly has on many occasions exercised its powers concurrently with the Council largely without any strong objection from member states.[13]

The second legal basis derives from Article 14 of the Charter, which provides (again, subject to the provisions of Article 12 of the Charter) that

> the General Assembly may recommend measures for the peaceful adjustment of any situation, regardless of origin, which it deems likely to impair the general welfare or friendly relations among nations, including situations resulting from a violation of the provisions of the present Charter setting forth the Purposes and Principles of the United Nations.

The General Assembly relied on Article 14 to respond to the Korean peninsula crisis in 1950. The Union of Soviet Socialist Republics (USSR) had exercised its veto against a United States draft resolution condemning North Korea's continued defiance of prior Security Council resolutions, which were adopted while the USSR was boycotting the Council and which imposed measures to protect the Republic of Korea. In response, the United States "succeeded in persuading the General Assembly that it should claim for itself

[13] See *Repertory of Practice of United Nations Organs* and its Supplement, including the most recent Supplement No. 10 covering the period 2000–2009. Between 2000 and 2009, the following situations, among others, were considered by both the General Assembly and the Security Council without Article 12 being invoked in the discussions: the "situation in Afghanistan"; the "situation in the Occupied Palestinian Territory, including East Jerusalem, and the occupied Syrian Golan"; and "measures to eliminate international terrorism." These agenda items and the dozens of resolutions adopted thereunder are in addition to the convening of successive emergency special sessions under UNGA resolution 377(V). *Repertory of Practice of United Nations Organs*, Supplement No. 10 (2000–2009), accessed June 16, 2024, https://legal.un.org/repertory/art12/english/rep_supp10_vol2_art12.pdf.

a subsidiary responsibility with regard to international peace and security, as enunciated by Article 14 of the Charter."[14] Taking up the United States' proposal, the Assembly adopted Resolution 377 (V)—the Uniting for Peace resolution.

The preamble to Part A of Resolution 377 (V) framed the resolution with three important observations. First, the General Assembly reaffirmed "the importance of the exercise by the Security Council of its primary responsibility for the maintenance of international peace and security, and the duty of the permanent members to seek unanimity and to exercise restraint in the use of the veto." Second, it stipulated that the failure of the Council to discharge its responsibilities "does not relieve Member States of their obligations or the United Nations of its responsibility under the Charter to maintain international peace and security." Third, it recognized that "such failure does not deprive the General Assembly of its rights or relieve it of its responsibilities under the Charter in regard to the maintenance of international peace and security." In the operative part of the resolution, the General Assembly

> resolved that if the Security Council, because of lack of unanimity of the permanent members, fails to exercise its primary responsibility for the maintenance of international peace and security in any case where there appears to be a threat to the peace, breach of the peace, or act of aggression, the General Assembly shall consider the matter immediately with a view to making appropriate recommendations to Members for collective measures, including in the case of a breach of the peace or act of aggression the use of armed force when necessary, to maintain or restore international peace and security.[15]

Resolution 377 (V) also introduced amendments to the rules of procedure of the General Assembly to set out the rules for the convening of the emergency special sessions. These sessions may take place either at the request of the Security Council by a procedural vote, or at the request of a majority of UN member states to the UN Secretary-General.

As mentioned above, pursuant to operative paragraph 1 of Resolution 377 (V), the General Assembly may recommend collective measures "including

[14] See Christian Tomuschat, "Uniting for Peace: Introductory Note," UN Audiovisual Library of International Law (Oct. 2008), accessed June 16, 2023, https://legal.un.org/avl/ha/ufp/ufp.html.

[15] A/RES/377 (V).

in the case of a breach of the peace or act of aggression the use of armed force when necessary, to maintain or restore international peace and security." Recommendations for preventive or enforcement action pursuant to that resolution are intended to provide a member state that is willing and able to act with a clear legal basis and the necessary legal authority to take the recommended measures up to and including the use of armed force if so recommended by the General Assembly in the event of a breach of the peace or act of aggression. Relying on Article 14, the Assembly's powers under the Uniting for Peace resolution[16] are arguably greater than its powers under Articles 10 and 11 of the UN Charter.

The reference to armed force in Resolution 377 (V) is highly controversial and has even been contested as *ultra vires*.[17] The latter contention is based on the presumption that, pursuant to Articles 39, 42, and 51 of the UN Charter, only the Security Council can authorize the use of force other than in the exercise of the inherent right of self-defense. In particular, Article 51 provides that

> Nothing in the present Charter shall impair the inherent right of individual or collective self-defence if an armed attack occurs against a Member of the United Nations, until the Security Council has taken measures necessary to maintain international peace and security. Measures taken by Members in the exercise of this right of self-defence shall be immediately reported to the Security Council. . . .

Article 51 explicitly preserves the inherent right of individual and collective self-defense in the event of an armed attack. As such, the General Assembly recommending collective measures to support a UN member state exercising the inherent right of self-defense in the event of an armed attack could reasonably fall within the terms of Article 51, at least "until the Security Council has taken measures necessary to maintain international peace and security." If a member state can turn to another UN member state for help, the UN Charter surely cannot intend to preclude it from seeking the support of all UN member states through the General Assembly. The latter

[16] See Mona Ali Khalil, *Reforming the UN Security Council*, Together First Campaign, United Nations Association – UK (2020), accessed June 16, 2024, https://una.org.uk/reforming-un-security-council.

[17] See Tomuschat, "Uniting for Peace." See also Larry D. Johnson, "'Uniting for Peace': Does It Still Serve Any Useful Purpose?" *AJIL Unbound* 108 (2014): 106–15.

understanding is reinforced in Part C of Resolution 377 (V), wherein the Assembly recommended that each UN member state

> maintain within its national armed forces, elements so trained, organized and equipped that they could promptly be made available, in accordance with its constitutional processes for service as a United Nations unit or units, upon recommendation by the Security Council or the General Assembly, without prejudice to the use of such elements in the exercise of the right of individual or collective self-defense recognized in Article 51 of the Charter.

Member states who use armed force on the recommendation of the General Assembly in collective self-defense would, in accordance with Article 51 of the UN Charter, have the same duty to report any measures, involving the use of force, they have taken to the Security Council. Article 51 does not, however, preclude them from taking such measures in the first place. Ultimately, however, the Assembly can only recommend such collective self-defense measures. Unlike the Security Council, it cannot oblige any member state to take them.

Section II: Exercising Authority and Assuming Responsibility (1950–1999)

Based on the foregoing, the General Assembly has enhanced its authority and arguably its responsibility to act in the face of aggression and other serious violations of international law when the exercise of a P5 veto prevents the Security Council from fulfilling its primary responsibility to maintain international peace and security. The architects of the UN Charter had entrusted the General Assembly with a measure of residual authority to respond to these threats. With the adoption of Resolution 377 (V), the General Assembly codified its residual authority and in the eleven subsequent emergency special sessions, it operationalized its subsidiary responsibility.

A. First to ninth emergency special session

After its inception in 1950, the General Assembly acted pursuant to the Uniting for Peace resolution for the first time in 1956 when Israel, with the support of France and the United Kingdom, invaded Egypt. The Assembly did not allow a veto by the two permanent members to block an international response to their and Israel's aggression. In its first emergency special session, the General Assembly, on the recommendation of the Secretary-General and with the support of the United States, called on all foreign troops to withdraw from Egypt. It established a UN command for one of the first UN peacekeeping forces, the UN Emergency Force (UNEF), to secure and supervise the withdrawal of all foreign troops from Egypt and the cessation of hostilities.[18]

In the subsequent eight emergency special sessions, the General Assembly continued to demonstrate that it is willing and able to recommend consequential measures in response to aggression and other serious violations of the UN Charter and international law. Having established a peacekeeping force in its first emergency special session, it went on to recommend a spectrum of collective measures, ranging from military and other assistance to the defending state(s), to arms embargoes and other sanctions on the aggressor state(s).

In its second and sixth emergency special sessions, the General Assembly called on the USSR to withdraw its forces from Hungary and Afghanistan, respectively; in its third, seventh, and ninth emergency special sessions, the Assembly called for the complete and unconditional withdrawals of Israeli troops from Jordan, Lebanon, the Occupied Palestinian Territory, and Syria, respectively.[19] In its fourth emergency special session, the Assembly adopted an arms embargo regarding the situation in the Democratic Republic of the Congo. In its fifth emergency special session, the Assembly called on member states to facilitate humanitarian assistance to alleviate the suffering of civilians and prisoners of war in the Middle East and called on Israel to rescind all measures to alter the status of Jerusalem. In its eighth emergency special session, the Assembly called on member states to provide military assistance to the front-line states and to the South West Africa People's Organization "to enable it to intensify its struggle for the liberation of Namibia."[20]

[18] See UN General Assembly, Resolutions 997(ES-I), A/RES/997(ES-1) (Oct. 30, 1956) and 1000(ES-I), A/RES/1000(ES-I) (Oct. 30, 1956), adopted in the General Assembly's first emergency special session.

[19] See "Emergency special sessions," accessed June 16, 2024, https://www.un.org/en/ga/sessions/emergency.shtml.

[20] Ibid.

The measures adopted by the first nine emergency special sessions of the General Assembly are recommendations that did not oblige any member state to act; they did, however, provide those member states that were willing and able to act with a legal basis to do so. Despite the robust precedents of the first nine emergency special sessions, the General Assembly has thus far failed to tap the full potential of the Uniting for Peace resolution in its tenth and eleventh emergency special sessions.

B. Tenth emergency special session (1997–Present)

The tenth emergency special session (ESS10) was first convened in 1997[21] to address the "illegal Israeli actions in Occupied East Jerusalem and the rest of the Occupied Palestinian Territory."[22] The ESS10 was the first to introduce a resumption mechanism, whereby the Assembly can adjourn temporarily and authorize its president to resume its meeting upon request from member states. It has been resumed twenty times between April 1997 and May 2024, during which it has adopted resolutions, *inter alia,* condemning the Israeli occupation and settlements as violations of international law and calling for the protection of the Palestinian civilian population.

Most notably, in 2003, the ESS10 requested an advisory opinion from the International Court of Justice (ICJ) on the "legal consequences arising from the construction of the wall being built by Israel, the occupying Power, in the Occupied Palestinian Territory, including in and around East Jerusalem."[23] In its advisory opinion of July 9, 2004, the ICJ confirmed the illegality of the wall and concluded that "Israel is under an obligation to make reparation for all damage caused by the construction of the wall."[24] Two years later, building

[21] See UN Secretary-General, Note by the Secretary-General, UN Doc. A/ES-10/1 (Apr. 22, 1997) (on the convening of the tenth emergency special session).

[22] *See* ibid., paras. 14–20. See also Legal Consequences of the Construction of a Wall in the Occupied Palestinian Territory, Advisory Opinion, 2004 ICJ 136 (July 9, 2004) (stating that the General Assembly had not exceeded its competence under Articles 10 and 11, as qualified by Article 12, paragraph 1, of the Charter). The ICJ also found that the conditions laid down by Resolution 377 A(V) had been met "after the rejection by the Security Council. . . as a result of the negative vote of a permanent member." Ibid. at 151.

[23] See UN General Assembly, Resolution ES-10/14, (Dec. 8, 2003). Nearly twenty years later, on 30 December 2022, the General Assembly adopted resolution 77/247, in which it requested a second ICJ advisory opinion on the legal consequences of Israel's "prolonged occupation, settlement, and annexation of the Palestinian territory occupied since 1967." UN General Assembly Resolution 77/ 247, (Dec. 30, 2022). The latter resolution is not of the tenth emergency special session but of the 77th regular session of the General Assembly.

[24] Legal Consequences of the Construction of a Wall, Advisory Opinion, 2004 ICJ 136.

on the Court's landmark advisory opinion, the ESS10 established the UN Register of Damage (UNROD) to serve as a record of the damage caused as a result of Israel's construction of the wall.[25]

While ICJ advisory opinions are not binding, it is generally accepted that they carry great legal and moral weight. In this particular case, to the extent that it rests on *jus cogens* principles, and invokes *erga omnes* obligations, the ICJ's 2004 opinion embodies existing legally binding obligations—not only on Israel but on all states. In particular, the Court called upon all states

- not to recognize the illegal situation resulting from the continuing construction of the wall and the expansion of the settlements in the Occupied Palestinian Territory, including in and around East Jerusalem;
- not to render aid or assistance in maintaining the situation created by such construction;
- to bring an end to any impediment, resulting from the construction of the wall and the settlements, to the exercise by the Palestinian people of its right to self-determination;
- to ensure compliance by Israel with international humanitarian law as embodied in the Fourth Geneva Convention;
- to ensure compliance by their nationals as well as legal persons and corporate entities under their jurisdiction to refrain from engaging in economic, commercial, or business activities that contribute to this illegal situation;
- to prevent further expropriation and exploitation of Palestinian territory and natural resources.[26]

Between October and May 2024, following the Hamas attack on 7 October 2023 and Israel's ongoing campaign of bombardment and starvation of Gaza thereafter, the tenth emergency special session has adopted three resolutions to date.[27] After several vetoes in the UNSC, the Assembly, by a majority of 120 UN member states, adopted the UN's first formal response calling, *inter alia*, for an "immediate, durable and sustained humanitarian truce leading to a cessation of hostilities". [28] With 153 UN member states voting in favor,

[25] UN General Assembly Resolution ES-10/17, (Dec. 15, 2006).
[26] Geneva Convention Relative to the Protection of Civilian Persons in Time of War (Aug. 12, 1949).
[27] See General Assembly resolutions in A/ES-10/21, A/ES-10/22 and A/ES-10/23.
[28] UN General Assembly Resolution ES-10/21 (Oct 27, 2023).

the Assembly adopted a second resolution reiterating the call for an immediate humanitarian ceasefire; demanding that all parties comply with their obligations under international humanitarian law, notably with regard to the protection of civilians; and demanding the immediate and unconditional release of all hostages as well as humanitarian access for the civilian population in Gaza.[29] Most recently, after the United States vetoed the State of Palestine's admission as a full member of the United Nations, the Assembly, with 143 UN member states voting in favor, adopted a third resolution calling on the Security Council to re-consider the matter favorably and upgraded the State of Palestine's rights of participation as an extraordinary interim measure.[30]

C. The eleventh emergency special session (2022–present)

Russia invaded Ukraine for the first time in 2014 when it occupied Crimea, and for the second time in 2022 when it purported to annex Ukraine's Donbas region. On February 24, 2022, Russia launched a full-scale invasion into Ukraine. On February 25, 2022, Russia vetoed a draft resolution condemning Russia's aggression. It was sponsored by more than eighty UN member states from all five regional groups, including three permanent members: France, the United States, and the United Kingdom. Ultimately, eleven Council members voted in favor and three, including China, abstained.[31] To the extent that the draft resolution did not invoke Article 39 or Chapter VII of the UN Charter, it ostensibly fell within the scope of Chapter VI. Accordingly, Russia should not have been able to vote on the resolution—much less veto it—by virtue of the explicit terms of Article 27(3) of the UN Charter. The latter article stipulates that in decisions under Chapter VI, "a party to a

[29] UN General Assembly Resolution ES-10/22 (Dec. 12, 2023).

[30] UN General Assembly Resolution ES-10/23, (May 10, 2024). Since the start of 2024, the International Court of Justice has issued several orders including provisional measures in the case "Application of the Convention on the Prevention and Punishment of the Crime of Genocide in the Gaza Strip (South Africa v. Israel)" See Order on Provisional Measures, 2024 ICJ Reports (Jan. 26, 2024); Order on Provisional Measures, (Mar. 28, 2024); and Order on Provisional Measures, (May 24, 2024). The Prosecutor of the International Criminal Court has also requested arrest warrants for three Hamas leaders as well as the Prime Minister and the Minister of Defense of the State of Israel for various war crimes and crimes against humanity.

[31] See UN Security Council, Draft Resolution S/2022/155 (Feb. 25, 2022); UN Security Council, 8979th mtg., UN Doc. S/2022/PV.8979 (Feb. 25, 2022).

dispute shall abstain from voting." Of course, other permanent and elected members have also violated the mandatory abstention rule in Article 27(3).[32]

On February 27, 2022, the Security Council adopted Resolution 2623 (2022) on the proposal of Albania and the United States,[33] calling for the convening of an emergency special session of the General Assembly after "taking into account that the lack of unanimity of its permanent members at the 8979th meeting [had] prevented it from exercising its primary responsibility for the maintenance of international peace and security." A Security Council resolution convening an emergency special session is a procedural matter requiring only nine affirmative votes to pass. While Russia vetoed the resolution, the resolution passed with eleven votes in favor and three abstentions including China.

In accordance with the Uniting for Peace resolution, the Secretary-General convened the eleventh emergency special session (ESS11) on February 28, 2022. The timing was significant: the session took place only four days after Russia invaded Ukraine, three days after Russia vetoed the substantive resolution deploring its aggression against Ukraine, and one day after the Security Council passed a procedural resolution requesting the convening of the emergency special session.[34] It had been twenty-five years since ESS10 was first convened in 1997 at the request of a majority of UN member states and forty years since an emergency special session was convened at the request of the Security Council itself.[35]

In the first and second resolutions of ESS11,[36] the General Assembly reaffirmed its commitment to the sovereignty and territorial integrity of Ukraine, and condemned the Russian aggression against Ukraine. The Assembly called for an immediate, complete, and unconditional withdrawal of Russian forces from Ukraine. Most important, it reaffirmed the fundamental principle of customary international law that "the territory of a State shall not be the object of acquisition by another State resulting from the threat or use of force."[37]

[32] See Security Council Report, "In Hindsight: Obligatory Abstention," (Mar. 31, 2014), accessed June 16, 2024, www.securitycouncilreport.org/monthly-forecast/2014-04/in_hindsight_obligatory_abstentions.php.

[33] See UN Security Council, Resolution 2623, (Feb. 27, 2022); UN Security Council, 8980th mtg., UN Doc. S/2022/PV.8980 (Feb. 27, 2022).

[34] See UN Secretary-General, Note by the Secretary-General, UN Doc. A/ES-11/1 (Feb. 27, 2022).

[35] See UN Security Council, Resolution 462, (Jan. 9, 1980); UN General Assembly, Resolution ES-6/2 (Jan. 14, 1980).

[36] UN General Assembly Resolutions A/RES/ES-11/1 (Mar. 2, 2022); and ES-11/2, A/RES/ES-11/2 (Mar. 24, 2022).

[37] A/RES/ES-11/1 and/RES/ES-11/2.

In the third resolution,[38] the General Assembly decided to "suspend the rights of membership in the Human Rights Council of the Russian Federation." In the fourth resolution,[39] the Assembly condemned "the organization by the Russian Federation of illegal so-called referendums in regions within the internationally recognized borders of Ukraine" and declared illegal the "annexation of the Donetsk, Kherson, Luhansk, and Zaporizhzhia regions of Ukraine, following the organization of the above-mentioned referendums."[40]

In the fifth[41] and sixth resolutions,[42] the General Assembly turned to the question of accountability. The fifth resolution recommended the creation of an "international register of damage," similar to the above-mentioned UNROD, to create a record of the damage, loss, or injury caused by internationally wrongful acts of Russia in or against Ukraine. The sixth resolution emphasized "the need to ensure accountability for the most serious crimes under international law committed on the territory of Ukraine through appropriate, fair, and independent investigations and prosecutions at the national or international level."[43] As it has with ESS10, the General Assembly has adjourned and resumed ESS11 several times.

Section III: A More Robust Response to the Situations in Palestine and Ukraine

While the tenth and eleventh emergency special sessions have been relatively active, they have yet to tap the full potential of the Uniting for Peace resolution. The powers and precedents described above can set the stage for a resurgent General Assembly willing and able to authorize a range of collective

[38] UN General Assembly, Resolution ES-11/3, A/RES/ES-11/3 (Apr. 7, 2022).
[39] UN General Assembly, Resolution ES-11/4, A/RES/ES-11/4 (Oct. 12, 2022).
[40] Ibid.
[41] UN General Assembly, Resolution ES-11/5, A/RES/ES-11/5 (Nov. 14, 2022).
[42] UN General Assembly, Resolution ES-11/6, A/RES/ES-11/6 (Feb. 23, 2023).
[43] See A/RES/ES-11/6, para. 9; see also Allegations of Genocide (Ukraine v. Russia), 2022 ICJ 211 (Mar. 16, 2022); ICC Prosecutor, Karim A. A. Khan, Statement on the Situation in Ukraine: Receipt of Referrals from 39 States Parties and the Opening of an Investigation (Mar. 2, 2022), accessed June 16, 2024, https://www.icc-cpi.int/news/statement-icc-prosecutor-karim-aa-khan-qc-situation-ukraine-receipt-referrals-39-states. The Pre-Trial Chamber II of the ICC has issued warrants of arrest for President of the Russian Federation and another Russian official for the alleged war crime of unlawful deportation and transfer of children from occupied areas of Ukraine to the Russian Federation.

measures to achieve a far more robust and consequential response to the situations in Palestine and Ukraine.

It bears repeating, however, that unlike the Security Council, the General Assembly can only provide a legal basis for action by member states that are willing to act; it cannot impose binding obligations on member states that do not wish to do so. Nonetheless, the General Assembly has the ability to do more than it has done to give effect to the collective will of the international community to end the occupation of Palestine and of Ukraine, to bring a just and comprehensive peace between Israel and Palestine, and to restore the territorial integrity of Ukraine.

If and when ESS10 resumes again, the General Assembly can consider recommending the following nonexhaustive list of concrete collective measures:

- encouraging member states to provide humanitarian assistance to Palestine;
- deploying a UN peacekeeping mission or civilian protection force to Gaza at the request or with the consent of the Palestinian Authority;
- establishing a Trust Fund for the Reconstruction of Gaza;
- calling upon states that are parties to the Rome Statute of the International Criminal Court (ICC) to provide the necessary resources to advance the investigation and prosecution of war crimes and crimes against humanity by Israel and other serious violations of international humanitarian law by armed Israeli settlers as well as by Palestinian militants including Hamas and Islamic Jihad and to enforce any arrest warrants issued by the ICC;[44]
- calling upon the high contracting parties to the Fourth Geneva Convention to convene a conference on the situation in Palestine; and/or
- recommending diplomatic, financial, and other sanctions, including an arms embargo, against Israel for its failure to comply with the

[44] It is worth noting that the General Assembly does not have the authority to make referrals to the ICC. Pursuant to Article 13 of the Rome Statute, the ICC may exercise jurisdiction by a referral to the prosecutor by the Security Council acting under Chapter VII of the UN Charter; there is no equivalent provision providing for referrals by the General Assembly.

provisional measures ordered by the International Court of Justice to prevent a genocide against the Palestinian people in Gaza[45]

Similarly, if and when the ESS11 is resumed again, the General Assembly can consider recommending the following nonexhaustive list of concrete collective measures[46]:

- authorizing member states to provide military assistance to Ukraine;
- authorizing the conduct of a referendum at the request or with the consent of the Ukrainian government;
- deploying a UN peacekeeping mission or civilian protection force to Ukraine at the request or with the consent of the Ukrainian government;
- recommending the establishment of a UN compensation commission for Russian aggression against Ukraine, similar to the UN Compensation Commission for Iraqi aggression against Kuwait;[47]
- calling upon states that are parties to the Rome Statute to provide the necessary resources to advance the investigation and prosecution of war crimes and other serious violations of humanitarian law by Russia and Ukraine and to enforce any arrest warrants issued by the ICC;[48] and/or
- recommending diplomatic, financial, and other sanctions, against Russia, for its failure to comply with the provisional measures ordered by the International Court of Justice.[49]

To the extent that Russia's armed attack against Ukraine falls within the meaning of "armed attack" under Article 51 of the UN Charter and constitutes an act of aggression within the meaning of Resolution 377 A (V), the General Assembly is not limited to providing military assistance to the defending state and sanctions against the aggressing state. The General Assembly may, within the explicit terms of Resolution 377 (V), consider

[45] Application on Convention on Prevention and Punishment of Crime of Genocide in Gaza Strip (South Africa v. Israel), Order on Provisional Measures, 2024 ICJ 1(Jan. 26, 2024); Order on Provisional Measures, (Mar. 28, 2024); and Order on Provisional Measures, (May 24, 2024).

[46] Mona Ali Khalil, "A Just Peace for an Unjust War in Ukraine," *Passblue*, May 2022, accessed May 25, 2024, https://www.passblue.com/2022/05/29/a-just-peace-for-an-unjust-war-in-ukraine/.

[47] The United Nations Compensation Commission established pursuant to UN Security Council, Resolutions 687, S/RES/687 (Apr. 3, 1991) and 692, S/RES/692 (May 20, 1991).

[48] Subject to the jurisdiction of the ICC, this should include the crimes committed by Russia in Ukraine since February 24, 2022, as well as any committed by Ukraine in the same period.

[49] Allegations of Genocide (Ukraine v. Russia) at 2022 ICJ 211. Order of Provisional Measures (Mar.16, 2022)

recommending the use of armed force in order to restore the territorial integrity of Ukraine. Beyond noting the option, it is not the author's intention here to suggest that the General Assembly should actually exercise that option.

Conclusion

Moments of crisis are also moments of opportunity. When unprincipled powers prevent the Security Council from fulfilling its primary responsibility, the General Assembly has shown its willingness and demonstrated its ability to uphold the power of the principles of the UN Charter. In order to overcome paralysis in the Security Council, the General Assembly has acted on its explicit powers under the UN Charter and expanded them; it has seized on implicit and implied powers and codified them; it has relied on legal and moral imperatives and operationalized them.

While the General Assembly cannot oblige any member state to take or to refrain from any action, it can recommend collective measures to give effect to the will of the international community. While such measures would be voluntary and not mandatory, they would arguably have more international legitimacy than unilateral sanctions or interventions. Abiding by and ensuring respect for the UN Charter and customary international law general, is not only a legal and moral imperative but also a practical and even existential one. The failure to do so may itself be a threat to international peace and security.

While all member states are required to fulfill their obligations under the UN Charter, the permanent members—to the extent that they are continuously and permanently entrusted with the primary responsibility for the maintenance of international peace and security—have a heightened obligation to respect and to ensure respect for those obligations. Using a veto—especially when genocide, crimes against humanity, and war crimes are being committed—not only violates the permanent members' obligations under customary international law, but it also prevents the Security Council from fulfilling its primary responsibility under the UN Charter.[50]

If the Responsibility to Protect and the responsibility to maintain international peace and security are to have any credibility in the twenty-first century, the General Assembly must be ready to exercise its full powers under the

[50] See Khalil, *Reforming the UN Security Council.*

Uniting for Peace resolution whenever and wherever the Security Council fails to prevent or reverse aggression; to prevent or punish genocide; or to prevent or respond to situations involving war crimes, crimes against humanity, and ethnic cleansing.

The General Assembly can and should do more than issue condemnations and call for ceasefires and troop withdrawals; it can and should authorize more consequential measures in response to aggression and mass atrocity crimes. Thus, when the Security Council is unable to fulfill its primary responsibility, "We the Peoples"—in whose name the UN Charter was adopted— can and should look to the General Assembly to maintain international peace and security in fulfillment of the purposes and principles of the United Nations..

8

Reinforcing the International Court of Justice

Catherine Amirfar and Floriane Lavaud

Introduction

The Charter of the United Nations envisions parallel, mutually reinforcing roles for the Security Council (or Council) and the International Court of Justice (or Court). Where the Security Council serves as the political executive pillar, the Court functions as the impartial judicial pillar of the UN system. While each has distinct mandates to fulfill in furtherance of international peace and security, there are important points of complementarity, where the Council can look to the Court for authoritative guidance on legal issues and to facilitate the peaceful resolution of legal disputes, and the Court, in turn, can rely on the Council to take steps to support effective enforcement of its judgments.

While intrastate and regional conflicts have dominated the Security Council's agenda of threats to international peace and security, over the past year alone, the Security Council and the Court have dealt with multiple interstate conflicts, including Russia's invasion and war of aggression against Ukraine, the conflict between Armenia and Azerbaijan, Venezuela's threats of a territorial war against Guyana, and the Israel-Palestine conflict.

This chapter explores opportunities for the Security Council to reinforce the authority of the Court. Section I addresses the Security Council's role in recommending referrals to the Court in Article 36 of the UN Charter, seeking advisory opinions (AOs) pursuant to Article 96, and other mechanisms that contribute to the promotion of international peace and security. Section II addresses the Security Council's authority to enforce the judgments of the Court judgments in accordance with Article 94(2) of the Charter.

Catherine Amirfar and Floriane Lavaud, *Reinforcing the International Court of Justice* In: *Empowering the UN Security Council.* Edited by: Mona Ali Khalil and Floriane Lavaud, Oxford University Press. © Oxford University Press 2024.
DOI: 10.1093/oso/9780197780602.003.0009

Section I: International Court of Justice and the Peaceful Settlement of Disputes

The Security Council can reinforce the Court's jurisdiction over legal disputes to advance the peaceful settlement of such disputes, which in turn can promote international peace and security. Over the years, states have increasingly come to view the Court as an institution capable of resolving disputes through fair and impartial adjudication. Indeed, at the time of writing, more than 100 states are participating in cases on the Court's increasingly busy docket.

This section explores, first, how the Security Council may facilitate the judicial settlement of disputes through the use of Article 36 of the UN Charter. It then discusses the Council's right to request AOs from the Court and their historical and potential impact on peace and security. Finally, it discusses additional mechanisms that support a complementary role between the Court and the Security Council in the maintenance of international peace and security.

A. Judicial settlement of disputes

The Security Council cannot directly refer legal disputes to the Court. Rather, it may request the relevant states to do so. Pursuant to Article 33 of the UN Charter, the Security Council may, when it deems necessary, call upon the parties to settle "any dispute" through negotiation, mediation, arbitration, or other peaceful means, if the continuance of that dispute "is likely to endanger the maintenance of international peace and security."[1] Article 36(3) further provides that, in making recommendations, the Council "should also take into consideration that *legal* disputes should as a general rule be referred by the parties to the International Court of Justice in accordance with the provisions of the Statute of the Court."[2]

Interestingly, the Security Council appears to have invoked this mechanism only once. In 1947, the Council passed Resolution 22 recommending that the United Kingdom and Albania immediately refer to the Court their dispute over the explosion of mines in the Corfu Channel.[3] The United

[1] UN Charter art. 33.
[2] UN Charter art. 36(3) (emphasis added).
[3] UN Security Council, Resolution 22, S/RES/22 (1947).

Kingdom subsequently brought a case before the Court, and Albania voluntarily accepted its jurisdiction, resulting in the 1947–1949 Corfu Channel case (*United Kingdom v. People's Republic of Albania*).

While the Security Council has not been inclined to call upon states to refer specific cases to the Court, the Council has instead consistently urged states to accept the compulsory jurisdiction of the Court over disputes more generally, most recently in 2012.[4] Under Article 36(2) of the Statute of the Court, states parties may "at any time declare that they recognize as compulsory *ipso facto* and without special agreement, in relation to any other State accepting the same obligation, the jurisdiction of the Court."[5] To date, seventy-four member states have made declarations accepting the Court's mandatory jurisdiction, including only one of the five permanent members (P5): the United Kingdom.[6]

B. Requests for advisory opinions

In addition to its role in contentious disputes, under Article 96 of the Charter, the Security Council "may request the International Court of Justice to give an advisory opinion on any legal question."[7] Initial texts proposed during the Dumbarton Oaks Conference suggested a more limited scope for AOs.[8] One draft proposal stated, "The Security Council should be empowered to refer to the court, for advice, legal questions connected with other disputes."[9] Ultimately, however, the language adopted under Article 96 paved the way for the Court to issue AOs broadly on "any legal question."

To date, the Security Council has requested an AO only once (in the *South West Africa* case), while the General Assembly has requested AOs in eighteen instances. The General Assembly's requests have covered a broad spectrum of international legal questions of great global significance, ranging from

[4] Press Release, Security Council, "Using Advisory Opinions Would Bolster Links between Security Council, World Court, Strengthen Rule of Law, Chief Justice Says in Open Debate," UN Press Release SC/14392 (Dec. 18, 2020).

[5] Statute of the International Court of Justice, Article 36(2).

[6] International Court of Justice, "Declarations Recognizing the Jurisdiction of the Court as Compulsory," accessedJune 20, 2024, https://www.Court-cij.org/declarations.

[7] UN Charter art. 96. See also Article 65 of the Statute of the International Court of Justice.

[8] The Dumbarton Oaks conference led to the establishment of a "general international organization"—later, the United Nations.

[9] United Nations Conference on International Organization (UNCIO) 3 (1945), 14, 370.

states' decolonization obligations, to the legality of the threat or use of nuclear weapons and other obligations.

Notwithstanding their nonbinding nature, AOs are authoritative statements of international law by the UN's highest judicial organ that "carry great legal weight and moral authority."[10] In particular, they allow the Court to provide comprehensive statements clarifying state obligations on issues of global consequence, and in some cases, these have significantly influenced states' conduct. Clarifying states' legal obligations can lead to greater predictability in the global order, which in turn strengthens peace and security. In addition, AOs can reinforce and frame ongoing negotiations by providing a legal analytical framework for the problem, as well as leverage for further diplomacy or legal action. In the words of former president of the Court, Judge Shi Jiuyong, advisory proceedings play "an 'indirect' part in preventing disputes and conflicts from developing, by clarifying the legal parameters within which a problem may be solved."[11] Finally, AOs can serve to increase or maintain global public attention on a particular problem, which also can be a catalyst for state action.

It is in this context that the contributions of AOs to the Security Council's primary responsibility for the maintenance of international peace and security must be assessed. Such contributions are perhaps most apparent in the postcolonial context. As noted, the only AO the Security Council has requested to date related to a dispute regarding South Africa's occupation of the Republic of Namibia (then, South West Africa). After adopting Resolution 276 condemning South Africa's illegal occupation,[12] the Council requested an AO on "the legal consequences for States of the continued presence of South Africa in Namibia, notwithstanding Resolution 276."[13]

In its 1971 opinion, the Court concluded, inter alia, that the General Assembly had terminated South Africa's mandate over Namibia; all UN member states were under the obligation to abstain from entering into dealings with South Africa that may further entrench its authority over Namibian territory; and any state entering into such a relationship could not

[10] International Court of Justice, "Advisory Jurisdiction," accessed June 20, 2024, https://www.Court-cij.org/advisory-jurisdiction.

[11] H. E. Judge Shi Jiuyong, "The Advisory Function of the International Court of Justice," speech to the Sixth Committee of the General Assembly of the United Nations, November 5, 2004, 4.

[12] See UN General Assembly, Resolution 276, S/RES/276 (Jan. 30, 1970).

[13] UN Security Council, Resolution 284, S/RES/284 (July 29, 1970).

expect the UN to recognize its validity or effects.[14] In respect of the last point, the Court noted an important exception—referred to as the "Namibia exception"—that "the non-recognition of South Africa's administration of the Territory should not result in the depriving the people of Namibia of any advantages derived from international co-operation."[15] As a result of the Court's decision, the Council adopted another resolution expressing its agreement with the AO and reaffirming its calls upon South Africa to withdraw and upon other states to comply with the Court's decision.[16] The Court's AO also had a broader impact on state conduct: the Namibia exception has since been invoked in subsequent conflicts where self-determination of populations is at issue, including in the Israel-Palestine conflict and Turkey's occupation of Northern Cyprus.

Another example of the consequential impacts of AOs and their contribution to peace and security arose in the context of the decolonization of Mauritius. In 2017, on the initiative of the African Group, the General Assembly adopted Resolution 71/292,[17] requesting the Court to advise on whether the process of decolonization of Mauritius had been lawfully completed and to opine on the legal consequences of the continued administration of the Chagos Archipelago by the United Kingdom. In its 2019 AO, the Court found that the process of decolonization was not lawfully completed and that the United Kingdom was obligated to end its administration of the Chagos Archipelago as soon as possible.[18] While the United Kingdom did not immediately comply, the AO provided an important legal framework that proved useful in ongoing attempts to facilitate a resolution. Indeed, Mauritius explicitly relied on the Court's decision in subsequent General Assembly debates. In particular, its characterization of the AO as a decisive confirmation of the United Kingdom's obligations under international law was a main focus of its argument for complete withdrawal.[19] Subsequently, the General Assembly adopted a resolution welcoming the Court's AO and again demanded that the United Kingdom withdraw within six months to

[14] Legal Consequences for States of the Continued Presence of South Africa in Namibia (South West Africa) notwithstanding Security Council Resolution 276 (1970), Advisory Opinion, 1971 ICJ 16, para. 133 (June 21).

[15] Ibid., para. 125.

[16] UN Security Council, Resolution 301, S/RES/301 (Oct. 20, 1971).

[17] UN General Assembly, Resolution 71/292, A/RES/71/292 (June 22, 2017).

[18] Legal Consequences of the Separation of the Chagos Archipelago from Mauritius in 1965, Advisory Opinion, 2019 ICJ 95 (Feb. 25).

[19] UN General Assembly, 83rd plenary mtg., A/73/PV.83, 5-7 (May 22, 2019).

allow Mauritius to complete decolonization.[20] In 2022, the United Kingdom began negotiations with Mauritius concerning the sovereignty of the territory, which remain ongoing.[21]

Examples of such contributions also exist outside the postcolonial context. For example, in 1996, the General Assembly requested the Court's opinion on whether the threat or use of nuclear weapons was, under any circumstance, permitted under international law.[22] The AO proceedings attracted broad state participation, with twenty-eight states filing written statements and twenty-two presenting oral arguments. Even as the Court held that it could not "conclude definitively whether the threat or use of nuclear weapons would be lawful or unlawful in an extreme circumstance of self-defence, in which the very survival of a State would be at stake,"[23] it took the opportunity to clarify that certain principles of international environmental law constitute customary international law.[24] The AO further "recognize[d] that the environment is not an abstraction but represents the living space, the quality of life, and the very health of human beings, including generations unborn,"[25] setting the stage for future legal developments surrounding the rights and obligations implicit in the principle of intergenerational equity.[26]

It is important to note that the Court has the authority to advise on an ongoing conflict even where the Security Council remains seized of the matter. The Court clarified this point in the advisory proceedings on Kosovo's declaration of independence. In 2008, General Assembly Resolution 63/

[20] UN General Assembly, Resolution 73/295, A/RES/73/295, ¶ 3 (May 24, 2019).

[21] James Cleverly, Secretary of State for Foreign, Commonwealth, and Development Affairs, "British Indian Ocean Territory/Chagos Archipelago: Statement made on 3 November 2022," Statement UIN HCWS354, accessed June 20, 2024, https://questions-statements.parliament.uk/written-statements/detail/2022-11-03/hcws354.

[22] See Legality of the Threat or Use of Nuclear Weapons, Advisory Opinion, 1996 ICJ Reports (July 8).

[23] Ibid., para. 105(e).

[24] In 2014, the Marshall Islands initiated a contentious case against nine states, accusing them of not fulfilling their obligations with respect to cessation of the nuclear arms race and nuclear disarmament in which it invoked the Court's 1996 AO as "the most authoritative recognition of the customary status of the obligation" "to pursue negotiations in good faith on effective measures relating to cessation of the nuclear arms race at an early date and to nuclear disarmament, and on a treaty on general and complete disarmament under strict and effective international control" under Article VI of the Treaty on the Non-Proliferation of Nuclear Weapons. Obligations concerning Negotiations relating to Cessation of the Nuclear Arms Race and to Nuclear Disarmament (*Marshall Islands v. United Kingdom*), Memorial of the Marshall Islands, 2015 ICJ (Mar. 16, 2015), para. 196. The Court ultimately decided that it lacked jurisdiction under Article 36(2) of the ICJ Statute to hear the case. Ibid., (*Marshall Islands v. United Kingdom*), Preliminary Objections, Judgment, 2016 ICJ 833 (Oct. 5, 2016).

[25] Ibid., para. 29 (emphasis added).

[26] UN General Assembly, Resolution 77/276, A/RES/77/276 (Apr. 4, 2023).

3 requested the Court to opine on the legality of Kosovo's unilateral declaration of independence from Serbia.[27] The AO considered the effects of Security Council Resolution 1244,[28] which provided a framework for the resolution of the Kosovo conflict. Certain states argued that Resolution 1244 circumscribed the Court's authority to act because that Resolution triggered Article 12(1) of the UN Charter.[29] Article 12(1) provides that the General Assembly may not make a recommendation about a dispute or situation while the Security Council is exercising the functions assigned to it by the Charter on the same situation.[30] The Court concluded that, while Article 12 may limit the scope of the action the General Assembly may take *subsequent to* the receipt of an AO, it does not limit its power to request an AO in the first instance.[31]

The potentially powerful role of AOs in recent years is perhaps best illustrated by the widespread participation of UN member states in AO proceedings relating to some of the most long-standing issues on the UN's agenda.[32] For example, in 2022, the General Assembly voted to request an AO from the Court on two legal questions relating to the Israeli policies and practices in the Palestinian territory occupied since 1967, in particular, how these policies and practices affect the legal status of the occupation and the legal consequences that arise for all states and the United Nations from this status.[33] More than fifty states and three regional organizations participated in the Court's advisory proceedings in 2024 on the "Legal Consequences Arising from the Policies and Practices of Israel in the Occupied Palestinian Territory, Including East Jerusalem."[34]

This development came some two decades after the General Assembly adopted Resolution ES-10/14, requesting an AO on the legal consequences

[27] UN General Assembly, Resolution 63/3, A/RES/63/3 (Oct. 8, 2008).

[28] See UN Security Council, Resolution 1244, S/RES/1244 (June 10, 1999).

[29] Accordance with international law of the unilateral declaration of independence in respect of Kosovo, Advisory Opinion, 2010 ICJ 403, paras. 24, 39–42. See also, e.g., Accordance with International Law of the Unilateral Declaration of Independence in Respect of Kosovo, Written Statement of the Government of the Republic of Albania (April 2009), paras. 48–53.

[30] UN Charter art. 12(1).

[31] Accordance with International Law of the Unilateral Declaration of Independence in Respect of Kosovo, Advisory Opinion, 2010 ICJ 403, para. 24.

[32] The Court's Statute permits member states to request to contribute written and oral statements in any AO. ICJ Statute, art. 66(2)–(3). The Court has discretion to decide whether to permit the state to submit a written or oral statement.

[33] UN General Assembly, Resolution 77/247, A/RES/77/247 (Dec. 30, 2022).

[34] International Court of Justice, "Legal Consequences Arising from the Policies and Practices of Israel in the Occupied Palestinian Territory, Including East Jerusalem," accessed June 20, 2024, https://www.icj-cij.org/case/186.

arising from the construction of the wall built by Israel in Occupied Palestinian Territory (OPT).[35] Those proceedings also attracted significant state participation, with forty-five states submitting written statements. In 2004, the Court found Israel had "severely impede[d] the exercise by the Palestinian people of its right to self-determination" with the construction of the wall[36]and violated its international humanitarian and human rights law obligations, as well as obligations of an *erga omnes* character that applied to other states and the United Nations, including the General Assembly and the Security Council.[37] It further held that Israel had the obligation to immediately end the violation by "ceas[ing] the works of construction of the wall,"[38] "dismantling . . . those parts . . . situated within the [OPT],"[39] and "mak[ing] reparation[s] for the damage caused to all the natural or legal persons concerned."[40]

Even more recently, a record-breaking ninety one written statements were filed in the Court's advisory proceedings on the "Obligations of States in Respect of Climate Change."[41] This unprecedented level of participation in an AO proceeding follows an equally unprecedented movement in the General Assembly, when in 2023, Vanuatu led a coalition of 132 UN Member states to adopt the resolution requesting the Court's AO.[42] The Court's forthcoming opinion is an opportunity to clarify a broad array of international legal obligations that have become increasingly fragmented, with a view to specifying the obligations of states across a spectrum of large emitters and climate-vulnerable states.

[35] UN General Assembly, Illegal Israeli Actions in Occupied East Jerusalem and the Rest of the Occupied Palestinian Territory, A/RES/ES-10/14 (Dec. 12, 2003).

[36] Legal Consequences of the Construction of a Wall in the Occupied Palestinian Territory, Advisory Opinion, 2004 ICJ 136, para. 122 (July 9).

[37] Ibid., paras. 137, 155. The Court elaborated on the *erga omnes* obligations of other states, as well as "the United Nations, and especially the General Assembly and the Security Council, . . . to bring to an end to the illegal situation" in question. Ibid., paras. 159–160.

[38] Ibid., para. 151.

[39] Ibid.

[40] Ibid., para. 152.

[41] International Court of Justice, "Obligations of States in Respect of Climate Change," accessed June 20, 2024, https://www.icj-cij.org/case/187.

[42] UN General Assembly, Request for an Advisory Opinion of the International Court of Justice on the Obligations of States in Respect of Climate Change, A/77/L.58 (Mar. 1, 2023). Co-author Catherine Amirfar and other lawyers at Debevoise & Plimpton LLP represent certain states and international organizations (IOs) in these proceedings, and note that observations made throughout this chapter are personal and not attributable to Debevoise & Plimpton LLP or its clients.

C. Additional mechanisms

At least two additional mechanisms exist to support a complementary role between the Court and the Security Council to maintain international peace and security.

First, the Court's jurisdiction over a legal dispute exists notwithstanding decisions of the Council or the General Assembly that arguably already address the underlying merits of that dispute. The 1992 *Lockerbie* case is deemed to have significant implications in this regard. The *Lockerbie* case examined the interplay between the Court's competence in the context of Security Council action taken in response to Libya's involvement in the civilian aircraft bombing of Pan Am Flight 103 over Lockerbie. Libya had filed its application before the Court against the United Kingdom and the United States after the Security Council adopted Resolution 731 (1992), but before the Council adopted Resolutions 748 (1992) and 883 (1993) under Chapter VII of the UN Charter[43]; Libya alleged that the United Kingdom and United States had violated its rights under the Montreal convention even though the resolutions in question did not mention that convention. The Court rejected preliminary objections by the United Kingdom and the United States that the case was inadmissible due to the subsequent Security Council resolutions and upheld the Court's jurisdiction.[44] The case, however, did not proceed to the merits of the case as the three states notified the Court of their agreement to discontinue the proceedings with prejudice in September 2003.[45]

Second, in addition to the annual presentation by the president of the Court to the Council,[46] more informal interactions between the Court and the Security Council can serve as important confidence-building measures. For example, as another former president of the Court, Judge Abdulqawi

[43] UN Security Council, Resolution 731, S/RES/731 (Jan. 21, 1992), UN Security Council, Resolution 748, S/RES/748 (March 31, 1992) and UN Security Council, Resolution 883, S/RES/883 (Nov. 11, 1993).

[44] "Questions of Interpretation and Application of the 1971 Montreal Convention Arising from the Aerial Incident at Lockerbie *(Libyan Arab Jamahiriya v. United States of America)*," Preliminary Objections, Judgment, ICJ Reports 1998, 115.

[45] *Lockerbie (Libya v. United Kingdom)*, Order, Removal from the List, ICJ GL No. 88, 2003 ICJ 149 (Sept. 10); *Lockerbie (Libya v. United States)*, Order, Removal from the List, ICJ GL No. 89, 2003 ICJ 152 (Sept. 10).

[46] Security Council Report, "Annual Briefing by ICJ President," (Oct. 25, 2014), accessed June 20, 2024, https://www.securitycouncilreport.org/whatsinblue/2013/10/annual-briefing-by-icj-president.php ("The [Court president's] briefing, which has been held annually since the practice was first established in 2000, normally coincides with the presentation of the annual report of the ICJ to the General Assembly.")

Yusuf, has suggested,[47] a scheduled visit once every three years could encourage interaction between the two bodies and facilitate the Security Council's increased use of the AO procedure. The last official Council visit to the Court was in 2014.[48]

Section II: UN Security Council Enforcement of the Judgments of the International Court of Justice

The authority of the Security Council to enforce the Court's judgments stands out as the most significant mechanism for reinforcing the work of the Court. Such action by the Security Council is intended to ensure that states comply with the judgments of the Court when they fail to do so. A 2021 study found that in approximately 77% of cases where compliance was easy to assess, state behavior was "partly or wholly consistent" with the operative part of the Court's decision.[49] This section explores the basis for the authority of the Security Council to ensure state compliance as a matter of principle under the UN Charter and through the lens of the Council's actual practice.

A. Scope of Article 94(2)

Article 94(2) of the Charter provides that "[i]f any party to a case fails to perform the obligations incumbent upon it under a judgment rendered by the Court, the other party may have recourse to the Security Council, which may, if it deems necessary, make recommendations or decide upon measures to be taken to give effect to the judgment."[50]

At least initially, the drafters of the Charter hesitated to include any provision for Security Council enforcement of Court decisions in the Charter. The United States, for example, argued such "enlargement of the Council's

[47] Security Council, "Using Advisory Opinions Would Bolster Links between Security Council, World Court, Strengthen Rule of Law, Chief Justice Says in Open Debate," UN Press Release SC/14392 (Dec. 18, 2020).

[48] See International Court of Justice, "United Nations Security Council Pays Visit to the International Court of Justice," (Aug. 11, 2014), accessed June 20, 2024, https://www.Court-cij.org/multimedia/56e93a6288fa3fe1450a7959.

[49] Tom Ginsburg, "The Institutional Context of the International Court of Justice," *University of Chicago Public Law & Legal Theory Working Papers* (2021): 9.

[50] UN Charter art. 94(2).

powers . . . had already been criticized as being too wide."[51] Other states expressed concerns that the phrase "if it deems necessary" in Article 94(2) "might tend to weaken the position of the Court."[52] To overcome these concerns, proponents "pointed out that the action to be taken by the Security Council was permissive rather than obligatory and that the addition . . . merely made more clear the discretionary power of the Security Council."[53]

And indeed, while states may request the Council to enforce a Court judgment pursuant to Article 94(2), it is entirely within the Security Council's discretion whether or not to do so. Should the Council wish to accede to a request under Article 94(2), it would call upon the party concerned to comply with the Court's judgment and impose measures in the event that the party fails to comply. Council action could include recommendations under Chapter VI or enforcement measures under Chapter VII.

B. Article 94(2) in practice

Despite at least seven state requests, the Council has never acted under its Article 94(2) authority.[54] The following case studies nevertheless demonstrate the history and potential of the provision.

1. Provisional measures

Of the seven state requests made pursuant to Article 94(2), four requested the Security Council to enforce provisional measures ordered by the Court. The text of Article 94(2) explicitly refers to "judgments" of the Court. While the Court itself consistently confirms that its provisional measures have binding effect,[55] thus far, states invoking this provision have not succeeded in obtaining action in the Security Council to enforce provisional measures.

[51] UNCIO 11 (1945), 396. The delegate of the United States continued that it seemed "unwise... to give additional powers to the Council" beyond "those powers necessary for meeting threats to peace or suppressing them."

[52] UNCIO 13 (1945), 459.

[53] Ibid.

[54] See Security Council Report, "In Hindsight: The Security Council and the International Court of Justice" (Dec. 28, 2016), accessed June 20, 2024, https://www.securitycouncilreport.org/monthly-forecast/2017-01/in_hindsight_the_security_council_and_the_international_court_of_justice.php.

[55] See Application of the Convention on the Prevention and Punishment of the Crime of Genocide (*The Gambia v. Myanmar*), Order on Provisional Measures, ICJ Reports (Jan. 23, 2020); Allegations of Genocide under the Convention on the Prevention and Punishment of the Crime of Genocide

The first invocation of Article 94(2) occurred in 1951, when the United Kingdom requested that the Security Council address the Iranian government's failure to comply with provisional measures issued in the *Anglo-Iranian Oil Company* case.[56] The United Kingdom sent a letter to the Security Council including a draft resolution in which the Council would "call[] upon the Government of Iran to act in all respects in conformity with the provisional measures indicated by the Court."[57] In the course of debate on the request, the United Kingdom invoked Article 94(2) of the Charter.[58] Iran responded that Article 94 did not apply because the provisional measures issued did not qualify under Article 94(2) as a "judgment" because they were not "final and binding."[59] The Council postponed further discussion until the Court determined whether it had jurisdiction, which it subsequently found lacking. The issue was not taken up again in the Security Council.[60]

The next invocation of Article 94(2) took place decades later in the context of the Bosnian War. In April 1993, the Court ordered Yugoslavia to immediately "take all measures within its power to prevent commission of the crime of genocide."[61] That same month, Bosnia and Herzegovina requested that the Security Council enforce the Court's provisional measures order pursuant to Article 94(2).[62] The Security Council passed two resolutions: Resolution 819 explicitly took note of the Court's order and "demand[ed]" Yugoslavia cease the supply of military arms and equipment to Bosnian Serb military units,[63] and Resolution 820 increased financial and economic sanctions against

(*Ukraine v. Russia Federation*), Order on Provisional Measures, ICJ Reports (March 16, 2022); and Application of the Convention on the Prevention and Punishment of the Crime of Genocide in the Gaza Strip (*South Africa v. Israel*), Order on Provisional Measures, ICJ Reports (Jan. 26, 2024).

[56] United Nations, *Repertoire of the Practice of the Security Council*, Chapter VI: Relations with Other UN Organs, 235–38 (1946–1951), accessed June 20, 2024, https://www.un.org/securitycouncil/sites/www.un.org.securitycouncil/files/en/sc/repertoire/46-51/46-51_06.pdf#page=23.

[57] Ibid. at 236.

[58] Ibid.

[59] Ibid.

[60] Edgardo Sobenes Obregon, "Recourse to the Security Council under Article 94(2) of the United Nations Charter," Max Planck Encyclopedia of International Procedural Law (Apr. 2017) para. 44, accessed June 20, 2024, https://opil.ouplaw.com/display/10.1093/law-mpeipro/e3166.013.3166/law-mpeipro-e3166.

[61] Application of the Convention on the Prevention and Punishment of Genocide (*Bosnia and Herzegovina v. Yugoslavia (Serbia and Montenegro)*), Order on Provisional Measures, 1993 ICJ 3 (Apr. 8).

[62] Permanent Rep. of Bosnia and Herzegovina to the UN, Letter dated Apr. 16, 1993, from the Permanent Rep. of Bosnia and Herzegovina to the United Nations addressed to the President of the Security Council, S/25616 (Apr. 16, 1993).

[63] UN Security Council, Resolution 819, S/RES/819 (Apr. 16, 1993).

Yugoslavia to "strengthen the implementation of the measures imposed by its earlier relevant resolutions."[64] Neither resolution referenced Article 94(2). Bosnia and Herzegovina later requested a meeting with the Security Council, again invoking Article 94(2),[65] but the Security Council took no further action.

In March 2022, one day after the Court indicated provisional measures ordering Russia to immediately suspend its military operations in Ukraine,[66] Ukraine made a statement before the Council encouraging its members "to exercise their duty, envisaged by Article 94, paragraph 2, of the UN Charter, to make recommendations or decide upon measures to be taken in the case of Russia's failure to comply with the obligations incumbent upon it under the judgment."[67] At the time of writing, the Council has not taken action in response to this request.

Finally and most recently, Article 94(2) has been invoked in the context of *South Africa v. Israel*, a contentious case brought under the Convention on the Prevention and Punishment of the Crime of Genocide in relation to the Palestinians in the Gaza Strip. In January, March, and May 2024, the Court indicated provisional measures against Israel in that context.[68] On May 29, 2024, the South African Ambassador invoked Article 94(2) in an address to the UN Security Council, urging the Council to "give effect to the Court's judgments" and arguing for the uniform application of international law.[69] At the time of writing, the Security Council has taken no action on the matter.

[64] UN Security Council, Resolution 820, S/RES/820 (Apr. 17, 1993).

[65] Permanent Rep. of Bosnia and Herzegovina to the UN, Letter dated Sept. 15, 1993, from the Permanent Rep. of Bosnia and Herzegovina to the United Nations addressed to the President of the Security Council, S/26442 (Sept. 15, 1993).

[66] Allegations of Genocide under the Convention on the Prevention and Punishment of the Crime of Genocide (*Ukraine v. Russia Federation*), Order on Provisional Measures, ICJ Reports (March 16, 2022).

[67] UN Security Council, 8998th mtg., S/PV.8998, 20–21 (Mar. 17, 2022).

[68] Application of the Convention on the Prevention and Punishment of the Crime of Genocide in the Gaza Strip (South Africa v. Israel), Order on Provisional Measures, ICJ Reports (Jan. 26, 2024); Application of the Convention on the Prevention and Punishment of the Crime of Genocide in the Gaza Strip (South Africa v. Israel), Order on Provisional Measures, ICJ Reports (March 28, 2024); Application of the Convention on the Prevention and Punishment of the Crime of Genocide in the Gaza Strip (South Africa v. Israel), Order on Provisional Measures, ICJ Reports (May 24, 2024).

[69] Statement by Ambassador Mathu Joyini, Permanent Representative of South Africa to the United Nations at the meeting of the United Nations Security Council on the situation in the Middle East (May 29, 2024), p. 2.

2. Preliminary objections

Only one state has invoked Article 94(2) in an attempt to enforce the Court's ruling on preliminary objections. In the above-mentioned *Lockerbie* case, Libya instituted proceedings before the Court, alleging that the United Kingdom and the United States breached the Montreal convention by seeking Council action and that, in accordance with Article 27(3) of the Charter, they should have recused themselves from voting on the related Security Council resolutions under Chapter VI of the UN Charter due to their involvement in the dispute.[70] In 1998, the Court issued a ruling dismissing the preliminary objections raised by the United Kingdom and the United States and confirming its jurisdiction to adjudicate Libya's claims.[71] Libya subsequently invoked Article 94(2), requesting the Security Council to give effect to the Court's ruling, but the United Kingdom and the United States objected on the basis that the Court's ruling on preliminary objections had "a purely procedural character affecting future proceedings on the case" and "does not, and cannot constitute a final 'judgment' of the kind referred to in" Article 94(2).[72] The United States and United Kingdom nevertheless made clear their intention to "proceed in light of [the Court's] findings that it has jurisdiction."[73] The Security Council took no further action.[74]

3. Merits

States have invoked Article 94(2) to enforce Court judgments on the merits in two instances. One of these, Nicaragua's attempt to enforce the Court's judgment in *Military and Paramilitary Activities in and against Nicaragua (Nicaragua v. United States of America)*, is the only instance where the Security Council actually voted on a resolution pursuant to Article 94(2), although a resolution never passed.

[70] Observations and Submissions of the Great Socialist People's Libyan Arab Jamahiriya on the Preliminary Objections of the United States of America, *Lockerbie (Libya v. United States)*, 1995 ICJ, 89–90 (Dec. 22, 1995); Reply of the Great Socialist People's Libyan Arab Jamahiriya, *Lockerbie (Libya v United States)*, 2000 ICJ, 82 (Jun. 29, 2000).

[71] *Lockerbie (Libya v United States)*, Judgment, Preliminary Objections, 1998 ICJ 211 (Feb. 27); *Lockerbie (Libya v. United Kingdom)*, Judgment, Preliminary Objections, 1998 ICJ 9 (Feb. 27).

[72] Permanent Rep. of the United Kingdom and Acting Permanent Rep. of the United States, Letter dated Mar. 16, 1998, from the Permanent Rep. of the United Kingdom and Acting Permanent Rep. of the United States addressed to the President of the Security Council, S/1998/239, para. 7 (Mar. 16, 1998).

[73] Ibid.

[74] Obregon, "Recourse to the Security Council under Article 94(2) of the United Nations Charter," para. 49 (based on the United States and United Kingdom's opinion that Article 94(2) was inapplicable to the Court's order on preliminary objections, "the UNSC decided not to take action on Libya's requests, which seems to be in line with the previous practice of the UNSC").

In 1984, Nicaragua instituted proceedings against the United States concerning the responsibility of the United States for using armed forces in and against Nicaragua in violation of Nicaragua's sovereignty, including by allegedly directing a mercenary army against Nicaragua in Honduras and mining Nicaraguan ports.[75] In 1986, the Court found in favor of Nicaragua and ordered the United States to cease unlawful actions and pay reparations.[76] After the United States did not comply, Nicaragua requested that the Security Council schedule a meeting to consider the dispute, but without explicitly invoking Article 94(2).[77]

The Security Council held a debate and drafted a resolution calling for full compliance with the Court's judgment, which was vetoed by the United States.[78] Subsequently, Nicaragua "request[ed] an emergency meeting of the Security Council, in accordance with the provisions of Article 94 of the Charter, to consider the non-compliance" of the United States with the Court's judgment.[79] During the emergency meeting of the Security Council, Nicaragua stated that it had not previously invoked Article 94(2) "in order to give the United States the benefit of the doubt with respect to the ruling of the Court, in order to keep open the last possibility that it would decide to comply with and do justice to its international obligations."[80] At this meeting, the Security Council voted on a second draft resolution that "[u]rgently call[ed] for full and immediate compliance" with the Court's judgment.[81] The United States again exercised its veto,[82] despite the Article 27(3) abstention provision. Nicaragua's invocation of Article 94(2) led to four General Assembly resolutions, although ultimately, the United States never complied.[83]

[75] Military and Paramilitary Activities in and against Nicaragua (*Nicaragua v. United States of America*), Memorial of Nicaragua (Questions of Jurisdiction and Admissibility), 1985 ICJ 361 (June 30).

[76] Military and Paramilitary Activities in and against Nicaragua (*Nicaragua v. United States of America*), Judgment, 1986 ICJ 14 (June 27).

[77] Permanent Rep. of Nicaragua, Letter dated July 22, 1986, from the Permanent Rep. of Nicaragua addressed to the President of the Security Council, S/18230 (July 22 1986).

[78] UN Security Council, Draft Resolution S/18250 (July 31, 1986).

[79] Permanent Rep. of Nicaragua, Letter dated October 17, 1986, from the Permanent Rep. of Nicaragua addressed to the President of the Security Council, S/18415 (Oct. 20, 1986).

[80] UN Security Council, 2715th mtg., S/PV.2715, 18 (Oct. 21, 1986).

[81] UN Security Council, Draft Resolution S/18428 (Oct. 28, 1986).

[82] UN Security Council, Provisional Verbatim Record of the 2718th Meeting, S/PV.2718 (Oct. 28, 1986), 57. See also "UN Security Council Meetings and Outcomes Tables," Dag Hammarskjold Library (2024), accessed June 20, 2024, https://research.un.org/en/docs/sc/quick (United States exercised veto of Security Council Resolution S/18428 on October 28, 1986).

[83] UN General Assembly, Resolutions 41/31, A/RES/41/31 (June 27, 1986); 42/18 A/RES/42/18 (Nov. 12, 1987); 43/11 A/RES/43/11 (Oct. 25, 1988); 44/43 A/RES/44/43 (Dec. 7, 1989).

The second instance arose sixteen years later, when Honduras invoked Article 94(2) in an attempt to enforce the Court's judgment on the merits against El Salvador in the contentious case between the two states.[84] The Court's 1992 judgment decided the dispute over the frontier line between the two states and the legal situation of certain islands and maritime spaces.[85] Following the Court's judgment, the conflict between the parties persisted for almost a decade. In 2002, Honduras alleged that El Salvador had failed to comply with the Court's judgment and requested Security Council intervention for enforcement pursuant to Article 94(2).[86] El Salvador denied Honduras's allegations, yet did not object "to the Council's considering the request."[87] The Security Council did not respond to either state's request to address the issue, and El Salvador and Honduras eventually resumed negotiations and began a new demarcation regime.[88] Despite the Council's inaction, commentators considered that Honduras's invocation of Article 94(2) "was sufficient to trigger a more conciliatory tone from El Salvador" and "prompt[ed] renewed vigour in negotiations that diffused tensions and ultimately speeded up compliance with the ICJ's delimitation of their common border."[89]

In short, the Security Council's practice with respect to Article 94(2) suggests that there are structural barriers to comprehensive and full-throated action by the Council in support of better enforcement of compliance with the judgments of the Court. Further, the impact of the P5 veto looms large in how effective the Council can be in this respect, especially where a P5 member has a direct stake in the underlying case. It could be that the much-discussed proposed reforms of the Security Council to, inter alia, restrain the veto power and encourage abstention by the P5 would also improve the ability of the Security Council to effectively enforce Court judgments. It is

[84] Land, Island, and Maritime Frontier Dispute (*El Salvador v. Honduras: Nicaragua intervening*), Judgment, 1992 ICJ 51 (Sep. 11).

[85] Ibid.

[86] Permanent Rep. of Honduras, Letter dated Jan. 23, 2002, from the Permanent Rep. of Honduras addressed to the President of the Security Council, S/2002/108 (Jan. 23, 2002).

[87] Permanent Rep. of El Salvador, Letter dated Sep. 24, 2022, from the Permanent Rep. of El Salvador to the President of the Security Council, S/2002/1102 (Sep. 24, 2002).

[88] Aloysius P. Llamzon, "Jurisdiction and Compliance in Recent Decisions of the International Court of Justice," *European Journal of International Law* 18 (2007): 828.

[89] Ibid. at 848; see also Maria Otero, "Problems in the Caribbean: The Absence of Finality to the Territorial Dispute in Nicaragua v. Colombia Will Have Negative Impacts in the Region," *University of Toledo Law Review* 46 (2015): 643; Laurence Boisson de Chazournes and Antonella Angelini, "After the Court Rose: The Rise of Diplomatic Means to Implement the Pronouncements of the International Court of Justice," *Law and Practice of International Courts and Tribunals* 11 (2012): 23.

also significant that these prior examples demonstrate that the mere act of invoking Article 94(2) and the process of responding to such requests and holding debates in the Security Council can encourage state compliance even when no resolution is adopted. In *El Salvador v. Honduras*, the threat of Security Council action arguably was enough to bring the states to the negotiating table and reach a diplomatic solution. Thus, even in the absence of an adopted resolution, the Security Council's discussion of a dispute can be a powerful tool working in favor of compliance with Court judgments.

Conclusion

While the Security Council and the Court each have unique roles and responsibilities to promote international peace and security, the Council has many means to support the Court in fulfillment of both their respective mandates. Articles 36(3), 94(2), and 96 of the UN Charter offer tools to advance the peaceful settlement of disputes and enforce the rights and obligations of states under international law. While to date the Security Council has rarely availed itself of these tools, it is well placed to reinforce the Court by increasing its resort to, support of, and cooperation with the Court as part of a more effective strategy to ensure the rule of law and the maintenance of international peace and security, including by encouraging states to accept the mandatory jurisdiction of the Court and to refer their disputes to the Court, seeking AOs on significant legal questions, and taking steps to ensure the effective enforcement of the judgments of the Court.

9

Enforcing the Rome Statute and the Geneva Conventions

Fatou Bensouda

Introduction

Throughout the twentieth century, significant developments in the field of international criminal justice culminated in the creation of the permanent International Criminal Court (ICC). A diplomatic conference of state representatives took place in Rome from June 15 to July 17, 1998; on the last day, states adopted the Rome Statute by 120 votes to 7, with 21 states abstaining.

The Rome Statute establishes the ICC's jurisdiction over the crimes of aggression, genocide, war crimes, and crimes against humanity for individual perpetrators (as opposed to states parties). The ICC seeks to ensure accountability for the most heinous acts that are of concern to the entire international community. It upholds individual accountability so that no one is above the law, up to and including heads of state, who are criminally responsible for violations of international humanitarian law. Consequently, it serves as an instrument for reinforcing the four Geneva Conventions and three additional protocols that together form the core of international humanitarian law.

As such, the ICC plays an essential role in combating impunity, preventing and punishing mass atrocities, and seeking justice for victims and accountability for perpetrators around the world. Given the Council's essential role in maintaining international peace and security, the Council benefits under the Rome Statute from considerable powers, including a role in the determination of the crime of aggression, the authority to refer situations to the ICC even if the state concerned is not a party to the Rome Statute, and the power to defer cases.

Lacking its own police forces, the ICC relies on the good faith, compliance, and cooperation of states parties to discharge its duties. This includes

Fatou Bensouda, *Enforcing the Rome Statute and the Geneva Conventions* In: *Empowering the UN Security Council*. Edited by: Mona Ali Khalil and Floriane Lavaud, Oxford University Press. © Oxford University Press 2024.
DOI: 10.1093/oso/9780197780602.003.0010

the provision of evidence (testimonies, seizure of documents or assets, onsite visits, etc.) and the apprehension of the accused individuals. To this end, the ICC also relies on the Security Council's enforcement power to compel compliance with the ICC's indictments, arrest warrants, and judgments.

The Rome Statute provides

> Where a State Party fails to comply with a request to cooperate by the Court contrary to the provisions of this Statute, thereby preventing the Court from exercising its functions and powers under this Statute, the Court may make a finding to that effect and refer the matter to the Assembly of States Parties or, where the Security Council referred the matter to the Court, to the Security Council.[1]

This chapter focuses on the Security Council's role in the enforcement of international criminal law. Justice is essential for achieving sustainable peace and preventing cycles of violence and retribution. Ensuring criminal accountability for violations of the Rome Statute and the Geneva Conventions is not only necessary for purposes of punishing perpetrators, but also serves as a deterrent to prevent genocide and other mass atrocity crimes. Despite the setbacks and challenges, the international community has made great progress advancing international criminal justice. The universal values of human rights and calls for ending impunity increasingly define this new century. This chapter advocates for strong, consistent, and tangible support for the ICC and other transitional justice mechanisms. These goals are not only laudable but necessary for the sake of international peace and security.

Section I discusses the enforcement authority of the UN Security Council and charts the evolution of enforcement powers from states, to the Council itself, to criminal courts. It also discusses the important role that commissions of inquiry play in holding perpetrators of international crimes accountable. Section II focuses on how the Security Council can achieve greater justice and accountability through more consistent referrals to the ICC, more tangible support of the ICC, and more effective enforcement of the Rome Statute and the Geneva Conventions and their additional protocols.

[1] Rome Statute of the International Criminal Court art. 87(7), July 17, 1998, 2187 UNTS 90.

Section I: Enforcement Authority of the UN Security Council

A. The evolution of enforcement: state, Council, and Court

The international community has aspired to establish an international criminal court since the founding of the United Nations, but it took fifty years to achieve that goal. In the 1990s, the Security Council established several ad hoc international criminal tribunals, including the International Criminal Tribunal for the former Yugoslavia (ICTY) and the International Criminal Tribunal for Rwanda (ICTR) to prosecute persons responsible for serious international humanitarian law violations committed in these specific conflicts during specific time frames. These ad hoc tribunals confirm the Security Council's prevailing "consensus that impunity is unacceptable."[2] They upheld the principle of individual accountability, including for heads of state, and paved the way for a permanent criminal court. On July 17, 1998, the international community reached a historic milestone when 120 states adopted the Rome Statute, establishing the International Criminal Court. The Rome Statute entered into force on July 1, 2002.

The four Geneva Conventions and their additional protocols together constitute the foundation of international humanitarian law and set out the crimes falling within the jurisdiction of the ICC.[3] The first and second Geneva Conventions protect wounded and sick soldiers during war on land and at sea, respectively, while the third and fourth Geneva Conventions set forth responsibilities for and protections applicable to prisoners of war and civilians. In response to the proliferation of noninternational armed conflicts following the initial enactment of the four Geneva Conventions, states adopted two additional protocols in 1977. Additional Protocols I and II strengthen protections for victims of international and noninternational armed conflict respectively, and provide limitations on conduct during wars. In 2005, states parties adopted a third additional protocol affirming the "Red Crystal," in addition to the Red Cross and Red Crescent, as an emblem that

[2] International Criminal Court, "The ICC at a Glance," ICC-PIOS-FS-01-007/19_Eng, 1, accessed June 16, 2024, https://www.icc-cpi.int/sites/default/files/Publications/ICCAtAGlanceENG.pdf

[3] See Hortensia D. T. Gutierrez Posse, "The Relationship between International Humanitarian Law and the International Criminal Tribunals," *International Review of the Red Cross* 88, no. 8691 (Mar. 2006).

signifies neutrality, international humanitarian law protection, and the provision of medical relief for military personnel.[4]

The Geneva Conventions and additional protocols frequently position states as their primary enforcer and therefore include provisions on penal sanctions for their violations.[5] Similarly, Additional Protocol I provides for state repression of breaches and grave breaches, while naming additional acts that constitute violations of international humanitarian law.[6] On the other hand, Additional Protocol II does not contain any provision on repression of breaches.[7]

The Security Council has several roles and responsibilities relating to international criminal justice under the UN Charter and the Rome Statute.[8] Pursuant to Article 24 of the UN Charter, the Security Council is entrusted with the primary responsibility for the maintenance of international peace and security.[9] Under Article 34 of Chapter VI of the Charter,[10] the Council has the authority to investigate any conflict or potential threat to international peace and security. In carrying out this responsibility, the Council can establish fact-finding missions or commissions of inquiry. Such missions and commissions can gather evidence and establish facts and circumstances relating to the crimes under the ICC's jurisdiction.

Under Chapter VII, in the event of threat to the peace, breach of the peace, or act of aggression within the meaning of Article 39 of the Charter, the Council may make recommendations, or decide what measures shall be taken in accordance with Articles 41 and 42, to maintain or restore international peace and security. The Council's role in determining the existence of

[4] International Committee of the Red Cross, "Protocol Additional to the Geneva Conventions of 12 August 1949, and Relating to the Adoption of an Additional Distinctive Emblem (Protocol III), 8 December 2005," (2024), accessed June 16, 2024, https://ihl-databases.icrc.org/en/ihl-treaties/apiii-2005. The symbol was adopted as an alternative to the commonly used red crescent, lion, sun, and cross symbols, and devoid of political and racial connotations.

[5] Convention for the Amelioration of the Condition of Wounded and Sick in Armed Forces in the Field arts. 49 and 51, Aug. 12, 1949, 75 UNTS 31; Convention for the Amelioration of the Condition of the Wounded, Sick, and Shipwrecked Members of Armed Forces at Sea arts. 50 and 51, Aug. 12, 1949, 75 UNTS 85; Geneva Convention Relative to the Treatment of Prisoners of War arts. 129 and 130, Aug. 12, 1949, 75 UNTS 135; Geneva Convention Relative to the Protection of Civilian Persons in Time of War arts. 146 and 147, Aug. 12, 1949, 75 UNTS 287.

[6] Protocol Additional to the Geneva Conventions of 12 August 1949, and Relating to the Protection of Victims of International Armed Conflicts (Protocol I) art. 85, June 8, 1977, 1125 UNTS 3.

[7] See Hans-Peter Gasser, "The Changing Relationship between International Criminal Law, Human Rights Law and Humanitarian Law," in *The Legal Regime of the International Criminal Court*, eds. Jose Doria et al. (Boston: Martinus Nijhoff, 2009), 1115.

[8] Rome Statute art. 1. See also Rome Statute art. 5.

[9] UN Charter art. 24.

[10] Chapter VI requires states to peacefully settle their disputes.

an act of aggression is set out in Article 39 of the UN Charter, as well as in Article 15bis and 15ter of the Rome Statute. The Security Council may make referrals to the ICC pursuant to Article 13(b) of the Rome Statute. It can also impose enforcement measures to ensure compliance with the indictments, arrest warrants, and judgments of the Court. Such enforcement measures can include sanctions against the individual concerned under Article 41 of the Charter (such as a travel ban and freezing the individual's assets) and measures against any state failing to comply with the requests, orders, or judgments of the Court under Article 41 (measures not involving the use of force) or under Article 42 (measures involving the use of force).

In recent times, the Council has repeatedly failed to come to a consensus regarding the use of its Chapter VII powers in situations where both the spirit and letter of the UN Charter and the Rome Statute warranted intervention—in particular, where perpetrators committed crimes on the territories of states not party to the Rome Statute.[11] The Council must have the necessary political will to uphold the rule of law and ensure criminal accountability, especially for acts of aggression, genocide, war crimes, and crimes against humanity—all crimes within the jurisdiction of the ICC. The Council's political will, or lack thereof, can have a significant effect in ensuring peace, justice, security, and accountability.

A powerful Council that leverages its political will to maintain international peace and security will inevitably encounter the paralysis that accompanies an inherently political organ. A successful international legal framework will create space for the Council to flex its political powers, while providing for alternative mechanisms when political stalemates prevent the Council from preventing or responding to mass atrocities. This chapter expands on two tools that the international community may exploit in pursuit of a more effective UN framework: first, more frequent use of commissions of inquiry; second, stronger engagement with the ICC.

B. Establishment of commissions of inquiry

Before the entry into force of the Rome Statute, the Security Council had established certain commissions of inquiry to carry out tasks designed to maintain international peace and security, including to investigate gross violations

[11] See Rome Statute preamble.

of international humanitarian law and human rights. Notably, commissions of inquiry were set up in the context of the conflicts in Rwanda[12] and the former Yugoslavia.[13] In the context of the former Yugoslavia, thc final report of the commission was instrumental in establishing the ICTY.[14]

The Council's critical role in initiating investigations was also evident following the 1993 military coup and ensuing massacres in Burundi, during which political extremists assassinated then-President Melchior Ndadaye. In 1995, the Council passed Resolution 1012 "request[ing] the Secretary-General to establish, as a matter of urgency, an international commission of inquiry," while noting that "impunity creates contempt for law and leads to violations of international humanitarian law."[15] The commission submitted its final report to the UN Secretary-General in 2002, concluding after interviews with 667 witnesses that acts of genocide took place in Burundi against the Tutsi minority following the assassination of the president, and that indiscriminate killings of Hutus were carried out by various groups.[16] Although the Council and government of Burundi engaged in long negotiations to establish a truth commission and hybrid court to "prosecute those bearing the greatest responsibility for genocide, crimes against humanity, and war crimes," neither project came to fruition.[17]

In 2004, the Council likewise set up a commission of inquiry in Sudan.[18] Specifically, the Security Council requested the establishment of a commission of inquiry to investigate reports of violations of international humanitarian law and human rights law committed in Darfur by all parties to the armed conflict.[19] The commission was also tasked with determining whether acts of genocide had occurred in Darfur.[20] Following the transmission of the report of the commission to the Security Council in 2005,[21] the situation in Darfur was referred to the prosecutor of the ICC.[22]

[12] UN Security Council, Resolution 935, S/RES/935 (July 1, 1994).
[13] UN Security Council, Resolution 780, S/RES/780 (Oct. 6, 1992).
[14] Ibid.
[15] UN Security Council, Resolution 1012, S/RES/1012, 1, para. 1 (Aug. 28, 1995).
[16] United States Institute of Peace, "Commission of Inquiry: Burundi," (Sept. 1, 1995), accessed June 16, 2024, https://www.usip.org/publications/1995/09/commission-inquiry-burundi.
[17] Ibid.
[18] UN Security Council, Resolution 1564, S/RES/1564 (Sep. 18, 2004).
[19] See Rep. of the Int'l Commission of Inquiry on Darfur to the Secretary-General (2005), transmitted by Letter dated 31 January 2005 from the Secretary-General Addressed to the President of the Security Council, S/2005/60 (Feb. 1, 2005). See also United Nations, *Repertoire of the Practice of the Security Council: Supplement 2004-2007*, (September 2014) accessed June 16, 2024 , https://www.un-ilibrary.org/content/books/9789210563062.
[20] S/RES/1564, para. 12.
[21] S/2005/60.
[22] UN Security Council, Resolution 1593, S/RES/1593 (Mar. 31, 2005).

In 2013, the Council established a commission of inquiry on the Central African Republic (CAR). Resolution 2127 was responsive to the "continuing deterioration of the security situation in CAR, characterized by a total breakdown in law and order" brought about by conflict between two military insurgent groups (the Seleka and anti-Balaka forces) that wreaked havoc upon the small central-African state.[23] The Council requested that the Secretary-General "rapidly establish an international commission of inquiry," ensuring the inclusion of experts in both international humanitarian law and human rights law.[24]

The primary objective of the commission was to promptly investigate reports of violations of international humanitarian law, international human rights law, and human rights abuses in the CAR by all parties to the conflict since January 1, 2013. Under its mandate, the commission is tasked with gathering pertinent information, aiding in the identification of perpetrators of such violations and abuses, indicating their potential criminal liability, and facilitating the accountability of those responsible. The resolution called upon all parties involved to fully cooperate with the commission. Emphasizing the imperative of accountability, the resolution noted that certain actions may constitute crimes under the Rome Statute of the International Criminal Court.

More recently, in 2017, the Council set up an investigative team to promote accountability for crimes committed by Da'esh/ISIL.[25] The Council requested the Secretary-General to establish an investigative team to support domestic efforts in Iraq to hold Da'esh/ISIL accountable by collecting, preserving and storing evidence in Iraq of acts that may amount to war crimes, crimes against humanity, and genocide committed by the terrorist group in Iraq.[26]

Despite the powers of the Security Council to contribute to the enforcement of the Rome Statute and the Geneva Conventions, the use of the veto power by the permanent members has impeded the international community's efforts to ensure accountability and end impunity. For instance, following the armed conflict in Syria, the UN Human Rights Council established the commission of inquiry on the Syrian Arab Republic.[27] In

[23] UN Security Council, Resolution 2127, S/RES/2127, para. 1 (Dec. 5, 2013).
[24] Ibid., para. 24.
[25] UN Security Council, Resolution 2379, S/RES/2379 (Sep. 21, 2017).
[26] Ibid., paras. 2–3, 11.
[27] UN Human Rights Council, Resolution 17/1, A/HRC/S-17/1 (Aug. 22, 2011).

its report, the commission recommended the Council take appropriate action by referring the situation to the prosecutor of the ICC. Efforts to refer the situation to the ICC failed due to a double veto at the Security Council from Russia and China.[28] This was the fourth time that the states had jointly vetoed resolutions on Syria since the beginning of the Syrian crisis in 2011.[29]

Section II: Security Council Engagement with the International Criminal Court

The entry into force of the Rome Statute marked a new phase in the global fight against impunity for the commission of atrocity crimes.

Today, the cardinal issue remains enforcement of the Rome Statute and the Geneva Conventions. There are currently about 110 ongoing armed conflicts[30] in the world involving mass atrocity crimes on the territories of both states parties and non–states parties to the Rome Statute. At the time of writing, there are 123 states parties to the Rome Statute: 33 African states, 19 Asia-Pacific states, 18 Eastern European states, 28 Latin American and Caribbean states, and 25 Western European and other states.[31]

Part 2 of the Rome Statute sets forth the Court's three jurisdictional trigger mechanisms:[32] first, referrals by states parties;[33] second, referrals by the Security Council;[34] and third, the Prosecutor's *proprio motu* initiation of an investigation.[35] Furthermore, states not party to the Rome Statute could unilaterally accede to the jurisdiction of the Court by way of declaration.[36] For the purposes of this chapter, we will focus on the powers of the Security Council through the Statute. During the drafting of the Rome Statute, one of the key issues relating to the jurisdiction of the ICC was the nature of the

[28] Human Rights Watch, "UN Security Council: Vetoes Betray Syrian Victims," May 22, 2014, accessed June 16, 2024, https://www.hrw.org/news/2014/05/22/un-security-council-vetoes-betray-syrian-victims.

[29] Ibid.

[30] Geneva Academy of International Humanitarian Law and Human Rights, "RULAC: Rule of Law in Armed Conflict," accessed June 16, 2024, https://www.rulac.org/.

[31] International Criminal Court, "The States Parties to the Rome Statute," accessed June 16, 2024, https://asp.icc-cpi.int/states-parties.

[32] Rome Statute art. 17.

[33] Ibid..

[34] Ibid., art. 13(b).

[35] Ibid., art. 15.

[36] Ibid., art. 12(3).

ICC's relationship with the Security Council.[37] As mentioned above, the Rome Statute grants the Council the power of referrals.[38] Article 13(b) of the Statute permits the Council to refer a situation to the prosecutor where international crimes "appear to have been committed."[39] The Statute also accords the Council the power of deferral; Article 16 allows the Council to suspend ICC investigations or prosecutions for twelve months with a resolution adopted under Chapter VII. The Council may renew the request through the same procedure. The Rome Statute also grants the Council powers to enforce state cooperation with the ICC.[40]

The Negotiated Relationship Agreement between the ICC and the United Nations regulates the relationship between the ICC and the Council. For instance, Article 17(1) of the relationship agreement provides:

> When the Security Council, acting under Chapter VII of the Charter of the United Nations, decides to refer to the Prosecutor pursuant to article 13, paragraph (b), of the Statute, a situation in which one or more of the crimes referred to in article 5 of the Statute appears to have been committed, the Secretary-General shall immediately transmit the written decision of the Security Council to the Prosecutor together with documents and other materials that may be pertinent to the decision of the Council. The Court undertakes to keep the Security Council informed in this regard in accordance with the Statute and Rules of Procedure and Evidence. Such information shall be transmitted through the Secretary-General.[41]

Procedurally, when following a Council referral, the Court must apply its normative statutory framework during investigations and prosecutions.[42] This provision also requires the Court to keep the Security Council informed about the status of proceedings by the Office of the Prosecutor (OTP). Since the entry into force of the Rome Statute, the Council has referred two

[37] John-Mark Iyi, "Re-thinking the Authority of the UN Security Council to Refer Nationals of Non-party States to the ICC," *Netherlands International Law Review* 66, no. 391 (2019): 395–97.
[38] Rome Statute art. 16.
[39] Ibid., art. 13(b).
[40] Ibid., art. 87(5)(b).
[41] Negotiated Relationship Agreement between the International Criminal Court and the United Nations art. 17(1), Oct. 4, 2004, ICC-ASP/3/Res.1.
[42] Alexandre Skander Galand, "Security Council Referrals to the International Criminal Court as Quasi-Legislative Acts," *Max Planck Yearbook of United Nations Law* 19 (2015): 150.

situations to the ICC: Libya and Darfur.[43] The Libya and Sudan referrals are notable as neither state is a party to the Rome Statute.

A. Referrals of the situations in Darfur and Libya

Commissions of inquiry help establish that crimes within the ICC's jurisdiction have been committed. Indeed, the 2004 report of the International Commission of Inquiry on Darfur played a key role in the Security Council's referral of the situation to the ICC.[44] The Council commissioned the report in the context of the mass atrocities in Darfur, a major internal armed conflict that began in 2003 between rebel groups and the government of Sudan, which was rooted in allegations of the Sudanese government's oppression of Darfur's non-Arab population. According to the report, violations of international humanitarian law that could amount to war crimes—including rape and other forms of sexual and gender-based violence, indiscriminate attacks against civilians and civilian property, killings of civilians, torture, and enforced disappearances—had been committed in Darfur.[45] Based on the Commission's report, the Security Council, acting under Chapter VII of the UN Charter, adopted Resolution 1593 referring the situation in Darfur to the ICC.[46]

The ICC's investigation opened in June 2005 and led to cases against state and nonstate actors, including government officials, Janjaweed leaders, and leaders of the Resistance Front.[47] The ICC has issued seven arrest warrants with four suspects at large.[48] Two of the seven warrants named former president of Sudan, Omar Al Bashir, as a perpetrator.

[43] UN Security Council, Resolution 1970, S/RES/1970 (Feb. 26, 2011); S/RES/1593.
[44] See S/2005/60.
[45] Ibid.
[46] S/RES/1593 (China and the United States abstaining).
[47] International Criminal Court, "Situation in Darfur, Sudan," accessed June 16, 2024, https://www.icc-cpi.int/darfur.
[48] Warrants of arrests have been issued against Ahmad Muhammad Huran (suspect at large), "Warrant of Arrest for Ahmad Harun," International Criminal Court, accessed June 16, 2024, https://www.icc-cpi.int/court-record/icc-02/05-01/07-2; Omar Hassan Ahmad Al Bashir (suspect at large), "Warrant of Arrest for Omar Hassan Ahmad Al Bashir," International Criminal Court, accessed June 16, 2024, https://www.icc-cpi.int/court-record/icc-02/05-01/09-1; Abdallah Banda Abakaer Nourain (case closed), "Warrant of arrest for Abdallah Banda Abakaer Nourain," International Criminal Court, accessed June 16, 2024, https://www.icc-cpi.int/court-record/icc-02/05-03/09-606; Bahar Idriss Abu Garda (Case closed), "Abu Garda Case," International Criminal Court, accessed June 16, 2024, https://www.icc-cpi.int/darfur/abugarda; Abdel Raheem Muhammad Hussein (suspect at large), "Warrant of Arrest for Abdel Raheem Muhammad Hussein," International Criminal Court, accessed June 16, 2024, https://www.icc-cpi.int/court-record/icc-02/05-01/12-2; and Ali Muhammad Ali Abd-Al-Rahman (suspect in custody), "Case Information Sheet Ali Muhammad

In the ICC prosecutor's recent report to the UN Security Council on the situation in Darfur, he informed the Council of the ICC's investigative efforts with respect to crimes committed as part of the current hostilities between the Sudanese Armed Forces (SAF) and the Rapid Support Forces (RSF), which began in 2023.[49] The prosecutor also informed the Council of the status of arrest warrants issued against Omar Al Bashir and other alleged perpetrators.[50] Amidst some positives, the OTP's report identifies noncooperation between the government of Sudan and the OTP as a major challenge to the fulfillment of the Court's request for assistance, including a lack of access to documentary evidence.[51]

In 2011, following the uprising in Libya and events that unfolded thereafter, the Security Council passed Resolution 1970,[52] referring the situation to the ICC. To date, five arrest warrants have been issued in the Libya investigation.[53] The ICC's investigation has broadened to include events beyond those associated with the 2011 Libyan uprising, including the subsequent Libyan civil war (2014–2020) and associated international crimes. Currently, the OTP is engaged in four key lines of inquiry: 2011 violence; crimes in detention facilities; crimes related to the 2014–2020 operations; and crimes against migrants.[54] The OTP has faced two major challenges in the Libyan investigation, namely the lack of adequate cooperation of the Libyan authorities and budgetary limitations.

Ali Abd-Al-Rahman," International Criminal Court, accessed June 16, 2024, https://www.icc-cpi.int/sites/default/files/CaseInformationSheets/abd-al-rahmaneng.pdf (collecting multiple arrest warrants).

[49] Office of the Prosecutor, International Criminal Court, *Thirty-Eighth Report of the Prosecutor of the International Criminal Court to the United Nations Security Council Pursuant to Resolution 1593 (2005)* (January 2024), accessed June16, 2024, https://www.icc-cpi.int/sites/default/files/2024-01/OTP-38th%20Report-Darfur-ENG.pdf.

[50] Ibid., paras. 21, 22, 25.

[51] Ibid., paras. 40–46.

[52] S/RES/1970.

[53] Warrants of arrest were issued for Saif Al-Islam Gaddafi (pretrial stage), "Warrant of Arrest for Saif Al-Islam Gaddafi," International Criminal Court, accessed June 16, 2024, https://www.icc-cpi.int/court-record/icc-01/11-01/11-3-0; Al-Tuhamy Mohamed Khaled (case closed), "Warrant of Arrest for Al-Tuhamy Mohamed Khaled," International Criminal Court, accessed June 16, 2024, https://www.icc-cpi.int/court-record/icc-01/11-01/13-1; and Mahmoud Mustafa (case closed), "Warrant of Arrest for Mahmoud Mustafa Busayf Al-Werfalli," International Criminal Court, accessed June 16, 2024, https://www.icc-cpi.int/court-record/icc-01/11-01/17-2.

[54] Office of the Prosecutor, International Criminal Court, *Twenty-Sixth Report of the Prosecutor of the International Criminal Court to the United Nations Security Council Pursuant to Resolution 1970 (2011)* (November 2023), paras. 31–55, accessed June 16, 2024, https://www.icc-cpi.int/sites/default/files/2023-11/2023-11-08-report-prosecutor-unsc-libya-eng.pdf.

B. Enforcing cooperation for Security Council referrals under Article 13(b)

Under international law, when a legal obligation is viewed from the lens of a treaty-based, normative system, states are bound by the texts of a treaty to the extent that they have expressed their consent to be bound.[55] This also applies to states parties to the Rome Statute, with one important exception. For states not party to the Rome Statute, when the Council refers a situation to the ICC, the states concerned have an obligation to comply not under the Rome Statute, but under Article 25 of the UN Charter pursuant to which "Members of the United Nations agree to accept and carry out the decisions of the Security Council," especially those adopted under Chapter VII of the Charter.[56]

States' national mechanisms are instrumental in facilitating cooperation of the tribunals. However, the Security Council's formulation of current referral notifications urging state cooperation with the ICC occasionally contains language that states may interpret as nonbinding or not sending a strong signal of support to the Court. For instance, Resolution 1593, "while recognizing that States not party to the Rome Statute have no obligation under the Statute, urges all States and concerned regional and other international organizations to cooperate fully."[57] While the language of referral requires Sudan to cooperate with the Court, cooperation may be more effective if the referral resolution contained more potent language—including language indicating the Council's readiness to consider enforcement measures in an event of noncooperation. Amending existing referral resolutions with a strong emphasis on pragmatic cooperation steps could achieve this outcome. The benefits for the Court would be immense in its pursuit to end impunity and ensure accountability.

C. Enforcement through financing and victim-centered approach

A combined reading of the operative texts of Resolution 1593 and Resolution 1970 reveals that the Security Council put the burden of financing

55 Vienna Convention on the Law of Treaties art. 34, May 23, 1969, 1155 UNTS 331.
56 See S/RES/1593, para. 2; S/RES/1970, para. 5.
57 S/RES/1593, para. 2.

investigations on the Court and on states willing to provide voluntary contributions.[58] The crimes captured under Article 5 of the Rome Statute deeply shock the conscience of humanity. To the extent that the General Assembly holds the purse strings in the United Nations, its support for the financing of the Court's work on cases referred by the Security Council will contribute to its own efforts to ensure accountability for serious violations of international humanitarian law. This is evidenced, for example, by its establishment of the International, Impartial, and Independent Mechanism to Assist in the Investigation and Prosecution of Persons Responsible for the Most Serious Crimes under International Law Committed in the Syrian Arab Republic.[59] Successive ICC prosecutors have thus far unsuccessfully advocated for the Assembly's provision of financial support for Council referrals to the ICC.

Relatedly, the Rome Statute incorporates a restorative justice dimension by embracing a victim-centered approach. Article 68(3) of the Rome Statute underscores this commitment, affirming survivors' rights to present their perspectives and concerns directly to ICC judges during judicial proceedings. This participatory right extends throughout the entirety of legal proceedings, including appeals. Furthermore, survivors retain the opportunity to seek reparations in cases where an accused is convicted. Ratification of the Rome Statute implies a commitment on behalf of the state to enforce the Statute's obligations on the national level. As formulated by the UN Secretary-General, the Rome Statute serves "as a catalyst for enacting national laws against the gravest international crimes."[60]

Consistent with this victim-centered approach, the legal framework of the ICC provides for the establishment of the Trust Fund for Victims and gives details about the two mandates of the trust fund.[61] The Assembly of States Parties has also passed several resolutions relating to the Trust Fund for Victims.[62] For instance, in the Libyan context, the referral resolution contained aspects which froze assets of Libyan nationals—some of whom have been indicted by the ICC. Currently missing in the existing referrals regime is the willingness of the Security Council, acting under its Chapter VII

[58] See S/RES/1593, para. 7; S/RES/1970, para. 8.
[59] UN General Assembly, Resolution 71/148, A/RES/71/248 (Dec. 21, 2016).
[60] Ibid., para. 49.
[61] See Rome Statute art. 79; Rules of Procedure and Evidence of the ICC, r. 98.
[62] See ICC Assembly of States Parties, Resolution ICC-ASP/1/Res.6, (Sept. 9, 2002). See also ICC Assembly of States Parties, Resolution ICC-ASP/3/Res. 7 (Sept. 10, 2004); ICC Assembly of States Parties, Resolution ICC-ASP/4/Res.3 (Dec. 3, 2005).

powers, to manage the assets of these individuals in a manner consistent with the existing framework of the Rome Statute. There are compelling arguments in favor of unfreezing the assets of individuals convicted by the ICC to provide compensation or reparation to their victims.

By embracing these proposals, the Security Council, through its referral and enforcement authority, and the General Assembly, through its financial authority, can reinforce the jurisdiction of the ICC and ensure accountability for violations of the most serious violations of international humanitarian law. In so doing, they can ensure individual accountability for the perpetrators and justice for the victims, laying the foundations for peaceful resolutions of conflict that are more just and more sustainable.

Conclusion

The conventional emphasis on retributive justice has evolved, giving way to a contemporary paradigm where restorative justice holds greater resonance in fostering peace-building and reconciliation usually embedded in transitional justice processes.

In his report before the UN Security Council on the rule of law and transitional justice in conflict and post-conflict societies, former Secretary-General Kofi Annan explained that the notion of transitional justice "comprises the full range of processes and mechanisms associated with a society's attempts to come to terms with a legacy of large-scale past abuses, in order to ensure accountability, serve justice, and achieve reconciliation."[63] In this sense, transitional justice seeks, through a holistic approach, the easing of tensions in the form of a healing process of national catharsis with the aim of reconciliation through truth-seeking, nonrepetition, accountability, and reparation to the victims and affected communities.

The ICC does not supersede national courts. Its jurisdiction is governed by the principle of complementarity. This principle dictates that states hold the primary responsibility and right to prosecute the most serious crimes of international concern. The ICC only intervenes when national legal systems are deemed unwilling or genuinely unable to conduct investigations and prosecutions. Indeed, Security Council Resolution 2090 emphasizes that the ICC is only "*complementary* to the national criminal jurisdictions."[64]

[63] UN Security Council, Resolution 616, S/2004/616, para. 8 (Aug. 23, 2004).
[64] UN Security Council, Resolution 2090, S/RES/290 (Feb. 13, 2013) (emphasis added).

The Security Council should reinforce the ICC. It can adopt a multipronged approach seeking the peaceful settlement of disputes, with concurrent judicial and nonjudicial actions each playing an important role. Consider, for example, the situation in Darfur. In Resolution 1593, the Council—even while referring the situation to the ICC—emphasized the imperative of fostering "healing and reconciliation" and endorsed the establishment of "institutions . . . such as truth and/or reconciliation commissions . . . to complement judicial proceedings."[65] The Security Council thus seems to promote the coexistence of both judicial and nonjudicial processes, especially in a post-conflict setting where the return to peace and the establishment of the rule of law and democracy requires strong commitment to justice and reconciliation.

The commissions of inquiry for the former Yugoslavia and Darfur illustrate the Security Council's efforts to end impunity under Chapter VI of the UN Charter; they were also precursors to the Security Council's establishment of the ICTY and ICTR. The Libya and Sudan referrals to the ICC are important instances of the Security Council using its Chapter VII powers to ensure criminal accountability for mass atrocity crimes in furtherance of international peace and security. The Security Council should exercise its powers under the Charter to reinforce the ICC and to enforce the Rome Statute and the Geneva Conventions and their additional protocols in territories of state and nonstate parties. The Council has not come close to exercising the full extent of its authority in this regard. One thing is clear: while the referrals of the situations in Libya and Sudan are laudable, more can be done to ensure effective enforcement and consistent accountability. Security Council referrals are also a means to another end—creating a clear and consistent pathway for a just and sustainable peace.

[65] S/RES/1593, para. 5.

10

Strengthening Regional Cooperation

Boštjan Malovrh[*]

Introduction

The sheer magnitude of global challenges our world faces today requires a review of the international peace and security architecture. In particular, regional arrangements—as envisioned under Chapter VIII of the UN Charter—have been instrumental in the past and can carry enormous potential for the future.

The UN Charter foresees the need for regional arrangements by design (in instances where the Security Council calls upon regional arrangements to act) and by default (when regional arrangements are in a position to act more promptly than the Council). Great Power politics affect and even determine whether a particular crisis will appear on the Council's agenda. Moreover, the Council's shifting focus on *selective* versus *collective* security interests and its frequent deafening silence or paralysis in the face of serious threats present additional challenges to the maintenance of international peace and security. Resort to regional arrangements is therefore now more important than ever and constitutes an underused yet potentially powerful mechanism to share the burden of peacekeeping and peace enforcement.

Despite the urgent need for regional arrangements to contribute to the maintenance of international peace and security, and the fact that there are significant differences between individual regional arrangements, with some notable exceptions, they generally face significant structural, political, and financial challenges that limit their effectiveness. The Council has been inconsistent in its cooperation with the regional arrangements, and the arrangements themselves, like other intergovernmental organizations, often

[*] The views expressed in this chapter are exclusively the author's views in his personal capacity and do not reflect any opinion of or attribution to the Republic of Slovenia's Ministry of Foreign and European Affairs.

Boštjan Malovrh, *Strengthening Regional Cooperation* In: *Empowering the UN Security Council*. Edited by: Mona Ali Khalil and Floriane Lavaud, Oxford University Press. © Oxford University Press 2024.
DOI: 10.1093/oso/9780197780602.003.0011

suffer from their own internal issues. Moreover, the Council does not treat regional arrangements with the attention they deserve, nor does it provide the level of support sufficient for their success—even when that success is clearly in the interest of collective security.

This chapter charts the rise of regional arrangements and provides practical proposals to improve their effectiveness in maintaining international peace and security. Section I discusses the evolution of Chapter VIII of the UN Charter, which provides for the structure and scope of regional arrangements, and explores present-day challenges to regional cooperation. Section II sets forth proposals for a more effective use of the regional arrangements, as Chapter VIII envisions. The chapter concludes with some forward-looking thoughts on broader cooperation with regional arrangements in furtherance of international peace and security.

Section I: The Rise and Evolution of Chapter VIII

Articles 52 through 54 of the UN Charter are the main provisions governing regional arrangements and their relationship with the UN Security Council.

Article 52 states that the Security Council shall "encourage the development of pacific settlement of local disputes" through regional arrangements or by regional agencies.[1] In order for the activities of a regional arrangement to fall within the scope of Chapter VIII, the activities must "relat[e] to the maintenance of international peace and security," and both the arrangement and its activities must be "consistent with the Purposes of and Principles of the United Nations."[2]

Article 53, in turn, provides that "the Security Council shall, where appropriate, utilize such regional arrangements or agencies for enforcement action under its authority. But no enforcement action shall be taken under regional arrangements or by regional agencies without the authorization of the Security Council."

Finally, Article 54 provides that regional arrangements shall keep the Security Council fully informed, at all times, of the activities they have undertaken or are contemplating for the maintenance of international peace

[1] For a detailed discussion, see Christian Walter, "Chapter VIII Regional Arrangements, Article 52" in *The Charter of the United Nations: A Commentary*, eds. Bruno Simma et al. (Oxford: Oxford University Press, 2012).

[2] UN Charter art. 52(1).

and security. In practice, this provision has provided room for early action by regional arrangements.

A. Scope of regional arrangements envisioned within Chapter VIII

Regional arrangements that fall within the scope of Chapter VIII today include the Organization of American States (OAS), the African Union (AU), and the League of Arab States (LAS). In practice, the North Atlantic Treaty Organization (NATO) and the Organization on Security and Co-operation in Europe (OSCE) have also functioned as Chapter VIII regional arrangements. Article 52 makes clear that the use of regional arrangements does not impede the rights of the Council and General Assembly under Articles 34[3] and 35.[4] Primary responsibility for peace and security stays with the Council, in accordance with Articles 24 and 53.

Article 53 mandates Council authorization for any enforcement measures undertaken by regional arrangements,[5] but the definition of "enforcement action" remains an open question. While the question used to revolve around the mandatory or nonmandatory nature of a given regional measure,[6] the debate now largely focuses on whether enforcement actions can include nonmilitary measures as well as military force.[7]

If a state invites a regional peacekeeping force within its borders, the Security Council need not authorize the operation. However, "in civil war situations in which no reliable peace agreement has been concluded and in

[3] In particular, the reservation of the Council's right to investigate under Article 34 makes clear that the Council may investigate even if a regional arrangement is already seized of a dispute, or a "situation which might lead to international friction or give rise to a dispute." UN Charter art. 34.

[4] Article 35 permits any member state to "bring any dispute, or any situation of the nature referred to in Article 34, to the attention of the Security Council or of the General Assembly": even if a regional arrangement is already involved in a particular situation or dispute, a member state may still choose to turn to the United Nations. UN Charter art. 35.

[5] UN Charter art. 53(1). There is, however, a historical exception for measures against aggressive policies by "any state which during the Second World War has been an enemy of any signatory of the present Charter." UN Charter art. 53(2).

[6] The argument that an action must be mandatory in order to qualify as an enforcement action largely stems from the ICJ's advisory opinion in the *Certain Expenses* case. Certain Expenses of the United Nations (Article 17, Paragraph 2, of the Charter), Advisory Opinion, 1962 ICJ 151, 165 (July 20) (holding that the measures taken did not constitute an enforcement action due to the fact that they were merely "recommendatory").

[7] For a further discussion of this debate, see Christian Walter, "Chapter VIII Regional Arrangements, Article 53" in *The Charter of the United Nations: A Commentary*, eds. Bruno Simma et al. (Oxford: Oxford University Press, 2012).

which military force is used on the basis of governmental consent the legitimacy of which is doubtful, [Security Council] authorization is necessary."[8] The Council has not been consistent: sometimes it authorizes regional action before the fact,[9] other times after.[10]

B. Historical evolution of Chapter VIII

Chapter VIII represents an international compromise of states' visions on the desired structure of the international legal system. During drafting, the architects of the Charter found themselves at a crossroads between the dueling concepts of universalism and regionalism. While universalists advocated for a strong, centralized international system, regionalists preferred the creation of a system that would allow for the settlement of local disputes by regional organizations. In drafting the Charter, states representing both schools of thought reached a compromise that allowed for the regional settlement of disputes while maintaining the primacy of the Security Council and the United Nations.[11]

In the years following the establishment of the United Nations, political blocks in the Security Council meant that the Council rarely resorted to Chapter VIII. As former UN Secretary-General Boutros Boutros-Ghali observed, the "cold war impaired the proper use of Chapter VIII."[12] On a number of occasions, members of the permanent five (P5) blocked attempts to engage with Chapter VIII in the Security Council.

In the post–Cold War era, the Security Council gradually began to cooperate with regional arrangements. Since the early 1990s, the Council has utilized regional arrangements in the former Yugoslavia,[13] Somalia,[14]

[8] Ibid., para. 30.

[9] See, e.g., UN Security Council, Resolution 2628, S/RES/2628 (Mar. 31, 2022) (authorizing member states of the African Union to support peace and reconciliation efforts in Somalia for an initial period of twelve months in light of the threat posed by the Al-Shabaab terrorist group).

[10] See, e.g., UN Security Council, Resolution 2123, S/RES/2123 (Nov. 12, 2013) (authorizing multinational stabilization force to respond to conflict in Bosnia and Herzegovina).

[11] The compromise resulted in the inclusion of the inherent right of collective self-defense in Article 50 of the Charter. UNCIO 12 (1945), 849.

[12] UN Secretary-General, *An Agenda for Peace: Preventative Diplomacy, Peacemaking and Peace-Keeping*, para. 60, A/47/277-S/24111 (June 17, 1992).

[13] UN Security Council, Resolutions 1160, S/RES/1160 (Mar. 31, 2008); 1203, S/RES/1203 (Oct. 24, 1998).

[14] UN Security Council, Resolution 1744, S/RES/1744 (Feb. 21, 2007).

Burundi,[15] Liberia,[16] and Haiti[17] (among others). During this time, a practice of annual consultative meetings emerged. In 2003, former Secretary-General Kofi Annan noted that the United Nations needed to "move toward creating a network of effective and mutually reinforcing mechanisms—regional and global—that are flexible and responsive."[18]

As the Security Council became overburdened, the benefits of turning to and working with regional arrangements became increasingly apparent. The Security Council's July 2004 presidential statement recognized this overburdening, noting that "effectively addressing the numerous conflict situations confronting the international community . . . require[s] an increased level of cooperation with regional organizations, where appropriate."[19]

Today more than ever, there is a crucial need for deeper cooperation between the Security Council and regional arrangements under Chapter VIII of the Charter. In 2023, Secretary-General António Guterres published "A New Agenda for Peace," calling for strong partnerships between the United Nations and regional frameworks as part of "networked multilateralism."[20] And since 2000, the Security Council has increasingly recognized and relied upon regional arrangements to prevent the escalation of and to respond to numerous threats to peace and security facing our world today.

According to the "Repertoire of the Practice of the Security Council,"[21] since 2000 the Council has increasingly encouraged efforts undertaken by regional and subregional arrangements in the pacific settlement of disputes. For example, the Council supported the efforts of the Economic Community of West African States (ECOWAS) to promote a peaceful settlement of the conflict in Côte d'Ivoire and welcomed the commitment of the African Union in supporting the process of national reconciliation in

[15] UN Security Council, Resolution 1545, S/RES/1545 (May 21, 2004).

[16] UN Security Council, Resolution 1497, S/RES/1497 (Aug. 1, 2003).

[17] UN Security Council, Resolutions 1529, S/RES/1529 (Feb. 29, 2004); 1780, S/RES/1780 (Oct. 15, 2007).

[18] UN SCOR, 4739th mtg. at 4, S/PV/4739 (Apr. 11, 2003).

[19] SC Pres. Statement 2004/27, 1 (July 20, 2004).

[20] UN Secretary-General, "Our Common Agenda Policy Brief 9: A New Agenda for Peace," 12 (July 2023), accessed June 16, 2024, https://www.un.org/sites/un2.un.org/files/our-common-agenda-policy-brief-new-agenda-for-peace-en.pdf.

[21] UN Security Council, "Repertoire of the Practice of the Security Council, Regional Arrangements (Chapter VIII of UN Charter)," accessed June 16, 2024, https://www.un.org/securitycouncil/content/regional-arrangements-chapter-viii-un-charter#:~:text=Chapter%20VIII%20of%20the%20Charter,Security%20Council%20is%20primarily%20responsible.

that country.[22] With respect to the situation in Somalia, the Council repeatedly welcomed and commended the efforts of the African Union, the League of Arab States, the European Union, and others for their persistent efforts in support of the peace process in Somalia.[23] Regarding Haiti, the Council emphasized the role of regional organizations in the ongoing process of the state's stabilization and reconstruction, and called upon the UN Stabilization Mission in Haiti (MINUSTAH) to continue to work closely with OAS and the Caribbean Community (CARICOM) in the implementation of its mandate.[24] The Council also commended and expressed strong support for the efforts of the OSCE in the pacific settlement of the dispute in Georgia.[25]

The Security Council has increasingly authorized regional arrangements to deploy peacekeeping operations, most of which were also authorized to take all necessary actions up to and including the use of force under Chapter VII of the UN Charter. For example, the UN Operation in Burundi (ONUB) was initially composed of existing forces of the African Mission in Burundi (AMIB), which were rehatted as ONUB troops. With regard to the situation in Georgia, the Commonwealth of Independent States (CIS) operated side-by-side with the UN Observer Mission in Georgia (UNOMIG). The cooperation with regional arrangements in peacekeeping culminated in the deployment of the United Nations–African Union Hybrid Operation in Darfur (UNAMID).[26]

The Security Council has also authorized the engagement of regional arrangements with enforcement actions beyond the context of regional peacekeeping operations. In 2007, the Council authorized the European Union Force (EUFOR) "to take all measures necessary to effect the implementation of" its mandate as a multinational stabilization force for Bosnia and Herzegovina.[27] (EUFOR was the legal successor to the multinational stabilization force led by NATO.) The Council also authorized the use of

[22] UN Security Council, Resolutions 1527, S/RES/1527 (Feb. 4, 2004); 1528, S/RES/1528 (Feb. 27, 2004).

[23] See, e.g., UN Security Council, Resolution 2628, S/RES/2628 (Mar. 31, 2022) (endorsing a decision of the AU Mission in Somalia); UN Security Council, Resolution 2554, S/RES/2554 (Dec. 4, 2020) (welcoming and commending the efforts of numerous regional arrangements for their efforts in Somalia).

[24] UN Security Council, Resolution 1542, S/RES/1542, paras. 5–6 (Apr. 30, 2004).

[25] UN Security Council, Resolution 1554, S/RES/1554, para. 2 (July 29, 2004).

[26] United Nations Security Council, "Repertoire of the Practice of the Security Council, Regional Arrangements (Chapter VIII of UN Charter)."

[27] UN Security Council, Resolution 1785, S/RES/1785, para. 14 (Nov. 21, 2007).

force by regional arrangements in Mali and Somalia,[28] and requested the cooperation of regional arrangements in the implementation of enforcement actions in the Central African Republic,[29] Haiti,[30] the Middle East,[31] Sudan and South Sudan,[32] and Burundi.[33]

The Security Council's most significant authorization of the use of force came in 2011 with respect to Libya. For the first and only time, the Council invoked the third pillar of the Responsibility to Protect, "authorizing Member States that have notified the Secretary-General, acting nationally or through regional organizations or arrangements, and acting in cooperation with the Secretary-General, to take all necessary measures to protect civilians and civilian populated areas under threat of attack."[34] The Council specifically referred to Chapter VIII, recognizing "the important role of the League of Arab States in matters relating to the maintenance of international peace and security in the region."[35] NATO and LAS worked together to fulfill their mandate to protect civilians in Libya, although concerns were later raised about the regime change that allegedly culminated from the regional groups' operations.

The Security Council has also cooperated with NATO in Kosovo and Afghanistan. With Resolution 1244 in 1999, the Council authorized NATO participation in Kosovo under Chapter VII of the Charter, with an invitation to take all necessary means to fulfill its responsibilities.[36] In Afghanistan, the Council also authorized the International Security Assistance Force (ISAF) led by NATO in the stabilization process of Afghanistan. Acting under Chapter VII of the Charter, several of the Council's resolutions authorized the participatory ISAF member states to "take all necessary measures" to fulfill its mandate.[37]

[28] UN Security Council, Resolution 2480, S/RES/2480, para. 37 (June 28, 2019) (Mali); UN Security Council, Resolution 2472, S/RES/2472, para. 8 (May 31, 2019) (Somalia).
[29] UN Security Council, Resolution 2648, S/RES/2648, para. 10 (July 29, 2022).
[30] UN Security Council, Resolution 2653, S/RES/2653, para. 23 (Oct. 21, 2022).
[31] UN Security Council, Resolution 2624, para. 18 (Feb. 28, 2022).
[32] UN Security Council, Resolutions 2625, S/RES/2625, preamble, para. 20 (Mar. 15,2022); 2633, S/RES/2633, paras. 17, 20 (May 26, 2022).
[33] UN Security Council, Resolution 2303, S/RES/2303 (July 29, 2016).
[34] UN Security Council, Resolution 1973, S/RES/1973, para. 4 (Mar. 17, 2011).
[35] Ibid., para. 5.
[36] UN Security Council, Resolution 1244, S/RES/1244 (June 10, 1999), para. 7.
[37] United Nations Security Council, "Repertoire of the Practice of the Security Council, Regional Arrangements (Chapter VIII of UN Charter)."

C. Present-day challenges to regional cooperation

While there are many successful examples of Security Council cooperation with regional organizations under Chapter VIII, several limitations of the states, the regional organizations, and the Council itself prevent Chapter VIII from reaching its full potential. In particular, challenges to successful regional cooperation arise in six areas.

First, states and the Council hold fragmented views about the use of Chapter VIII. On one hand, there is a group of states that selectively choose which situations the Security Council should be addressing. Instead of promoting collective action consistently, the Council's agenda is in certain situations faced with a selective focus on matters of specific interest to individual states or their allies. On the other hand, there is a faction of states that oppose regional or international action in certain situations on the Council's agenda, on the pretext that the Council has failed to decisively address *any* conflict situation. Each group contributes to deficiencies in the effectiveness of Security Council action. The first group's selective choice of certain crises the Council should address further entrenches the perception of a biased Council, while the second group of states effectively bars the use of Chapter VIII, a potentially powerful tool for peace and security.

Second, some individual regional organizations face challenges to their legitimacy and credibility.[38] The legitimacy of a political organ is a precondition to its enforcement power and political influence. A number of regional organizations suffer from leadership crises and decision-making paralysis. Regional organizations also often have difficulty coming to agreement on statements, draft resolutions, and other texts. Even when an organization reaches agreement on a sufficiently strong choice of words regarding a particular issue, its consideration at the Council frequently results in a diluted text with platitudes of condemnation and humanitarian appeals. The limited results of the organizations' efforts thus undermine their perceived credibility in addressing international threats to peace and security.

Another factor that can have an impact on the effectiveness of regional peacekeeping efforts is troop loyalty. Divided loyalties between the state and the regional organization can hinder mission leadership and unity. In rare cases, peacekeeping contingents have even rejected commands in the

[38] See generally Berthold Rittberger and Philipp Schroeder, "The Legitimacy of Regional Institutions," in *The Oxford Handbook of Comparative Regionalism*, eds. Tanja A. Börzel and Thomas Risse (Oxford: Oxford University Press, 2018).

absence of approval from the contributing state's government.[39] States in distress often prefer to seek the assistance of powerful allies instead of using the comparatively weaker regional organizations as envisioned in Chapter VIII. The credibility challenge of regional organizations may affect their efforts undertaken pursuant to Chapter VIII. No peace process can be successful, and no regional arrangement can fulfill its mandate, if states do not genuinely try to pursue the collective interest and instead continue to pursue unilateral or bilateral agendas.

Third, the ability of the Security Council to actively promote, support, or facilitate dialogue with regional organizations is limited. When regional organizations do express their views on an issue, the Council sometimes does not acknowledge the statements of regional arrangements and does not always respond to requests to support their ongoing efforts.[40] In some circumstances, the Council's inaction has led the actors who are responsible for the continuation of a conflict to find alternative fora to support their policies and cease reliance on Council or regional arrangements—for example, by turning to their allies at the Security Council for diplomatic protection and bilateral assistance.

Fourth, the deficiencies in the effectiveness of the Council affect conflict development and at the same time can undermine the ability of regional arrangements to operate effectively. When the Council fails to ensure the implementation of its resolutions that have already been adopted, conflicts become protracted and then entrenched. As noted above, the prioritizing of selective over collective interests as well as the competition and lack of trust among the Great Powers further erodes the credibility of the Council. In particular, the perception that some states support double standards in the Council and act with bias in addressing conflicts can also sound a death knell for the credibility and legitimacy of the multilateral collective security system. When states sit in both regional organizations and on the Council, there is a possibility of further conflicts of interest. As a result, the Council

[39] Emmanuel Kotia, "In Multinational Missions, Preparation and Discipline Are Key," *Africa Defense Forum*, Jan. 20, 2016, accessed June 14, 2024, https://adf-magazine.com/2015/12/professionalism-in-peacekeeping/.

[40] States commented on this issue, among other challenges to the effectiveness of regional organizations, at a recent Security Council meeting. See "Peace through Dialogue: The Contribution of Regional, Subregional, and Bilateral Arrangements to the Prevention and Peaceful Resolution of Disputes—Security Council, 9448th Meeting," *United Nations*, Oct. 20, 2023, accessed June 14, 2024, https://webtv.un.org/en/asset/k1d/k1d2qgqeb7.

cannot effectively act through Chapter VIII and provide the leadership essential for coordinated efforts with regional organizations.

Fifth, UN support for regional troops raises risks under the Human Rights Due Diligence Policy (HRDDP), while rehatting those troops as UN peacekeepers has implication under the UN's human rights screening policy. At the core of the HRDDP is this principle:

> Support by United Nations entities to non–United Nations security forces must be consistent with the Organization's Purposes and Principles as set out in the Charter of the United Nations and with its obligations under international law to respect, promote and encourage respect for international humanitarian, human rights, and refugee law. . . . Consistent with these obligations, United Nations support cannot be provided where there are substantial grounds for believing there is a real risk of the receiving entities committing grave violations of international humanitarian, human rights, or refugee law and where the relevant authorities fail to take the necessary corrective or mitigating measures.[41]

Further, when the Council rehats a military or formed police contingent from a regional or subregional operation into a UN operation, they immediately become subject to the UN's human rights screening policy, whereby member states that nominate or provide personnel to serve with the United Nations are requested to screen their personnel and to certify that they have not committed, or are alleged to have committed, criminal offenses or violations of international human rights law and international humanitarian law.[42] Moreover, the United Nations lacks the resources to verify the certifications except in respect of the most senior appointments.

Sixth, and finally, the Security Council has often preferred to rehat regional troops—thereby transferring authority from regional operations to UN operations—to bring the funding and financing frameworks under UN auspices, rendering them subject to UN standards, financial regulations, and rules. To the extent that the financial power in the United Nations rests with the General Assembly, states are reluctant to authorize funding for external

[41] UN Secretary-General, Identical Letters dated Feb. 25, 2013, from the Secretary-General addressed to the President of the General Assembly and the President of the Security Council, UN Doc. A/67/775–S/2013/110, 2 (Mar. 5, 2013).

[42] UN Police, "United Nations Policy on Human Rights Screening of United Nations Personnel," (Dec. 11, 2012), accessed June 16, 2024, https://police.un.org/en/united-nations-policy-human-rights-screening-of-united-nations-personnel-11-december-2012.

actors, including regional arrangements over which the UN cannot exercise oversight or control.

Section II: Proposals for More Effective Use of Chapter VIII to Advance International Peace and Security

While acknowledging the achievements and learning the lessons of the past, the Security Council can recognize the contributions of and strengthen its partnerships with regional arrangements. In doing so, the Council can benefit from the full potential of regional arrangements. Efforts to achieve more effective action under Chapter VIII should focus on better coordination, greater burden sharing, and more mutually reinforcing cooperation.

As a preliminary point, proposals to improve regional cooperation and diplomacy are unlikely to make much difference unless the Security Council pays greater attention to the views of regional arrangements and consistently translates its commitments to action. Consider the Council's March 2022 presidential statement, where the Council recognized the unique capabilities of regional organizations in understanding the root causes of regional armed conflicts, and the benefits such expertise could yield to influence the prevention or resolution of conflicts.[43] In other statements made the same year, the Council even went so far as to envision a role for regional and subregional organizations with respect to nonproliferation of weapons of mass destruction and the use of sanctions—typically, two thematic areas firmly within the Council's ambit.[44]

These statements and resolutions are certainly important contributions to strengthening regional cooperative frameworks. Still, mere rhetorical support for regional arrangements falls short of the support the Council must provide to ensure effective cooperation under Chapter VIII.

Each of the five proposals outlined below should facilitate more effective cooperation between the Council and regional arrangements. With greater Council support, regional and other security arrangements can achieve much more than they already do.

[43] SC Pres. Statement 2022/1, paras. 3, 4 (Mar. 23, 2022).
[44] See UN Security Council, Resolutions 2663, S/RES/2663 (Nov. 30, 2022); 2664, S/RES/2664 (Dec. 9, 2022).

A. Council delegation to regional organizations

Whenever a situation arises that clearly has the potential to undermine international peace and security, the Council should offer quick, decisive, collective, and unanimous support to relevant regional initiatives. In particular, the Council should provide more concrete and tangible support to encourage the efforts of regional arrangements with respect to peaceful settlement of disputes and peacekeeping operations. This requires taking preventive action on a regional level well before resorting to the deployment of UN forces. Only then will these regional arrangements work as Chapter VIII envisioned.

In assessing the performance of regional arrangements in this context, states must temper expectations to arrive at realistic projected outcomes that regional arrangements can achieve. As Secretary-General António Guterres recently observed, "[N]o single organization can alone ensure peace, security, and development in a complex and rapidly changing world. It requires partnership across all levels—from the local to the regional to the global."[45] Where regional arrangements do not immediately succeed in quelling conflict, the Council should take care to make sober and fair assessments for future improvements in the conduct of those regional organizations and incorporate lessons learned into future planning and trainings.

B. Active involvement of the E10

Great Power politics within the Security Council often cause paralysis. In these instances, other States—especially the E10—should seek the active involvement of regional arrangements. Even without the veto, the E10 can act as a powerful bloc when working in concert. One of the most important aspects to promote successful coordination and greater alignment between the E10 and regional arrangements is abstaining from unilateral actions. Otherwise, as one delegation warned, "when Member States read from different scripts or take unilateral actions, conflicts become unnecessarily complex, protracted, internationalized, and certainly more destructive."[46] Acting

[45] UN SCOR, 8967th mtg. at 2, U.N. Doc. S/PV.8967 (Feb. 16, 2022).

[46] "Part VIII. Regional Arrangements," *Repertoire of the Practice of the Security Council, 25th Supplement (2022)*, p. 12 (recalling Kenya's statements on institutional cooperation with regional organizations).

in concert, the E10 can provide regional arrangements with clear guidance and help formulate a plan of action to increase the chances of building cohesive, collaborative frameworks for peacekeeping and peace enforcement.

The P5's permanency and veto power have led those states to develop entrenched positions committed to the status quo.[47] In contrast—and with full acknowledgment of its numerous drawbacks—the two-year term of the E10 encourages dynamic, nimble approaches to Security Council action, with ample room for change and flexibility. In the interest of peace, the E10 can step into the role of regional arrangement coordinators and breathe new life into Chapter VIII initiatives. This will not only increase the legitimacy of Chapter VIII efforts and improve approaches to international peace and security; the E10's new role and tradition of partnership with regional organizations may also increase those States' relative agency and power within the Council.

Finally, where regional organizations produce statements on a conflict, the E10 should commit to including the exact wording of the regional arrangements in the E10s' own statements and seek to incorporate and amplify those statements in the Council's own pronouncements. In so doing, the E10 may act as a conduit for views on-the-ground, broadcasting them through their position as states in the Council. At least in part, this will act as a counterbalance to the watering down of the language of regional organizations in the Council's official statements on the conflict.

C. Foresight and strategic use of on-the-ground visits

The E10 have term limitations at the Council and, with few exceptions, rarely have the opportunity to participate in on-the-ground visits in conflict situations. Nevertheless, they may proactively push the Council to partner with regional organizations to take part in such visits before the emergence of a hot war or conflict, and to prevent prewar situations from worsening.

This recommendation is particularly important since the COVID-19 pandemic, which reduced on-the-ground missions to a minimum. The E10 can push to change the perspective of key decision makers for greater hands-on

[47] "Concluding Debate on Security Council Reform, Speakers in General Assembly Urge More Representation for Developing Countries, Ending of Permanent Members' Power", GA/12473 (Nov. 18, 2022), accessed June 16, 2024, https://press.un.org/en/2022/ga12473.doc.htm (see in particular comments of Ghana).

involvement where conflict situations so require. In turn, the Council (and the P5 in particular) should provide support capabilities and security assistance to regional representatives, in particular at the highest political levels, ahead of conflict for early-stage prevention.

When the P5 do invoke the use of the veto to prevent Security Council response to humanitarian crises, the E10 could leverage their relationships with regional arrangements to arrive at a course of action that does not necessarily depend on or require Security Council authorization, but where E10 states can nevertheless lend Council support. In 1949, Resolution 267(III) outlined numerous actions that the General Assembly recommended the Council categorize as "procedural" rather than "substantive," and therefore not subject to the P5 veto power.[48] These include the establishment of subsidiary organs the Council deems necessary for the performance of its functions (chief among them, maintaining international peace and security); holding meetings at places other than the seat of the United Nations; and requesting convocation of a special session of the General Assembly.[49]

With these tools alone, the E10 could contribute to the creation of a fact-finding mission in the state of the conflict (subject to that state's cooperation); hold meetings at geographically strategic locations outside the seat of the United Nations to spotlight the conflict and raise awareness about urgency of action; and convene a special General Assembly session to discuss the dispute and advocate for on-the-ground visits.

D. Data collection and the principle of subsidiarity

Whenever threats to international peace and security arise, small states are often most at risk.[50] Regional and subregional organizations can insulate small states from this vulnerability, in particular when supported by the Security Council. The Council should employ the principle of subsidiarity

[48] UN General Assembly, Resolution 267(III), A/RES/267(III) (Apr. 14, 1949).

[49] A/RES/267(III), Annex.

[50] Adam Lupel and Lauri Mälksoo, "A Necessary Voice: Small States, International Law, and the UN Security Council," International Peace Institute (Apr. 2019): 2 ("Among UN member states, small countries are most at risk if the international system further deteriorates into an older model based on power politics and zero-sum games"); see also UNGA, Informal High-level Roundtable on "Small States, Multilateralism, and International Law" (Apr. 28, 2022) ("[I]t is often the smaller States that suffer the most when conflict prevails"), accessed June 16, 2024, https://www.un.org/pga/76/2022/04/28/informal-high-level-roundtable-on-small-states-multilateralism-and-internatio nal-law/.

in its Chapter VIII considerations, which holds that "a central authority should have subsidiary (less important than but related or supplement to something) function performing only those tasks that cannot be performed at a more local level,", or in short, "a rebuttable presumption for the local."[51]

Perhaps most important, subregional organizations can play a role in creating information awareness among small states to enhance early warning systems. Global early warning initiatives often rely on regional organizations to enhance data collection and, in turn, to better forecast future threats. Increasing regional and even subregional collaboration will develop and crystallize best practices for data collection, in turn allowing for richer conflict tracking and analysis.[52]

To achieve this, regional arrangements need support from the Council and the wider international community for their contributions to peace, justice, and security. The Council's role in bolstering regional arrangements' early warning capacity is to increase investment in those organizations. In a similar vein, UN member states should emphasize the importance of early warning systems through a subsidiarity lens, focusing on supporting the capacity of subregional organizations financially through bilateral investment and with public support for peace and security efforts.[53]

Chairs of regional and subregional organizations may also play a more active role. In particular, chairs can encourage the use of widely available technologies to their organizations' advantage, including mobile devices for real-time (pre)conflict information and monitoring. Capitalizing on real-time information-sharing will help regional arrangements to more effectively use virtual summits, diplomatic pressure, and other publicity exercises to enhance their relative strength through information awareness.

[51] Alena F. Douhan, "United Nations and Regional Organizations: Complementarity v. Subsidiarity," *Max Planck Yearbook of United Nations Law* 19 (2015): 268–69 (quoting J. Pearsall and P. Hanks (eds), Oxford Dictionary of English (revised 2nd ed., OUP 2006): 1761); Andreas Follesdal, "Subsidiarity and International Human-Rights Courts: Respecting Self-Governance and Protecting Human Rights—or Neither," *Law and Contemporary Problems* 79, no. 2 (2016): 148.

[52] Micah Zenko and Rebecca R. Friedman, "UN Early Warning for Preventing Conflict," *International Peacekeeping* 18, no. 1 (Feb. 2011): 33–34.

[53] See e.g., UN General Assembly, Resolutions 70/291, A/RES/70/290, cl. 2 (July 19, 2016); 47/120, A/RES/47/120 (Feb. 10, 1993).

E. Regional solutions for regional problems

Regional organizations contribute nuanced understandings of local conflict that might otherwise go unheeded. Making use of these pre-existing informational advantages is a simple way to encourage more comprehensive solutions for peace.[54] Indeed, when regional arrangements work well, they often offer early access to information through preliminary investigations that may not otherwise be accessible to the Council. While in rare cases states promote "regional solutions for regional problems" primarily to evade scrutiny or Council enforcement measures, the interest in regional solutions does correspond to an overall increase in peace operations undertaken by regional organizations.

Only functioning and effective regional security arrangements can successfully aid and promote international peace and security. The following proposals address actions that both the Council and the regional arrangements themselves may undertake.

1. Small states and regional arrangements

First, small states in at-risk regions should assume a greater leadership role in regional organizations and peacekeeping missions. Small states are less likely to hold entrenched power positions and are typically more risk-averse, as they stand to suffer the most from regional conflict. In a leadership position, small states may encourage common positions and caution against purely rhetorical stands of principle that might ultimately escalate or fail to deescalate security threats.

Additionally, small state leadership could be an answer to the criticism of lack of credibility and perceived biases by some more traditional actors. Preserving and encouraging greater leadership roles for small states could therefore help in alleviating the credibility deficit arising from the actual and perceived control by some states, which can sometimes aggravate already unstable situations. This is particularly so in peacekeeping missions, with complications arising out of intelligence-sharing, cooperation, and troop loyalty. For its part, the Council should support and encourage small states in these leadership roles.

[54] UN General Assembly, "A More Secure World: Our Shared Responsibility: Report of the High-level Panel on Threats, Challenges and Change," A/59/565 (Dec. 2, 2004).

2. Action by the UN Security Council
Regional arrangements are "well positioned in promoting confidence, trust, and dialogue among concerned parties" and, when given the space to do so, can better aid global efforts to limit security threats.[55] While the Council must provide regional arrangements with technical and financial support, it must also leave room for them to operate independently. Allowing regional organizations the flexibility to operate on their own terms is the best possible chance of those organizations adding value to international peace and security.[56]

In the event that regional organizations fail to produce tangible outcomes, an E10 state may initiate Council discussions. Less likely to have a vested interest in the outcome of a particular conflict, the involvement of E10 states lowers the risk of hidden power agendas or prerogatives that might hinder regional discussions. During a closed discussion with the regional arrangements in question, E10 states can assess the Council's prior involvement in the situation, and explore the steps the Council can take or the support it can provide to advance the regional organizations' efforts.

The closed-format meetings allow for focused briefings with practical assessments and provide a pathway to move forward after Council paralysis. To facilitate this process, the Council could also request a closed briefing from the regional organization or the Secretariat. In taking any action, the Council should focus on supporting the regional organizations' efforts, with a view to achieving peaceful resolutions. In so doing, the Council will avoid reverting to "vertical problem solving" and, in the end, arrive at more balanced, sustainable, and peaceful solutions.[57]

Conclusion

This chapter seeks to strengthen cooperation between the Security Council and the regional arrangements envisioned in Chapter VIII. Past successes and failures provide important lessons, as well as a greater understanding of the potential and added value of regional arrangements. The Council should

[55] SC Pres. Statement 2021/9 (Apr. 19, 2021) (emphasis added).
[56] SC Pres. Statement 2006/39 (Sept. 20, 2006).
[57] Bjorn Hettne and Fredrik Soderbaum, "The UN and Regional Organizations in Global Security: Competing or Complementary Logics," *Global Governance* 12, no. 3 (July–Sept. 2006): 230–31.

incorporate these experiential findings to lay stronger foundations for its cooperation with regional arrangements.

When regional arrangements are fully and proactively supported by the Council, they have immense capabilities. Such arrangements can prevent the escalation of disputes, advance the peaceful settlement of disputes, and act in a prompt and informed manner well before situations escalate to serious threats to international peace and security. In turn, regional peacekeeping and peace enforcement, under the guidance and with the support of the Council, can achieve more successful and sustainable outcomes.

Forward-looking, practical solutions will best support the furtherance of international peace and security through regional arrangements. And, if it becomes necessary for the Council to step in, it has the ultimate authority and responsibility to do so. Without regional security, there is no global security. By embracing the power and potential of regional arrangements, the Security Council can more effectively fulfill its primary responsibility to prevent and respond to modern threats to international peace and security.

Conclusion

As Mohamed ElBaradei said at the outset, we, the authors of this book, are among "those who wish to see the UN Security Council play its intended role in creating a more just, peaceful, and secure world based on international legitimacy and anchored in the rule of law."

We wish to see a Security Council composed of member states who represent the broader UN membership and carry out their duties in accordance with the Charter of the United Nations.

We wish to empower the ten elected members to act collectively to make the Security Council more responsive to the will of the international community and more accountable to "We the Peoples."

We wish to enable the Security Council to prevent aggression and mass atrocity crimes,to uphold the responsibility to protect and to end impunity and ensure accountability with greater urgency and automaticity.

We wish to inspire a less reactive and more proactive Security Council that promotes state responsibility through the International Court of Justice and individual accountability in the International Criminal Court.

We wish to restore the legitimacy of the Security Council, urging the five permanent members (P5) to act more responsibly; the elected members to participate more actively; and civil society to exercise more scrutiny.

We wish to restrain the use of the veto to the legal limits found in the UN's purposes and principles and *jus cogens* norms in situations involving genocide,war crimes, and crimes against humanity.

We wish to tap the full potential of the "Uniting for Peace" resolution to enable the UN General Assembly to take consequential action when the P5 veto paralyzes the Council.

We wish to reinforce the advisory and adjudicatory roles of the International Court of Justice in a world where states settle their disputes peacefully and respect the international rule of law.

We wish to hold accountable all perpetrators of aggression and mass atrocity crimes by enforcing the Rome Statute and Geneva Conventions and by ending impunity, including for heads of state and government.

Mona Ali Khalil and Floriane Lavaud, *Conclusion* In: *Empowering the UN Security Council*. Edited by: Mona Ali Khalil and Floriane Lavaud, Oxford University Press. © Oxford University Press 2024.
DOI: 10.1093/oso/9780197780602.003.0012

We wish to strengthen cooperation with regional arrangements to achieve a "networked multilateralism" capable of contributing to universal peace and collective security.

We wish to empower the Security Council to address modern threats to international peace and security in a manner that upholds international law equally for all peoples and protects the human rights equally of all persons.

We trust that UN member states are aware of the moral and practical imperative of recommitting to the UN's principles and fulfilling the UN's purposes for the sake of current and future generations.

We hope that UN member states will embrace the proposals made in this book and bring them to life in their work in the Security Council in particular, and the United Nations in general.

Index

For the benefit of digital users, indexed terms that span two pages (e.g., 52–53) may, on occasion, appear on only one of those pages.

accountability, 3–4, 5, 25, 42–43, 51, 55, 56, 57, 60–62, 64–65, 66–67, 68–69, 92–93, 102–4, 109, 122, 145, 146–47, 149, 151–52, 156–57, 158, 159, 179
Accountability, Coherence, and Transparency Group (ACT), 35–36, 48, 98–99, 100, 104–5
advisory opinion (AO), 5, 44, 48, 51, 118–19, 127, 128, 129, 130
Afghanistan, 32, 66–67, 117, 167
Africa, 1–2, 11, 36, 85–86
African, 28–29, 85–86, 151, 152
African Court on Human and Peoples' Rights, 66–67
African Group, 1–2, 85–86, 131–32
African Mission in Burundi (AMIB), 166
African Union (AU), 66–67, 85–86, 163, 165–66
Agenda for Peace, 165
aggression, 1, 2–4, 5, 11–12, 15, 19, 36–37, 42–43, 44–45, 46, 47, 49, 52–53, 65–66, 94, 96, 101–3, 105, 109, 110, 111, 112, 114–15, 116–17, 120–21, 124–26, 127, 145, 148–49, 179
Al-Qaeda, 27–28
Anglo-Iranian Oil Company case, 138
Annan, Kofi, 158, 164–65
armed force, 44–45, 114–15, 116, 124–25, 141
Asia, 11, 85–86
Asian Group, 1–2
Asia-Pacific, 36, 152
Association of Southeast Asian Nations (ASEAN), 85–86

Biden, President Joe, 101–2
Black Sea Grain Initiative, 50–51
Bosnian War, 138–39
Boutros-Ghali, Boutros, 164
Burundi, 150, 164–65, 166

Caribbean Community (CARICOM), 165–66
Chagos Archipelago, 51
China, 1–2, 10–11, 26–27, 28, 31, 35–36, 49, 73, 91–92, 101–2, 103, 110, 111–12, 120–21, 151–52
civilian, 46, 55, 56, 58–59, 62–64, 69, 73, 111, 117, 118, 119–20, 123, 124, 135, 147–48, 154, 167
climate change, 57, 65–66, 134
coalition, 2–3, 27, 28, 29, 44–45, 89, 134
Cold War, 2–3, 25–27, 59, 73, 77–78, 83, 164–65
compensation, 124, 157–58
compliance, 19, 21, 41–42, 52, 54, 62–63, 68, 119, 136, 141–43, 145–46, 148–49
Congo, the, 51, 63–64, 117
cooperation, 5, 21, 27, 35, 54, 58, 59, 68–69, 85–86, 143, 145–46, 152–53, 155, 156, 162, 163, 165, 166–67, 168, 171, 174, 176, 177–78, 180
COVID-19, 173–74
credibility, 1, 3–4, 10, 19, 20–21, 26–27, 65–66, 78, 84, 102–3, 109, 125–26, 168–70, 176
Crimea, 120–21

Darfur, 62, 150, 153–54, 155, 159

Economic Community of West African States (ECOWAS), 66–67, 165–66
eleventh emergency special session (ESS11), 121, 122, 124
enforcement authority, 146, 158, 162
erga omnes, 93–94, 95–96, 111, 119, 133–34
ethnic cleansing, 111, 125–26, 179
European Union Force (EUFOR), 166–67

France, 1, 10–11, 26–27, 28, 32, 33–34, 48, 49, 77, 91, 100–1, 103, 110, 116–17, 120–21
France-Mexico (initiative), 35–36, 88, 100–1
France, United Kingdom, & United States (P3), 26–27, 31, 32

Gaza, 46, 51, 102, 104, 119–20
Geneva Convention, Fourth, 119, 123, 147–48
Geneva Conventions, 5, 67–68, 96, 111, 123, 125–26, 145, 146, 147–48, 151–52, 159, 179
genocide, 11, 35–36, 48, 51, 55, 60–61, 65–66, 67–68, 76–77, 92–93, 96, 98–99, 100, 105, 111, 138–39, 145, 146, 149, 150, 179

Great Power, 1, 24, 44, 45–46, 49, 73, 91–92, 161, 169–70, 172–73
Group of Seven Plus (g7+), 85–86
Guterres, UN Secretary-General António, 50–51, 85, 165, 172
Guyana, 127

Haiti, 28–29, 32, 66, 164–67
Hamas, 3, 46, 111–12, 119–20, 123
Herzegovina, 138–39
Honduras, 141
human rights, 11–13, 14–15, 17, 22, 28, 41, 55–57, 58–61, 62–63, 64, 66–68, 69, 99, 100, 122, 133–34, 146, 149–52, 170, 180
Human Rights Due Diligence Policy (HRDDP), 170
Hungary, 117

Informal Working Group on Documentation and Other Procedural Questions (IWG), 34
intergovernmental negotiations (IGN), 97–98
International Commission on Intervention and State Sovereignty (ICISS), 78
international community, 1, 13, 14–15, 19–21, 22, 55, 56–57, 58–59, 60–61, 64–65, 66, 95–97, 98–99, 100, 102, 110, 111, 123, 125, 145, 146, 147, 149, 151–52, 165, 175, 179
International Court of Justice (ICJ), 44, 48, 51–52, 55, 66, 68, 118–19, 123–24, 142
international crime, 66–67, 146, 152–53, 155, 157, 158
International Criminal Court (ICC), 5, 55, 58–59, 61–63, 66, 68, 145–46, 147–49, 150, 151–59
International Criminal Tribunal for Rwanda (ICTR), 60–62, 147, 159
International Criminal Tribunal for the Former Yugoslavia (ICTY), 61–62, 147, 149–50, 159
international law, 1, 3–4, 5, 11–12, 19, 20–21, 41–43, 45, 46, 47, 51, 52–53, 54, 58, 59, 66, 68, 77–78, 83, 92–94, 95–96, 101, 102, 104–5, 111, 116, 117, 118, 121, 122, 125, 130, 131–32, 143, 156–57, 170, 180
International Law Commission (ILC), 95–96
Iran, 51, 138
Iraq, 2–3, 27–28, 32–33, 43–44, 73, 109, 111, 124, 151
Islamic State of Iraq and the Levant (ISIL), 27–28, 151
Israel, 3, 46, 50–51, 103, 111–12, 116–17, 118–20, 123–24, 127, 130–31, 133–34

Japan, 32, 34, 91–92
jus cogens, 5, 76–77, 93–94, 95–96, 119, 179

Kosovo, 66–67, 73, 77–78, 132–33, 167
Kuwait, 2–3, 34, 43–44, 73, 124

Latin America, 36, 85–86
Latin America and the Caribbean (group), 1–2, 11, 28, 85–86, 152
League of Arab States (LAS), 163, 167
League of Nations, 23, 53–54, 91, 92
least-developed countries (LDCs), 85–86
legal system, 10, 74, 158, 164
legitimacy, 1, 4, 5, 9, 12, 21, 24, 26–27, 28, 29, 65, 66, 68, 73–76, 78–80, 81, 83, 89, 125, 163–64, 168, 169–70, 173, 179
Libya, 27–28, 33–34, 66–67, 135, 140, 153–54, 155, 157–58, 159, 167
Liechtenstein, 35–36, 49, 103
Lockerbie case, 135, 140

mass atrocity crimes, 1, 3–4, 5, 11–12, 20, 35–37, 42–43, 56, 62–63, 64–66, 69, 92–93, 105, 110, 112, 146, 152, 159, 179
Mexico, 27–28, 48, 91, 98, 103–4
Middle East, the, 20, 117, 166–67
Montreal convention, 135, 140
multilateralism, 56, 65, 68, 69, 165, 180
Myanmar, 2–3, 51, 66

Namibia, 117, 130–31
Ndadaye, Melchior, 150
Nicaragua v. United States of America, 140
nonpermanent members (NPMs), 23–24, 25, 26, 27
North Atlantic Treaty Organization (NATO), 66–67, 163
nuclear proliferation, 33, 65
nuclear weapons, 129–30, 132

Occupied East Jerusalem, 118–19, 133
Occupied Palestinian Territory (OPT), 117, 118
Office of the Prosecutor (OTP), 153–54, 155
Organization of American States (OAS), 66–67, 163
Organization on Security and Cooperation in Europe (OSCE), 163

Palestine, 2–3, 20, 50–51, 69, 103, 112, 118, 119, 122–23, 127, 130–31, 133–34
Palestinian Authority, 123

peacekeeping, 2–3, 11, 15, 16, 25–26, 31, 44, 55, 58–59, 63–64, 66–67, 73, 84, 86, 116–17, 123, 124, 161, 163–64, 166–67, 168–69, 172–73, 176, 178
penholder, 30–32, 33–34

Rapid Support Forces (RSF), 155
reconciliation, 60, 158, 159, 165–66
reform, 4, 6, 9, 10, 14, 21, 22, 24–25, 26–27, 37, 42–43, 47, 48, 50, 73–74, 79, 89, 97–99, 102–3, 142–43
regime change, 167
regional conflict, 127, 176
regional group, 48, 85–86, 88, 99, 120–21, 167
regional organization, 5, 17–18, 30, 46–47, 69, 86–87, 133, 164, 165–66, 167, 168–70, 171, 172–73, 175–76, 177
reparation, 60, 118–19, 133–34, 141, 157–58
representation, 1–2, 97–98
Responsibility to Protect (RPT), 19–20, 57, 67–68, 78, 99, 125–26, 167
Rome Statute of the International Criminal Court (Rome Statute), 5, 55, 61–62, 67–68, 123, 124, 145, 146–47, 148–50, 151–54, 156–58, 159, 179
rule of law, 4, 27–28, 42–43, 54, 55–60, 61, 64–65, 66, 67, 68–69, 105, 111, 143, 149, 158, 159, 179
Russia, 1–2, 3, 10–11, 28, 31–32, 35–36, 42, 46, 49, 50–51, 73, 101–2, 103, 109, 110, 111–12, 120–22, 124–25, 127, 139, 151–52
Rwanda, 60–61, 63–65, 73, 77–78, 149–50

sanctions, 2–3, 5, 15, 19, 27–28, 32–34, 42–43, 44–45, 46–47, 52–54, 55, 58–59, 62–63, 76, 84, 109, 117, 123–25, 138–39, 148–49, 171
San Francisco, 77
security system, 10, 19, 21, 45, 47, 169–70
small island developing states (SIDS), 85–86
Somalia, 164–65
South Sudan, 63–64, 166–67
South West Africa, 117, 130
South West Africa case, 129–30
South West Africa People's Organization, 117
Sudan, 153–54, 159, 166–67
Sudanese Armed Forces (SAF), 155
Syria, 2–3, 32, 66–67, 111–12, 117, 151–52
system, 16–17, 30–31, 41, 42–43, 45, 47, 48, 52–53, 74, 99, 127, 156, 175

Taliban, 109
treaty, 43, 64–65, 69, 94, 95, 156, 163

Ukraine, 2–3, 32, 42, 43–44, 46, 49, 50–51, 66, 98, 103, 104, 109, 111–12, 120–23, 124–25, 127, 139
UN Charter, 3, 10–11, 18–20, 21, 44–45, 47, 48, 51, 58–59, 65–66, 93–94, 96, 98, 103–4, 110, 111, 113–14, 120–21, 124–25, 132–33, 136–43, 148, 154, 156
UN General Assembly resolutions, 36–37, 49, 50, 52–53, 88, 96–97, 103–5, 110, 113–15, 116, 124–25, 130, 131–34
UN Human Rights Council, 151–52
Union of Soviet Socialist Republics (USSR), 113–14, 117
United Kingdom, 1, 10–11, 26–27, 28, 32, 33–34, 43–44, 49, 91–92, 101, 103, 109, 110–11, 116–17, 120–21, 128–29, 131–32, 135, 138, 140
United Kingdom v. People's Republic of Albania (Corfu Channel case), 128–29
United Nations, 1, 4, 9, 10–11, 12–13, 14, 15, 16, 19, 20–21, 23, 36, 41, 42, 45–46, 47, 51, 54, 58, 66, 69, 91–92, 93, 94, 96–97, 98, 99, 100, 101–2, 103–4, 109–10, 111, 113, 114, 115, 116, 127, 133–34, 147, 153, 156–57, 162, 164–65, 166, 170–71, 174, 179, 180
United Nations–African Union Hybrid Operation in Darfur (UNAMID), 166
United States, 1, 3, 10–11, 26–27, 28, 32, 35–36, 43–44, 46, 49, 73, 91–92, 96–97, 101–2, 103, 109, 110–12, 113–14, 116–17, 120–21, 135, 136–37, 140–41
Uniting for Peace, 5, 50, 103, 110, 112, 113–15, 116–17, 118, 121, 122–23, 125–26, 179
UN Operation in Burundi (ONUB), 166
UN Security Council (UNSC), 5, 18, 47, 55, 56, 58–59, 60–61, 65–66, 68, 73, 75, 79, 80–81, 82, 83, 84–85, 101–2, 110, 146, 155, 158, 162, 179
UN Security Council resolutions, 27–28, 60–61, 121, 128–29, 132–33, 135, 138–39, 150, 151, 154, 155
UN Stabilization Mission in Haiti (MINUSTAH), 165–66

veto, 1, 3–4, 5, 9–10, 13–16, 18, 20, 21, 23–24, 26, 32, 34, 35–37, 42–43, 45–46, 47–49, 50, 65–66, 73, 74, 75, 76–78, 84–85, 86, 88, 91–95, 96–97, 98–99, 100–3, 104, 105, 109, 110–12, 114, 116–17, 120–21, 125, 141, 142–43, 151–52, 172–73, 174, 179
Vienna Conference, the, 59

Vienna Conventions on the Law of Treaties (VCLT) and its articles, 95–96

war crime, 122, 124, 125–26, 145, 149, 150, 151, 154, 179
West Africa, 32
Western European and Other States Group (WEOG), 11
World War II, 21, 23, 24, 41, 49, 91, 109

Yugoslavia, 61, 63–64, 73, 138–39, 149–50, 159, 164–65